It All Belongs

It All Belongs

Love, Loss, & Learning to Live Again

JUDY & ROY SMOOT

with MELINDA FOLSE

SparkPoint Press | Fort Worth, TX

Published by

SparkPoint Press | Fort Worth, TX

Publisher's Cataloging-in-Publication Data

Smoot, Judy.

It all belongs : love, loss, and learning to live again / Judy and Roy Smoot with Melinda Folse. –
Fort Worth, TX : SparkPoint Press, 2023.

p. ; cm.

ISBN13: 978-0-9826960-6-4

1. Smoot, Judy. 2. Women--Religious life. 3. Spiritual life. 4. Love--Religious aspects.
5. Grief--Religious aspects. 6. Creation (Literary, artistic, etc.)--Religious aspects.
I. Title. II. Smoot, Roy. III. Folse, Melinda.

BL625.7 S66 2022

204.082--dc23

Project coordination by Jenkins Group, Inc. | www.jenkinsgroupinc.com

Interior design by Mandy Gates

Printed in China

27 26 25 24 23 • 5 4 3 2 1

DEDICATION

To Judy Smoot,

In deepest gratitude and humble love for moments and memories
uncovered together, cherished as one, these pages are

Affectionately Dedicated

"Acquire the Spirit of Peace, and a thousand souls around you will be saved."

— ST. SERAPHIM OF SAROV

CONTENTS

PART I: HOW TO LIVE

PART II: ...AND HOW TO DIE

PART III: HOW TO SURVIVE

ACKNOWLEDGMENTS

These letters, thoughts, art, joys, and pains would not have been possible without our Creator bringing Judy and Roy together. For such beauty to be placed in their lives was and is an eternal gift from God. For this book to become a reality, many hearts were touched to push and encourage Judy and Roy to publish it—even as daunting a proposition as it was. We value each person who has walked with us courageously on the uncharted, unknown, sometimes terrifying paths to the completion of this book. We are grateful that these same paths have also provided surprising beauty, humor, and grace to everyone who listened with their heart and soul.

Encouragers included caregivers, our "Hide-A-Way Hills Fairies," "City Chicks," and close relatives including Judy's mom, my brothers and sister-in-law. We are so grateful for the shaping influence of spiritual directors, nuns of the Dominican Order of Peace in Columbus, Ohio, grief counselors, longtime friends, and Judy's "HAWKS," and expressive artists in Sarasota — as well as strangers who entered their lives in pubs, restaurants, national parks, coffee shops, and other "chance" encounters. (We know there is no such thing as a coincidence.)

Special thanks to the Jenkins Group, including Leah Nicholson who first helped imagine this project into fruition, the thoughtful guidance of Jerry Jenkins, the creative, patient design and production work of Yvonne Rohler, the wisdom of Jim Kalajian, and others whose names we may not know but to whom we are eternally grateful.

It All Belongs would not have happened without Melinda Folse's tireless, inspiring work and passion that led her sifting through over 1,000,000 words of journal entries and other writings and countless art pieces and original mandalas to paint this heart-wrenching and exquisite story of the journey traveled by Judy and Roy. She was also supported faithfully by her husband while she devoted countless hours, tears, and typing blisters to this mission. (Word has it he makes a mean cup of coffee, mysteriously provides perfect meals, and knows just when to show up with a glass of wine.)

Finally, Roy was passionately supported to move ahead with this project by June, his second wife, who knew Judy well. When they realized they were falling for each other, June told Roy that keeping his promise to Judy about publishing this book was another reason she fell in love with him. Roy has been eternally blessed with love from two amazing women and the gift of loving these two women beyond forever. How could he not strive to offer *It All Belongs* to lovers, loved ones, and life travelers everywhere?

HOW TO USE THIS BOOK

Judy often said that God placed lifelong friends in her life, broke her apart and put her back together in one breath, and equipped her to walk alongside people on their vulnerable, holy journeys. As a hospice worker, spiritual director, teacher, and retreat leader and founder of a nonprofit organization to support people with chronic pain and disease, she gained trust and open hearts of clients from coast to coast. Judy offers all she learned and all she became through her soulful explorations through art and writing within this book's pages.

Then from Roy, her husband, partner, and best friend, comes a rare opportunity to witness firsthand his pure, open, and raw vulnerability of devastating grief as he, after 42 years of observing Judy's work, teaching, and spiritual practices, learns to apply tools she provided to so many others. In Roy we find a relatable model as he struggles through his darkest days following Judy's sudden traumatic illness and death. Walking with Roy on his unwanted journey, we see healing's fits and starts and, at last, new life unfolding bit by tentative bit as he finds his own way forward.

IT ALL BELONGS IS A BOOK MEANT TO BE USED AS WELL AS READ

In this combined work, readers will be able to glean for themselves how to forge their own path, in their own way, through whatever challenge or darkness they are facing. Throughout this tender, thoughtful, and universal expression of love, grace, and redemption are many opportunities (wide margins, creative spaces, open pages) to serve as your invitation to experiment with a variety of creative expressions you'll find. You may wish to simply read and reflect, add notes or drawings as you go, or return another time (and as often as you like!) for further exploration of any sections drawing your attention, either in the spaces provided or in a separate journal or sketchpad.

Regardless of how you choose to experience *It All Belongs*, we encourage your first reading to be gentle and easy—simply allowing this book's themes, remembrances, observations, art, and poetry to wash over you—while staying open to discovery of ideas resonating with you in your own life and circumstance. While *It All Belongs* does not pretend to be an answer to your personal journey's ups and downs, perhaps you'll sense or recognize some familiar threads embedded in these reflections on emotions, trials, uncertainties, gratitude, decisions, joys, grief, and raw vulnerabilities woven into our journey—and yours.

SIMPLE GUIDELINES FOR GETTING THE MOST FROM THIS BOOK

Move gently into this material, neither asking nor expecting too much of yourself. This is material to be returned to again and again as you travel your own path. Trust you'll make new connections when you are ready to receive them.

Listen deeply—with all your senses—for anything in these pages speaking to you. These will be mile markers for your own path.

Explore purposefully, whether by journaling, creating art, reading, meditating, or listening to music. This book is meant to be used. Make it your own springboard for personal growth in your own circumstances.

Embrace fully this sacred time of exploration. Hold nothing back in your questions, rantings, thoughts, emotions. As this book's title affirms, everything you feel, think, ask, experience, live through, and release is a sacred part of your journey. *It all belongs*. Everything.

Seek freely any tools you want and need for your own journey. Allow this reading to spark your own ideas and permission for actions, explorations, and solitude, as well as to yield practical tools, practices, and processes for building skill sets and coping mechanisms to be yours and yours alone.

Consider intentionally the essence of your journey—hows, whys, and whats that may apply to you, your life, your comfort zones, your capabilities, your heart.

Express openly all thoughts, questions, and/or personal reactions bubbling up within your mind and heart as you read. FEEL FREE to write, create art, scribble in page margins, on blank spaces provided in this book, or in a separate journal.

WHAT IS ART? WHY IS IT IMPORTANT TO CREATE?

As Judy used to tell her expressive arts classes and spiritual direction clients, whether you believe yourself to be creative or not, the impulse to create is woven into each of us. Embracing and expressing in some way this gift of creativity is key to healing, a path to becoming whole. She loved to tell people, "Art can be anything expressing your deepest inner creativity." In addition to more obvious outlets, such as drawing, painting, writing, and composing music, art can take on many, many forms: cooking, sewing, gardening—even raising kids can be art. "Anything you deeply enjoy, anything putting light in your eyes, anything that makes you happy just to do it; that is your art."

CONNECT YOUR INNER AND OUTER EXPERIENCES IN A MANDALA

Judy chose mandalas as her creative outlet. Her process involved a daily discipline of meditative and scripture readings, deep reflections, writing, and prayer, and then, when so moved, she followed her creative impulses as she made a mandala.

HOW TO MAKE A MANDALA

Mandalas are used in many different cultures around our world. Although they can be quite elaborate, creating mandalas is a simple spiritual/expressive arts practice helping us process connections between our inner world and outer experiences.

While there are lots of ways to teach mandala making, both extremely simple and extremely complex, here's a basic primer to get you started:

~ Use a pencil to make a dot in the center of a plain white piece of paper.

~ Thinking of this dot as the center of a clock, go about 1/2 inch from the dot and add equidistant dots at 12:00, 3:00, 6:00, and 9:00.

~ Moving outward from the center dot, add as many dots as you want to, aligned with the first four, at 12:00, 3:00, 6:00, and 9:00. You'll have dotted lines radiating from your first dot.

~ Now draw a straight vertical line from your dots farthest away through the center from 12:00 to 6:00 and a straight horizontal line from 9:00 to 3:00.

~ Return to your first group of dots around the center and add new dots between each of the original four, equidistant from the center dot. (If this is the face of a clock, put these new dots between 1:00 and 2:00, 4:00 and 5:00, 7:00 and 8:00, 10:00 and 11:00.)

~ Now connect your new dots with diagonal straight lines that run through your center dot and extend both ends of the diagonal line across the whole circle in a great big X.

~ Add dots aligned along the X to correspond with those you added on your horizontal and vertical lines to lay out your concentric circles.

~ Moving around the face of the clock, connect the dots to form each row with curved lines to make series of concentric circles, starting with that first 1/2-inch set of dots, all the way to the outside edge. It's OK if your circles are not perfect; this is just a guide. Your mandala will likely remind you of a spider web.

NOW COMES THE FUN PART

~ Using your choice of colored pencil, ink, crayon, etc., create a series of lines, circles, loops, squiggles—whatever comes to you—between two of the circle guides (the horizontal, vertical, and diagonal lines) in the same row. Now you're going to replicate and repeat that same series of shapes and colors exactly, section by section, all the way around that row, then repeat this same process in each concentric row.

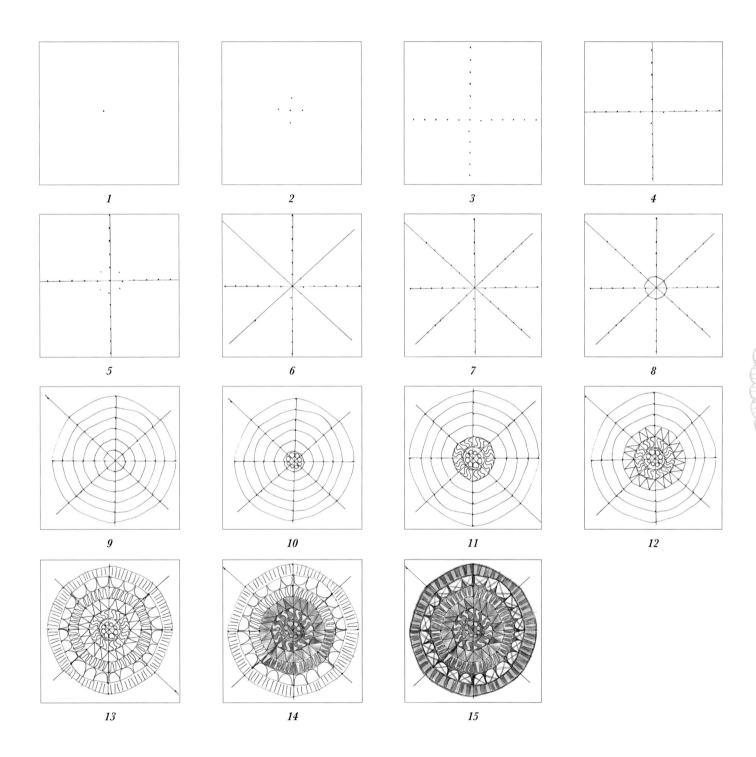

~ Take your time and repeat this process, row by row, working your way around the circle to repeat each random pattern in its row until all the rows are filled with your repeated patterns from the center to the outside edge.

~ Now you can go back and refine your repeating shapes within each row by drawing more shapes within them, taking care to repeat each addition, section by section, all the way around the circle. How many new shapes you add and repeat is completely up to you. Be sure to stay consistent within each row, but it's OK to add additional shapes to some rows and not all of them.

~ You can then color in the spaces or leave them more open like lace.

HOW THE MANDALA WORKS TO REVEAL YOUR SUBCONSCIOUS THOUGHTS AND REFLECTIONS:

In many cultures, creating a mandala is a spiritual practice providing us with a glimpse of deeply held information within us. We begin with a reading, a meditation, or a prayer with something specific in mind—and perhaps a request for illumination or application of this reading to our own lives or experience. As we draw in whatever shapes come to mind, these doodles are telling us something about our question or intent with which we began. And then, in repeating them over and over around each row of your circle, it provides opportunity to allow your mind to relax and allow new thoughts or understanding to surface.

Often, Judy would follow her mandala creation with a free-writing journaling exercise that would, more often than not, reveal new understanding, connection, or ideas for application of her opening meditation, prayer, or devotional reading.

UNLOCK YOUR HIDDEN AWARENESS THROUGH JOURNALING

While both Judy and Roy were avid journalers for years upon years, Roy chose journaling as his primary mode of creative expression when his journey through grief began shortly after Judy drew her final breath. Roy's journal began as a place to express his emotions coming in torrents, his questions with no answers, pure and searing pain permeating his day-to-day existence. Gradually, these pages also became a place for his observations of nature and people, as well as his own reflections, gratitude, poems, recollections, and stories he didn't want to forget, stories he had to capture on paper. Over time he began to unlock metaphors, find parallels in movies and music, and capture important conversations and connections. Slowly and surely, through his consistent exploration, striving, and writing, Roy found his path to healing and wholeness.

While there are more techniques for journaling than can be referenced here, the key is consistency, immediacy, and allowing words, phrases, thoughts, and observations to flow freely, inhibited, undirected, and uncensored. "Be all of who you are," Roy advises. "Give voice to every beautiful thought, raging flood of anger, gratitude, grief, flowing river of tears, fear, shock, feeling of helplessness, neediness, plea. Leave it all on the page; give it a place to be heard and recognized."

Ample space is provided in the pages of *It All Belongs* for recording simple observations as they bubble up into your awareness. Write in the margins. Underline words and phrases jumping out at you as you read. Ask questions, jot down ideas for future exploration or application, make this book your own healing workbook.

If you choose to use a separate journal, here are a few practical tips as well:

~ Choose a size, shape, type of paper, and writing instrument to make your writing easy and uninhibited. Choose something easy to carry, durable, and convenient for you. There are many designs, from cheap spiral notebooks in all sizes, to elaborate hardcover, to deckle-edged leather collectors' editions. (Some people even like to use notecards they carry in a wallet or shirt pocket; they start a new card each morning, record thoughts, feelings, and ideas in short form, and file it away each night before bed.)

~ It really doesn't matter what your journal looks like—just so you will feel free to write everything in it—even messy, regrettable, raw, and angry thoughts and rants. You can decide what to do with your journals later, whether locking them away for future reflection or posterity—or treating them to a fresh coat of fire once their job is done—but the key now is to write, write, write, in whatever feels most accessible. Release your pain, joys, screams, cradle-like sobs, moans, rage, grief.

~ Keep your journal with you and get in the habit of looking for places (coffee shops, restaurants, in your car, on a park bench or porch, on a hillside, on a beach or by a creek, in a garden, etc.) and opportunities to make time and space for this daily practice. Date each entry (and if it's a same-day entry, it can be helpful to add the time). You may or may not go back and reread your entries, but if you do, you will want and need this context of time; in these times of emotional turmoil, time markers can prove helpful.

~ Write every day, as many times a day as you can, whenever a thought, feeling, or emotion asks to be expressed. Short sentences or paragraphs, lists, bulleted points, poems, observations, descriptions of scenes, reactions to events, conversations, movies, stories, etc. Talking to other people can be helpful; however, writing allows your flow of thought and feeling into a safe, nonjudgmental space without need for the reciprocating rhythms of conversation.

~ Put your journals in a safe place once you've filled one and started another. Sometimes we don't know how far we've come till we look back; some of our greatest insights unfold over time and space if only we give them room to be recognized.

HOW TO JOURNAL USING THE "FREE-WRITING" TECHNIQUE:

~ Get still, whether through deep breathing, meditation, or prayer. Allow yourself a few minutes to relax and just be in this space of contemplation and reflection.

~ Begin with a statement, an idea, a topic, or a question. Where you are, what you see, a dream recalled, something you just experienced or felt.

~ Write what comes. Don't try to make sense of it; just keep writing as long as it flows. Allow one thought to lead to the next without question or censoring; just let your mind empty itself onto your page. You will almost always be surprised at what appears when invited. You are your thoughts' "first reader" as they flow from your mind and heart.

HOW TO "WORK" YOUR JOURNAL

~ Go back and reread a selected entry, allowing its words to settle within you, seeing what still resonates. Underline any words or phrases standing out and start a new dated entry to ask, "What else do I need to know about this?"

~ Follow the "free-writing" steps outlined above again. And again. Each time you go back over what you've written, you find new connections, new reflections, new ideas to explore.

Often, in drilling deeper on just a few thoughts, words, or phrases, you will learn much about why these things are important, what actions to consider next, and how to weight this observation in your overall journey and healing process.

INTRODUCTION

"You should publish your art and writings," Judy was told many times during her final years. At first, she was terribly reluctant. However, as she heard these comments repeated, nudges within told her to listen to them, consider their source. Was a hidden voice whispering to her heart through friends? Was something in her future reaching back through time, prompting her to give space to the quiet needs of people who would travel a similar journey—a journey Judy would never know? In her mixed-media journals kept over years of joys, fears, life-induced wisdom, prayers, gratitude, grief, art, and free-form mandalas, Judy's questions and anger flowed in color. On page after page, her unique expressions of raw, vulnerable, sweet, painful emotions flowed. She held nothing back.

"You should publish your journal writings for others to read," Roy was told by those few with whom he shared his grief journals. As he wrote and wrote and wrote, Roy felt as though he was etching words from deep within his dark, broken heart onto his dungeon's stone wall, a dungeon to which he was sentenced on October 10, 2016, when Judy left this world, leaving him to tread his own unwanted journey of grief. In restaurants and pubs, on his porch surrounded by woods, in parks, on Iona in Scotland, in the Grand Canyon and the Rocky Mountains, in shopping malls, in coffee shops, Roy's tears, rage, confessions, grief, prayers, pleas, memories—and even eventual healing—flowed from his heart, through his pen, onto the pages of his journals.

Judy and Roy were inseparable for more than 41 years, including 39 years of true wedded bliss. When they were asked how long they had been married, both often answered—even in their last years as wife and husband—"not long enough."

He adored her, always encouraging her to pursue her heart and dreams. She stood with him as they moved often in their early years together. In their 50s, Judy's past passion for art in various forms came alive, as did her love of serving people in crisis, both physical and spiritual. As Judy's past passion and growing love became seamless, Roy's smile was continuous as he watched her blossom into who she was created to become.

After completing a two-and-a-half-year spiritual direction program, Judy started a nonprofit organization devoted to helping those with chronic health challenges. To add the element of expressive arts to her offerings, she enrolled in an expressive arts school in Sarasota, Florida.

Realizing a dream that they had shared for more than a decade, Roy and Judy bought, renovated, and moved to their "Sunrise Ridge" cottage in southeastern Ohio's rolling hills. In this spectacular outdoor sanctuary, Judy created and offered retreats and programs in both spiritual direction and expressive arts.

Then life dealt them a tragic hand, an unforeseen and, at times, horrible journey. They remained inseparable through it all—chemotherapy, radiation treatments, two major brain surgeries, clinical trials, and hundreds of tests, blood draws, and doctors' appointments. Even in these most trying of times, Judy and Roy experienced gifts beyond measure.

On October 10, 2016, when Judy's spirit was guided to her eternal home by three hoots from a watchful owl, Roy entered a world he didn't know existed; a world he didn't want to know; a world of searing pain, grief, and grace beyond anything he could conceive. Just as art and writing were Judy's gifts to others, journaling became Roy's gift to himself, his therapy. Journaling became Roy's way to honor what they had, no matter how hard it was to put it to pen and paper.

It All Belongs details Judy and Roy's last four years together. It chronicles their lives' beautiful puzzle pieces falling perfectly into place—and then those same pieces violently ripped apart and scattered. This shockingly honest portrayal of love, anger, disappointment, joy, dashed hopes, growth, and ultimate acceptance—with a butterfly of healing-hope at last emerging from a shattered heart—is not new. It has been lived billions of times since the beginning of human love.

What is unique about *It All Belongs* is its infinite applicability to any kind of life-altering tragedy—diagnoses, shocking surprises, phone calls in the night, accidents, bad-news appointments with doctors, therapists, first responders, clergy, or military officers.

Whether a tragic journey with a loved one ends in her/his death or grace-granted recovery, the experience is most often marked with volcanic, emotional explosions. What are we to do with these?

While it was cancer (which really does suck) that invaded their lives and world, in sharing their story, their private journals, Roy and Judy extend their hope and prayer that through Judy's art, her processes and reasons for creating it, her words, Roy's words, and their combined learnings, will offer you, their reader, helpful whispers, images, and permission to travel your own road with authenticity, vulnerability, love, and compassion—for yourself and your loved ones.

Judy and Roy share their story as two "regular" people (not therapists or trained professionals) brought together by love and a higher power; two people who passionately treasured each other and life; two people who lived fully, not perfectly; two people who were separated long before they anticipated it ever happening.

Yet, they grasped life together, joining hands and hearts to face whatever came their way for four decades. Together, they experienced abysmally deep pain, fear, rage, and grief, as well as inconceivable moments of beauty, grace-filled acceptance, and deepening love. Many of these moments would not have been possible without those terrible, life-altering words quietly uttered in a southeastern Ohio emergency room: "Mrs. Smoot, you have a large mass in your right temporal lobe."

Above all, through the pages of *It All Belongs*, Judy and Roy want you to see life not as an either-or experience. It's a both/and adventure in which every moment is sacred.

It all belongs!

It All Belongs

November 2016

ROY: BAR HARBOR

A thick, heavy fog bank rolled into New England. I drove into it west of Boston, and it stayed with me, a serendipitous match with my heart, my soul. About five hours of fog, mist, and drizzle accompanied me on our way north to Bar Harbor.

We drove mostly in silence, with my one-sided conversation occasionally sprinkling the quiet. We also listened to country music on the radio—Judy's favorite—all stories of love, loss, fun, sadness, family. Stories of life.

We always anticipated our first view of the Bar Harbor Inn after we crossed onto Mount Desert Island. The fog bank made me wonder whether we would be able to see the inn's lights tonight.

Our first view was a pleasant welcome as the lights of the inn and Bailey Louise Todd's pier shone brightly, saying, "Welcome back!"

There is a second "first view" of the inn, just to be fair. That road leads to the island's edge.

Judy worked her magic on the second "first view." A full moon—I always call it the "Judy Moon" because she loves it so much— danced in and out of a high fog bank as it was breaking into pieces, reflecting gently on the water of Frenchman's Bay.

It was mystical, it was lovely, and I sobbed as I smiled. Her moon continued its playful dance with the rapidly moving clouds as they rushed to the northeast, driven by the breath of a Maine wind that seemed relentless.

The Judy Moon continued to shine down on me as I sat on our balcony after we checked in at the Bar Harbor Inn's Oceanfront Lodge.

Being exhausted, physically, mentally, and emotionally, I simply sat and gazed, drank in the dance above me, drank in Judy's love. The pain was still there but resting quietly. I, too, rested and absorbed her light, her love.

As the sun's early light colored our balcony and the wall opposite our room's broad French doors, I awoke, whispering, "Good morning, Judy." As I lay there, waves harmonized with my soft sobs, which happen each morning as I wake. They will subside in time, I know, but not any time soon.

Over our Bar Harbor Inn breakfast, we shared two pieces of their coffee cake, as we did so many times before. We toasted, and I smiled, choking up only slightly this time. We ate on the outdoor porch, watching people walk the shore path and relishing blue skies and bright sunshine.

We lingered as we did in previous years, no hurry to be anywhere, except with each other.

"There's a storm coming," said Mike, at the front desk.

I thought to myself, *It's already here—in my soul*.

Mike made his weather prediction after he heard the same from a few boat-owners he had called to find one who would take us into the bay today. He said it may be tricky to get a boat today—not only were captains and owners putting their boats away for the season but also others were prepping theirs for the storm.

Cheryl texted me during our conversation with Mike. While Mike was on the phone, she asked about whether we had found a boat to go out into the bay.

"Working on it," I replied.

"God will work it out," she responded.

Having no luck, Mike suggested I talk directly with the "Todd" Schooner owners to see whether we could get on their last afternoon cruise. Cheryl was right. Kelly, one of the owners, listened to my request and said she would see to it that the captain knew we would be aboard.

After acquiring a bottle of Pinot Noir for our cruise, I ordered a lobster roll at Testa's, where Judy and I often ate. While waiting for it, two elderly ladies entered the restaurant, with one wanting to introduce the other to her favorite waitress. She said to the waitress, "Judy, this is my dear friend, Phyllis." Judy and Phyllis! Phyllis is Judy's mother's name!

A smile crossed my lips in gratitude for this sweet reminder.

We watched as crew and guests raised the sails, and everyone applauded. We listened as diesel engines were silenced by the captain of the Bailey Louise Todd.

Our sails caught the wind, and we glided on Frenchman's Bay. Waiting just as I had over the past 40+ years for the best moment to give you gifts, I waited. The Todd was coming around, so winds would be at my back. As I waited, I read a few of Judy's favorite passages of scripture to her quietly; we chose them together for today: Psalm 91, Hebrews 12, the Rosary, and the Committal.

With the wind at my back and having raised a glass of Pinot Noir to Judy, to us, I quietly sobbed and released Judy's ashes, allowing the wind to carry her out over the waves. I watched through a curtain of tears as she flew freely and danced across her waves.

Now empty, her heart-shaped polished chrome keepsake urn reminded me of how I did not want to let go of her burial urn after the graveside service. The priest, after waiting a respectful amount of time, had reminded me gently, "Roy, it's time to let go."

After about 20 more seconds and three kisses, I gently lowered her urn into Frenchman's Bay's waves, about 100 yards from one of the Porcupine Islands.

The captain had come to stand beside me and put a rough hand on my shoulder. Then he pointed to the island straight ahead, in the direction you flew.

"That's Sheep Island," he said.

"Thank you," I whispered, realizing he told me so I would know its name. Then I chuckled, as I'm sure Judy did.

I looked at the captain. "She loved sheep."

A holy and sacred moment by Sheep Island. God smiled, for and with us. God shed a tear, for and with me.

Six o'clock dinner at a porch table at Galyn's, the place where we always ate our first dinner in Bar Harbor. Out of habit, I made the reservation for two, but now there is only one.

How does one dine alone?
    How do I dine without Judy?
    Whom do I give my maraschino cherry to?

Watching so many couples around me, how do I do this alone?

She's here, but she's not. She's not sitting across our table to laugh with, to gaze at until she tells me to stop, to hold hands with, to dream aloud with, to listen to, to adore.

It helped that I was writing in this journal, as though I was talking with her, which I suppose I was. It also helped when I asked for an extra empty wine glass and set it by her chair. It helped when I ordered crème brûlée, one of Judy's faves, with two spoons.

There was a woman at the table next to me, probably in her mid- to late 30s, also dining alone, also writing in a journal between bites of food. What was her story? Why was she alone?

No air of sadness about her. More one of contemplation or reflection. When I noticed she was leaving, I silently wished her well.

When I asked Jaime, our waitress, for my check, she told me that our dinner had been paid for "anonymously." She then confessed that it was our table neighbor. On the receipt she had written, "Wishing you peace and joy. Be well!"

I cried at this unexpected kindness from a stranger I'll never see again but will never forget. A blessed, kind, intuitive gift from an angel. Something Judy would do. Jaime touched my shoulder, telling me it was all right to cry.

This gift from a tender heart, this random act of kindness, was a model for me, something to pass on to others in the future. I am committed to honoring Judy, her "dive-in" heart, her compassion, as long as I live. Not sure how, but I will, with the help of God and Judy's spirit within me.

After dinner, I walked Bar Harbor's dark streets to avoid going back to our room alone. When at last I did, I sat on our porch beside Judy's empty chair. How do I do this with her gone?

Why, God, DID you allow her to die—and to leave me, to leave us? Why? WHY? Why couldn't we grow much older together? Why not keep her here—and healthy? So she could do more, teach more, love more, laugh more, hold us, and be held?

WHY DID THIS HAVE TO HAPPEN???

Reader's Notes

_____

_____

_____

_____

_____

_____

_____

_____

_____

_____

_____

_____

_____

_____

_____

_____

_____

_____

_____

_____

_____

2012: Genesis

JUDY: GENESIS

For many years now I have felt myself drawn to making art as a form of therapeutic expression. Study after study shows that people who are unable to communicate or articulate their emotions are able to allow them to emerge in different kinds of art.

I love art. I've dabbled in it for years, ever since my days at the Massey Fashion Institute in Atlanta, when being able to sketch and render an idea that came from within my imagination became a necessity rather than a hobby. I have tinkered and played with how this process of making art can release ideas, insights, emotions, and wisdom within.

Over about the past 10 years I've actively sought out workshops and programs that would help me better formulate what this prompting within me is trying to be. In other words, *God, where are you trying to lead me with this idea—and how can I best follow it?*

Roy and I have talked of this often. He is such an encourager and is so deeply sensitive to who I am and who I want to be in this world. I am blessed beyond words to have such a partner in this life.

For years I have felt called to help others who are facing hospice and the end-of-life transition. It is holy, sacred work that began when I cared for my sweet Aunt Ginny, who died of a horrible, aggressive, deadly form of brain cancer called glioblastoma. It was then that I entered the Wellsprings spiritual direction program.

Although Aunt Ginny wasn't sick for very long—that awful form of brain cancer hits hard and moves fast—the whole process was enough to show me this need and my particular aptitude for it.

It's not that death doesn't scare me. It does. I have a healthy fear of dying—of leaving this world and all I love within it behind—like everyone else, I suppose. It's just that when someone approaches eternity's door, it can be terrifying—and a calm, gentle, encouraging presence can go a long way toward making this transition the holy moment it is meant to be.

I witnessed it again and again in hospice workers who, noticing my interest and curiosity, took time to share thoughts, insights, and experiences with me. I am deeply intrigued about how I can and will use this experience in my own practice.

Another idea germinating in me is providing care and support to people who are facing chronic and/or debilitating illness—people who are not necessarily at the end-of-life stage with their disease or condition but those who have to cope with an escalating difficulty, day by day. Those who make the decision each and every morning to get up, get dressed, and do it for another day. To begin again, day after day, and to make the very most of the life and the ability they have left, rather than focusing on the disability and eventual death at the hands of whatever it is that has their life within its grip.

This passion, too, came about from my personal experience. When he was just a young man, Roy was diagnosed with multiple sclerosis. For about 10 years he lived with this diagnosis and the physical limitations we both knew were coming. Part of my role with him was helping him stay focused on beginning again, each day, to make the most of whatever quality time and ability he has left. Because MS can have a very slow progression that varies from individual to individual, we lived under that shadow for 10 years, just waiting for the other shoe to drop.

Miraculously, however, it didn't. Somehow, through a sequence of events I still don't fully understand, we learned that Roy had been misdiagnosed. His heart attack and other heart issues—and the testing required to diagnose and treat these things with a pacemaker, stents, and medications—somehow turned up the suspicion that he in fact did not have MS at all.

What a strange gift that was. And how it taught us how to live, really live, every moment we are given as the gift that it is. So easy to get caught up in the day-to-day and miss the miraculous in every moment we are able to remain on this earthly plane.

After making the extremely painful and difficult decision to leave my work with the church to which I had given so much time, attention, and creative energy, I found myself with a new capacity for ministry—and I continued to nurture the new ministry I felt growing within me.

The understanding dawned on me, at some point during my tenure in a different church, that our individual connection with God is what both calls each of us to and equips us for a unique ministry, as individual as we are. How we use our life to answer this call is our gift back to God to reflect our gratitude for all the blessings we are gifted with in this life.

In whatever way I am able, I now understand this call to assist people in adjusting, "beginning again," and reorienting their understanding of their end-of-life transition to help them accept this holy moment with peace and joy.

I wasn't too far into my work toward certification with Wellsprings to fully explore and develop how I would create and nurture my spiritual direction practice when I realized I wanted to offer people a place of retreat—an opportunity to unplug from their day-to-day life and focus on spiritual disciplines that would help them get in touch with God, themselves, and the voice of God within them.

Even with this decision to create and lead some sort of spiritual retreat as part of my spiritual direction practice, I knew there was still more I needed to do. As I prayed and contemplated and tried to discern this next part, I became aware of a woman named Sister Bridget, who worked in a place called the Boston Home, one of three such homes in the country, founded exclusively to care and support people living with progressive multiple sclerosis.

Becoming aware of Sister's Bridget work felt like the answer to my prayer for discernment and direction.

So I wrote her a letter. Out of the blue, just asking whether I could come and visit and perhaps "shadow her" in her work to see how she incorporates art and spiritual practices and how she makes this opportunity accessible to varying levels of ability.

"I've taken it to my committee, and we had a prayer about it," Sister Bridget wrote. "There have been many such requests, and we have never granted them, but there was something about your letter . . . and the answer is yes, come spend the day with us."

Roy was excited, for me, of course. He happened to be planning a trip to Boston for a national long-term-care convention, and now I would accompany him—and we'd be able to turn it into one of our "workcations" that were always a delightful way to mix business with fun in whatever random location the business part of the adventure called into play.

I remember rushing into our house, waving the letter from Sister Bridget, and throwing my arms around Roy, planting a loud kiss on his cheek.

He laughed. "What was that for?" he asked, pulling me close.

"They're going to let me!"

"Let you what?" he asked, leaning back a little, puzzled. "And who are 'they'?"

"Remember when I wrote to Sister Bridget at the Boston Home to see whether I could come and observe her work—shadow her for a day?"

"Yes."

"Well, the sisters, I suppose, had a *meeting* about it—apparently, they don't normally let people do that kind of thing—but for whatever reason, they decided to make an exception and let me come spend a day with Sister Bridget!"

"Well, I'd say that was very smart of them," he teased. "What do you think changed their mind? Have they heard of you?"

"I don't know!" I said, rereading the short letter from the sisters again. "They said it was 'something about my letter,' but I have no idea what that was."

"Probably that it came from *you*," Roy said, pushing my hair back and tucking it behind my left ear.

"Don't be silly," I said, rolling my eyes. "But I've been praying for some direction on this, some sort of model to follow—and I think this just might be it!"

I paused, then shrugged. "So I guess I'll be crashing your trip to Boston if that's OK with you."

"OK?" he asked, feigning incredulity. "Hmmm," he said, stroking his imaginary goatee for a ridiculously long time. "No, I'd say it's more like *spectacular*." He gathered me up in his arms. "Let's just see what kind of fun we can get into in Bean Town."

Oh, how I love that sweet, silly man.

We arrived in Boston late afternoon on the day before I was to meet Sister Bridget and the day Roy's conference began. After a lovely Italian meal in a tiny family-owned restaurant off the beaten path that our hotel concierge promised to be the most authentic Italian food this side of the Atlantic (I don't think he was wrong about that, but it bears more research and a trip to Italy, I think), we settled into our hotel room overlooking the Boston Commons, went up to the rooftop bar for a glass of port, and retired early to our wonderful hotel room Roy had sought out to make this "workcation" even more wonderful. He scoped out what's going on over the next few days in the theater district just around the corner and other restaurants and attractions to make our Boston experience complete while we're here.

After a fairly restless night (I was so excited I could hardly sleep, my mind teeming with questions I wanted to be sure and ask tomorrow), we got up early enough for breakfast together on the downstairs veranda before setting off on our separate adventures.

I took a cab to the Boston Home. I have to admit my heart began to beat a little faster as we arrived at its beautiful tree-shaded campus. What would I learn here? What new ideas and energy would become available to me after this day? Somehow, I knew it was going to be a pivotal experience.

And it was.

My visit began with a brief tour. I learned that the Boston Home, originally called the Home for Incurables, was founded in 1881 as a residential care facility for chronically ill young men and women with no place to live. Today, this visionary facility is a national model for the care of adults with advanced progressive neurological diseases, primarily multiple sclerosis.

The residents, all up and dressed and out of their rooms, were engaged in a variety of activities fit to their level of capability. Noting that the average age of its residents is 58 years old, the coordinator said, "Our mission here is to help our residents live as independently as possible."

When Sister Bridget arrived, she came with a cart filled with all kinds of expressive art tools—scarves, crayons, colored pencils, clay, sparkles, windmills—and we moved throughout the facility offering art sessions to groups and individuals. She engaged them gently and was respectful and kind regardless of their challenges.

It was easy to see that Sister Bridget really saw each person as a human being, a child of God who deserved her very best. And she gave it to them. All day long. We stopped for a few short breaks but would quickly "get back to it," as she said. It was magical to watch her use her expressive arts training in a way that helped them and brought them so much joy.

"It all feels so validating," I told Roy over dinner that evening at the little chowder place he found overlooking the Boston Harbor.

"Validating . . . how?" he asked through a mouthful of chowder. He knew. He just wanted me to articulate it. An annoying and yet endearing trait that always helps me crystalize my ideas.

I shared what I've learned and all I've done and all I've been wanting to do. "Connecting art with spiritual direction with retreats with chronic illness—it all connects here, in this work I observed today." I realized I was still holding my chowder-soaked chunk of bread, so I popped it in my mouth, chewing thoughtfully as I waited for his response.

"So you're saying," he began slowly, repeating my words back to me to further plant them into our shared consciousness, "that you're now thinking that there's a thing—a way—for you to bring together all these pieces into one mission, one overarching effort that uses creative processes to benefit others spiritually— especially, but not only, those with chronic illness. Is that pretty much it?"

"Yes," I said, smiling at the thought that popped into my head then, beckoned, of course, by this thoughtful exchange. "I want to form a nonprofit that is devoted to helping people work through their challenges, whatever they are, through art and spiritual practices."

"And what's the benefit to them?" he asked, continuing to help me jell this idea by asking questions.

"If I can use what I know as a spiritual director and somehow incorporate art and creativity, I will be able to offer them tools and practices that help them find moments of peace and joy and creative delight in every day. I want to help them make that decision every day to keep going, to keep trying, to keep creating. To begin again."

We let the silence hang between us as we finished our chowder and then pored over the dessert menu for something to split, as was our custom. It was a comfortable, thoughtful silence in which we each processed this idea and its viability—and possible impact on the lives of those this thing might be able to serve.

"Pie?" Roy said, looking up from the menu and smiling at me.

"Is that even a question?" I teased. "Of course, pie. Unless there's crème brûlée."

"Nope, no brûlée today," he quipped, grinning as he handed the menu to the server. "We'll have cherry pie, à la mode, two forks, and two coffees . . ." he looked at me, "with cream."

"I think what you have here is a wonderful idea," he said at last, reaching across the table to take my hand. "And I can't wait to see where this goes." He paused, looking deep into my eyes, my soul. "I'm just so amazed and in awe of how you can listen so deeply to God and to your own heart—and then come up with a way to serve both."

It's going to be interesting to see how all this comes together, but now that I know the path I'm on and where I ultimately want it to go, it will be at least a little bit easier to be patient, trust the process, and let each step unfold in its own time.

God, thank you for all the ways in which you're weaving together all the aspects of my work and purpose, beyond my awareness, and yet revealing each thing in its time so that I can take action and do the work you are equipping me to do.

And just like that, it was settled. In that moment in Boston, over cherry pie and with Roy's full support, my nonprofit organization, Always We Begin Again (AWBA), was born.

ART OF SPIRIT

The word "mandala" is Sanskrit for "circle" or "completion." Creating a mandala following a period of meditation is thought to be opening a window into our inner self.

From the moment I began dabbling in expressive art as a way of gaining insight into what's going on in my life, choices, attitudes, practices, relationships, and career, an enormous shift began within me. From almost the moment I began this exploration, I was drawn to the mandala for both its sacred roots and its current proven usefulness.

After learning more about this ancient tool for self-examination from Hindu and Buddhist traditions (and since adopted by many other spiritual seekers), I realized the power of this unassuming window for looking inside yourself for self-reflection, insight, accessing inner wisdom, and a deeper understanding about a situation, event, or emotion.

To my thinking—and I am by no means alone in this opinion—pairing this work with mandalas with various techniques of expressive arts could offer ever deepening layers of reflection, healing, and self-expression through the process of intentional and regular creation.

For the uninitiated, the mandala's outer circle and the repeating designs within appear simple. As an art form, it may even appear to be sort of elementary. The mandala, however, is first and foremost a tool, and even the most beautiful, intricate, and ornate mandala designs, quite obviously *also* works of art, are in fact a spiritual practice.

The crux of this simple geometric design based on a circle is that it represents the whole—and in every situation it is called upon to address, the process for creating it is as simple as it is revealing.

From my very first encounter with the mandala, I was absolutely fascinated, and I had to know more. And beyond that, I wanted to learn how to make this beautiful spiritual practice accessible to more people.

"I know which one I want to do," I told Roy one night as we sat on our porch with a glass of wine.

"Which one . . . what?" he asked, perplexed.

Roy and I are so connected that it's hard for me to remember that he's not always privy to my thoughts and up to speed on what's going on in my mind, which has been an awful lot lately.

"Expressive arts programs," I said, taking a sip. "I've looked at several really good programs, but the one I think offers the most of what I'm looking for is the one in Sarasota. Expressive Arts Florida Institute."

"Sarasota . . .Florida?" he asked. "Would you have to go there? How long a program is it?"

I laughed. "No, I'm not suggesting a long-distance relationship," I said. "It's two and a half years to get the level 1 and level 2 certification—they kind of overlap in the middle—and I'll need both if I'm going to add it to my curriculum. If I am accepted, I'll be assigned an advisor whom I'll work with via Skype to do the prep work and receive feedback. And then, there are what they call 'intensives' in January, April, and October when I'd have to go there for the course that runs Thursday through Sunday afternoon."

"I just have one question," Roy said, refilling his glass and loading another cracker with cheese. "Will you be needing a Sherpa?"

"An art Sherpa!" I replied with a grin. "I like it!" I paused. "But it's going to be four long, hard days of cramming a whole lot of material in a very small space of time," I warned. "I really won't have much time to play."

"In addition to my Sherpa duties, I'll be there as support staff," Roy replied, as if the plan was laying itself out perfectly in his own head as well. "I'll make sure you're fed and fanned, and I'll entertain myself during the days and make sure you have a good dinner and a decent bedtime each night."

"Sounds heavenly," I said, looking across at his adoring face and wondering what in the world I did to deserve this man.

"And when we're done, perhaps we could slip off to some resort down there for a couple days of R&R."

I smiled. "Perhaps we could," I said, shooting him a coy eye flutter. "A Sherpa's gotta have some reward for all his dedicated and backbreaking work."

And so it was settled. The next leg of my expressive arts journey began—and I knew it was going to be exactly what I needed to add to my offerings as a spiritual director and to lead AWBA in the direction it deserves to go.

I submitted my application the following week, along with the requisite pieces of art to the Expressive Arts Florida Institute (EAFI), excited beyond words that I was going to be able to integrate my love of making art with my deep and true calling to help those who desperately need the healing and peace this work will be able to offer.

The answer came back quickly. "I'm in!" I squealed as I read the letter that Roy had just brought in with the afternoon mail one lazy Saturday a few weeks later. "EAFI says, 'Come on down!'"

Roy put down the rest of the mail and scooped me up and twirled me in a circle. "Congratulations, my princess," he said. "I'll start gathering my Sherpa stuff!"

"You do that!" I laughed. "The first intensive is just a few weeks away!"

PART I
How to Live

Winter 2012-2013

JUDY: OVERWHELMED

As I prepare to begin this EAFI expressive arts training, and contemplate adding that to my already full to overflowing plate and the myriad of details entwined in my day-to-day life, I feel overwhelmed to the point of exhaustion.

Why am I doing this? What does it all mean? How will it connect? How can I continue to nurture my own soul while leading others to do the same?

With each step deeper into my spiritual direction, training, and exploration, the more I realize how much there is to do, to know, and to think about. Questions that continually plague me:
How will I get it all to work? How will I create a spiritual direction practice that is life giving for others? How will I continue this work at its deepest levels in a way that is also life giving for me?

Feeling agitated and overwhelmed, I need cerulean blue breath to enter and move through me. I need to slow and soften. I need to allow the swirling movement to quiet.

A PORTAL OPENING

Today finds me in a sudden and unexpected place of awareness that there is some sort of new portal opening for my work, and my task is to recognize all that surrounds it.

Still pondering this new awareness, I pick up today's lectionary reading (this has been my daily habit for as long as I can remember) from our Episcopalian denominational liturgy. The passage from Luke seemed to be speaking directly to me—and to this new awareness I've been pondering:

> *The Spirit of the Lord is on me,*
> *because he has anointed me to proclaim good news to the poor.*
>
> *He has sent me to proclaim freedom for the prisoners*
> *and recovery of sight for the blind, to set the oppressed free,*
>
> — LUKE 4:18 (NIV)

And then, a few hours later when we arrived at church for Sunday worship, I heard this same passage again; later that day Roy and I decided to visit a second worship service—and there it was once again.

Although logic dictates, of course, that this repetition was merely because the passage was from the daily lectionary, each time I heard it, I reflected a little more deeply on its bearing on my work in spiritual direction. Toward the end of the afternoon, my thoughts turned to how, through expressive arts, I might be able to, figuratively speaking, set free those who have been imprisoned by their thoughts and limiting beliefs. How might learning the tools and techniques of expressive arts help those whose outlook has become tired or jaded to see things in a new way—and free those who are oppressed by their past experiences to find hope and renewal? What good news might I be able to proclaim to the poor in spirit through art?

Finally, the deep significance of this passage—and its repetition throughout this day—dawns as a new affirmation that my upcoming studies of expressive art will create this portal for me and, through my guidance, for others to find freedom and renewal.

Meeting with my own spiritual director today—nearly a week since this insight, I was able to work more deeply with my earlier feelings and created image of "overwhelmed."

To be consistently overwhelmed with joy vs. hardship is a new thing for me. I don't know how to be in that space. My body wants to stay in that uncomfortable, burdened place.

So many ideas and possibilities are coming at me. There have been four interactions in recent months where others have said the same phrase to me: "Write a book."

Two of them were this week. That is like some very obscure, floating-on-the-horizon idea that I can't wrap my arms around.

"I am the fiery life of the essence of God."

— HILDEGARD OF BINGEN

Like so many others on this kind of spiritual path who seek a kind of poetic visionary influence for our time, I often call upon Hildegard of Bingen for inspiration, especially for finding ways to connect nature and theology.

Hildegard of Bingen, or Hildegard von Bingen, also known as Saint Hildegard, is a twelfth-century German Benedictine philosopher and Christian mystic who is considered by many to be a patron saint of musicians and writers. She has always intrigued me, as she does most others who know her story.

One Soul Petal

ONE SOUL PETAL

"But the body is the garment of the soul and it is the soul which gives life to the voice."

— HILDEGARD'S LETTER 41 TO THE
PRELATES OF MAINZ

As I reflect on the words of Hildegard of Bingen, I can't help but wonder whether, as I have always assumed, our voice informs our soul or, considering Hildegard's words, it is our soul that informs—or "gives life to"—our voice.

From the depths of the familiar, one piece of the soul makes itself known. Its light breaks through the other petals, slowly pushing its way to the surface.

~How will it reveal itself?
~What does it have to say?
~What does it need most to be nurtured and coaxed from its secret place into the world's expanse?

IN TIMES OF DRYNESS

"One who now receives my word and now refuses to accept it is like a field that is sometimes green and sometimes dried up, but this person does not perish utterly; his soul suffers hunger, but he has some greenness, though not much."

— HILDEGARD OF BINGEN, SCIVIAS III.10.4

I know that just as I experience the hunger that tells me I need to eat, God's grace will not allow me to perish in this dryness.

Even as I move back into the day-to-day work of building Always We Begin Again (AWBA), my nonprofit organization founded for people who suffer

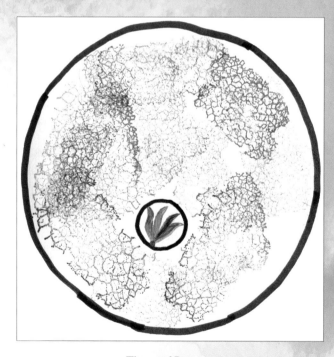

Times of Dryness

A Holy Birthing

Promise of Dawn

from chronic illness, I am also determined to continue my early-morning artistic theme with a daily observation.

Today I will intentionally try to eat the spiritual food given to me.

A HOLY BIRTHING

*"You have made everything beautiful in its time.
You have also set eternity in human hearts; yet they cannot fathom
what You have done from beginning to end."*

—ECCLESIASTES 3:11

Over the years, one of my most sustaining spiritual disciplines has been to begin each day with quiet time, often including devotional reading. Drawing first from the Episcopal church's daily lectionary, and then a reading from another text, sometimes two, I find that this almost always puts my mind in a good place to tackle whatever that day might bring.

Today this reading of Ecclesiastes 3:11 was first to greet me, and I followed it, as I often do, with Fr. Richard Rohr's devotional that today concludes with "the truth will set you free, but first it must make you miserable."

I dislike this, as I am sure every living being does. But at the same time, it does affirm my experience.

Moving on to Hildegard's Scivias, I discover an odd connection with the first two selections:

*"a person contains both likenesses of heaven and earth...
a head in which there is clarity, inspiration, and reason (and)...
the means to bring forth new life and the desire to do so..."*

—SCIVIAS II.1.2

This truth does lead me to misery sometimes. This "holy birthing" pushes into my psyche whether I want it there or not. Now that this vision is created, I can't not know it. Clarity and reason give it feet. Then it is on the move.

How are we called to make room for holy birthing?

TO STIR A NEW STORY

It's so interesting how participation in this "Promise of Dawn" movement meditation by Denise Pyles opens an expanse within me and helps me become more aware of my breath as a gentle, natural process.

When I am stretched, open, and available, my breath flows through me without effort. The promise of dawn seems to be more of a reality than a dream. There is much room now within me in which God may stir a new story.

The "Promise of Dawn" mandala is what came forth.

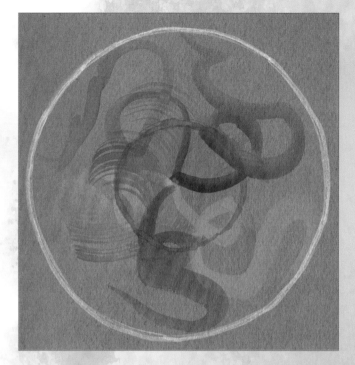

Convergence of Soul, Body, and Sense

THREE PATHS WITHIN US

"A person has within himself three paths . . .
The soul
The body, and
The senses
And all human life is led in these . . . .

The soul vivifies the body and conveys the breath of life to the senses;
body draws the soul to itself and opens the senses;
and the senses touch the soul and draw the body."

—HILDEGARD OF BINGEN, SCIVIA I 4.18

I am three in one. Soul, body, and sense, each unique with its own purpose in human life. The place where they gather, in the center, is where the greatest energy is to be found.

It can be tiring in that place, though, so I must move to the outskirts sometimes for respite. I will continue to hold all of it, all of you, in a safe place.

MORE THAN THE BODY CAN BEAR

"A person who toils more than her body can bear is rendered
useless and her spirit by ill-judged roil and abstinence,
living hopelessly and joylessly, that person's sense often fails."

—HILDEGARD'S LETTER TO ANOTHER ABBESS

The question that comes to mind first after today's reading of Hildegard's letter is: What actually happens when you "bear more than your body can bear"?

In answer, this piece of art shows how beauty becomes pressed down, all clarity and distinction gone but with color still evident.

As the final burden is placed, the colors begin to give in under the weight, and the container begins to bulge at its seams.

I don't see how clarity can be found in this tension-filled environment.

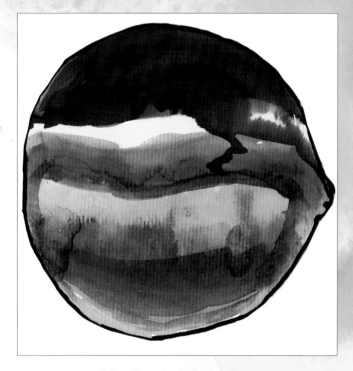

More than the Body Can Bear

THE GREENING OF THE SOUL

My creativity feels more embodied at our cottage than it does here in the city. And, even though we've created a wonderful art studio here for me that plays a significant role in our weekend "getaways" to the breathtaking natural beauty of Hide-A-Way Hills, most of my inspiration comes from sitting on our porch, walking the hills of our surrounding neighborhood, and breathing in peace and tranquility that most often elude us at home in the city.

More use of all the senses, perhaps?

In answer, I began this piece with no vision except for the strong color of oil pastels. I like swirling the colors together with the water. It looks like scarves, or ribbons, dancing in a snow globe.

Returning to my daily reading, this time in *The Book of Divine Works*, I am struck by the parallels to my earlier thoughts.

Toward the end of this day, I returned to my studio and this piece and considered anew its relevance to the feelings stirring inside me.

Innately, I suddenly realized that this creative work is not something I "do"... but rather how I allow my soul to become the "green life force" of my flesh so that I don't dry out.

These colors appear separate from the greening of the soul—and certainly distinct from the browning of the body, the earth.

"Embodied Creativity"

Using All the Senses

WALKING THE EDGES

After every period of deep contemplation, I write whatever thoughts or questions come to me, and then I move quickly into a visual creation that allows me to continue processing and building upon the insights, reflections, and deepening understanding of this sacred spiritual path I'm on.

I walk this winding path, carrying only what is essential so that my load remains light. My arms swing to and fro, dancing to the internal melody of my own voice. Although I can't see what lies ahead, I trust Spirit, who placed this path beneath my feet. I believe in who I am now and trust that even more awaits me.

Although I feel certain that harrowing challenges will be embedded in my path, I continue to walk the edges of this world. I know all too well the anxiety that can enter into the journey of "edge dwellers." Melancholy can grip your ankles, causing you to stop walking and to lose sight of the open horizon. Your breath becomes shallower and your sighs deeper.

But here's the antidote to these toxins lying in wait:

Name the experience and quickly detach from it. Reframe it. Play in the rain.

The horizon has not left me. God's path continues to pull me forward. Following God's path is my choice to make.

I will remain limp and flexible in the tornados of my day. I will release anxiety and melancholy to make room for the beauty to break through the temporary winds. I will trust the God who created both and who holds both for my eternal good.

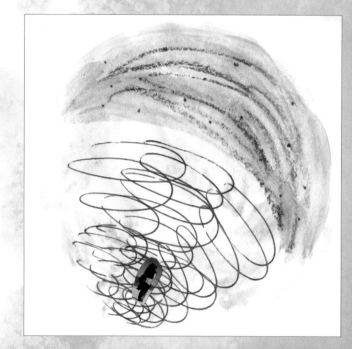

Tornadoes of My Day

LET YOURSELF BE FREE

Returning to one of my early Sarasota expressive arts exercises to play a little further with these deeper emotions I feel stirring within me. I personify them, with voice and perspective and the context of my new explorations and understandings:

Stepping my toe now into the darkest of emotional landscapes:

> *"I am doom. Melancholy and desperation are my center.*
> *They swirl and overlap in a contained center that holds*
> *an abundance of negative energy. I take from you.*
> *I do not give. As long as I can keep you in this web of confusion,*
> *you will have time for little else."*

Let Yourself Be Free

Goodness From Destruction

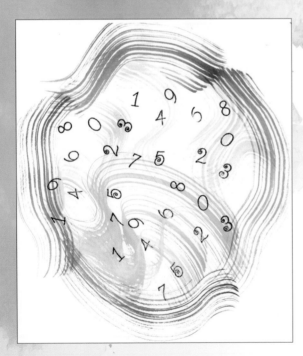

Don't Go by the Numbers

And then, as always, came both solution and reassurance:

*"I am Salvation, Hope, and Heavenly Joy.
I nurture and sustain you through those times of negativity.
I call forth goodness from the destruction brought about in
the tornado of negative thought. I will keep you moist and healthy.
Let me regenerate your soul and slow the tornado to gentle movement."*

*"[Virtues] are the antidote to sin,
because they have the might to make anything whole.
They nurture and sustain the world, and they bear all things.
Everything on earth steeps in the moisture of the virtues
and is made strong in the same way that the soul
makes the body moist and healthy, regenerating it."*

— HILEDGARD OF BINGEN, *THE BOOK OF LIFE'S MERITS*

Continuing this expressive arts exercise, I now personify the virtues, creating art to help express their insights:

"I am Wisdom, the circling encompassing energy of Mother God.
I am Strong as earth and light as air.
I am Expansive as a horizon.

I understand that you desire the seeming safety of a formula—steps that flow in a predictable sequence. Where is the joy and magic in that?

Let yourself be moved. Let yourself be free. Trust the process. You think you know how the numbers align . . .

You don't."

THE LIVING FOUNTAIN

Today, as always, the blank page reminds me that sometimes just showing up is all it takes to let loose the creative flow:

Returning now to my EAFI journal to see what further might come of it following my series on the virtues and the darkness, I run right into yet another "trust the process" moment.

Sitting down with the blank page, today I do not want to create anything. I feel blank. Totally void of a creative idea.

Returning to the words of Hildegard of Bingen, I am immediately overwhelmed with the sum of emotions expressed in my previous pieces, and then, suddenly, I feel compelled to create yet another piece along this theme.

Feeling the elation of my own Living Fountain breaking through, I joyfully created this mandala of love, wisdom, and humanity (that carries it all into the darkness) to complete the final work in this series.

BEING PRESENCE IN THE DARKNESS

Continuing my reflection on this piece later in the day, I am struck by how it expresses my own emotional landscape.

This is backbreaking work that I do. I'm bent over much of the time, praying for strength while providing plenty of breathing space and leaning space for the other.

And the other is usually bigger than me. Although I can't see it, I feel its larger presence around me.

Contemplating the meaning of this imagery, I look again—and I see that it is not actually leaning on me . . . there is space between us. Is it Spirit's space?

I listen now with all my senses and intuitive discernment attuned for the answer.

Spirit provides the cushion; Spirit provides the presence. I can relax into this pose. While this relaxed pose can protect, lift, and hold the other, I do not do it alone. Spirit enfolds both of us. Spirit keeps us steady while her healing movement works its wonder and mystery.

After taking a short break to rejuvenate and contemplate this further, I return to these pages to finish this entry with a new statement of being:

This need not be backbreaking work. I am not as much carrying the Other as simply being a presence in the darkness.

CAST YOUR BURDENS

"Cast your burden upon the Lord and he will sustain you;
he will never let the righteous stumble."

—PSALMS 55

In contemplating my scripture reading this morning, I can't help but relate it back to my own life—my own burdens, the day-to-day worries that are all part of this life—full, complicated, messy, and very heavy some days.

Following my inner prompt to create an expressive art piece to more thoroughly process this idea of casting burdens upon the Lord, I needed to depict this image of "casting."

The Living Fountain

Spirit Provides the Cushion

Cast Your Burdens

I send my burdens out to the Lord, out to the Trinity. I am still a companion to the hardship, but the bulk of the load is carried by God, not by me.

I settle back, allowing my thoughts and emotions about this burden casting to intermingle. My heart sits open and receptive to God's light shining down on me. It is in the act of casting my burdens that I am sustained and have space in which to receive.

As we remove this junk—these burdens—from our hearts and our life, we create empty space and can receive whatever God wants to put in its place.

Feeling like a child who had finally worked a difficult puzzle, I sigh a huge sigh of relief as I reach the point of all this wandering, exploring, reflecting, and contemplating I've been doing lately.

We cannot receive what God has planned for us if our space is full of burdens.

STOP. BREATHE. BE.

I was so weary from setting up blogs and Flickr groups for AWBA. With my eyes tired and brain fried, I forced myself to drop it all for an hour and drive to the Franklin Park Conservatory in Columbus.

Once at Franklin Park, I found myself waiting in line with a multitude of clamoring children. Seeing the tranquil escape I imagined evaporating, I entered with greatly lowered expectations, and yet I still found a sanctuary in the orchid garden—and a man playing guitar.

Thank you, God. Stop. Breathe. Be.

SARASOTA
THE BEGINNING

Just arrived at the Expressive Arts Florida Institute (EAFI) in Sarasota with no idea of what to expect. Its literature promised that the certificate training it offered in "six weekends and Skype" will fully equip me to tap into the "positive power of creativity for personal, professional and social change."

My goal in all of this, of course, was to add expressive arts—art therapy— to what I could offer others through retreats and spiritual direction. And in order to fully open this world for others, I first needed to open it for myself.

Stop. Breathe. Be.

ROY: SARASOTA

We arrived in Sarasota today for Judy's intensive in expressive art at EAFI. It's so much fun watching her arrive, giddy, and then willing herself to settle in, to center herself for the upcoming days of exhausting and exhilarating work ahead.

This is such an amazing process to watch, to be part of. Judy's settling in on the use of art as a way of encouraging self-expression and spiritual growth is the clearest example I've ever seen of finding one's calling.

My role here is clear, and it's one that I relish. As this fascinating world opens to her, bit by bit, I am here for her, to help keep her steady, focused, open, and settled with quiet company, good, nourishing food, scenic breaks (I touch the dog-eared guidebook in my pocket as I made a mental note of supplies I need to gather while she's in class for tomorrow's beach picnic).

Just enough of a break to give that whirling mind a rest but not so much as to distract or deter. That will be my dance for the next four days, and I feel like I've trained for this in all of the time we've spent together so far! If this is Judy's mountaintop experience, I want to be right there beside her, drinking in the view of what she sees and of her seeing it.

JUDY: SARASOTA
THE WORK

Over the course of this two and a half year process of discernment and training curriculum, I will move steadily toward this certification. Between the four-day intensives in Sarasota, there will be classwork via Skype and individual work from home in Ohio.

Through official and unofficial prompts of this work, I will explore at great depths the inner landscape that tends to blossom under the care of spiritual direction and training.

"Who am I?" prompts will ask me to ask myself, over and over. Each exercise, each answer in a new context will reveal a new layer. The goal of all this, of course, is for me to coax my deepest essence to the surface, emerging onion-like, paper-thin layer by paper-thin layer.

Excited, a little nervous, and ready to begin this new journey.

I AM PHYSICAL

I am both energy and passion. I am peace and gentle movement. I feel the tension of carrying both:

~   energy and passion that keep me moving and stretching and

~   peace and gentleness that keep me soft and balanced.

What I need is to remember the value of both and the support that each provides the other.

IF I WERE:

~   a kind of water .... The soft, fluid aqua of Gasparilla

~   a physical sensation............. Soft, flowing breath

~   a geography .... Lush, deep, embracing forest

~   a body part.......................... Hands

~   a piece of furniture............. A large, soft chair

~   a flavor .... Honey

I AM EMOTION

I travel within a sea of circumstances, sometimes barely holding on to the life I believe I know.

~   Some pieces are pleasant and peace filled;
others come at me unexpected, with sharp edges that hurt.

~   I feel small, almost like it could all totally engulf me;
what I need is to stop fighting so deeply as though I am in control.

~   I need to lie back and fix my gaze on the ever-changing horizon.

IF I WERE:

~   an emotion.......................... Exuberant

~   an instrument...................... Harp

~   an artform........................... Dance

~   a season.............................. Spring

~   a way of moving .... Unhurried, with intention

~   a scent................................ Lavender

I am bursting forth with energy from a grounded place.

I AM CREATIVE

I am feet moving to a melody created by God uniquely for me. I am color and fluid movement. I am scarves floating in rhythm to my inner music. I am paintbrush, clay, chalk, and watercolor. I am poetry. I am outward expression of a landscape words cannot capture. I feel both contained and free.

What I need is a sanctuary in which to learn how to express all that has been unsaid and unhurried time in which to explore the creative depths of my soul.

IF I WERE:

~ A gemstone .... Aquamarine

~ An animal .... Lamb

~ A time of day .... Twilight

~ A tree .... Weeping willow

~ An element .... Water

~ A climate............................. Crisp

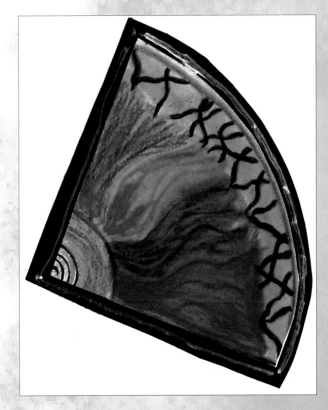

I Am Creative

I AM SPIRITUAL

I am life's energy pulsing through barriers to share God's light.

I am perpetual motion coming from the Source.

I feel fearless.

What I need is to anchor to the source and places and people to accept this healing gift of Spirit.

IF I WERE:

~ A fairy tale .... Cinderella

~ An historical period .... '60s

~ A mystical creature .... Unicorn

~ Weather .... Warm and balmy

~ A tool .... Screwdriver

~ A liquid .... Water

As I worked my way through these prompts, I also tried to imagine, to visualize not only what they were awakening within me but also what they could open up within others.

I know that in discovering again and again how the "I am" within each of us is anything that brings peace and creativity, I am so excited to be able to learn anew how to immerse and revel in my own uniqueness—and at the opportunity to learn how to teach others to tap into this amazing gift that lies, too often buried, deep within all of us.

Dormant, unsuspected, quietly present, it waits for us to do this joyful discovery. With every step of my own journey here, I am excitedly making plans for how I will incorporate this work into my own day-to-day life—and show others how to access this potential within themselves and their own lives.

ALWAYS HELD

This interplay between my emotions, writing, and art making seem to have found a flow of its own, and I'm grateful!

Working steadily—sometimes feverishly—to complete my "home" assignments before the second EAFI intensive session. As I contemplate all that this recent work has uncovered and conveyed—and how with this flow has come a new feeling of calm settled-ness—I struggle with how to adequately express this newness I feel coming into my life and awareness.

What is it, exactly?

I feel the words coming, so I grab a pen and set them free onto the page, allowing them to tumble out, more or less on their own:

I am the greening of your life. I have been nurtured and held within as you claimed your authentic self until the time came for me to push into your world.

I am always amazed when the words come this way; phrases come forth fully formed without thought or intervention from me. I want to wonder where they are coming from, but I think deep down I know. But is this really real?

As if in answer, the words begin to flow again, and again I release them onto the page:

You may not feel that I am anchored, but I assure you that my roots are deep. You don't see them, so you must work to remember that you are always held.

Always held.

Is this how art and writing flow and work through me? Are the images now springing forth all part of this "greening" within me? Again my pen lets its ink flow into new words on the page, as if the art tucked deep within me is speaking to my soul.

As I receive air in which to breathe, I become more expressive. Reaching into the unknown, I am certain of finding a new container.

This word tumult continues, and there is no time for thought as I concentrate only on getting them onto the page.

I am the red womb that has held you for so long. The denseness of my energy has shaped and nurtured you for new life. I will continue to nourish you in hidden ways. Your past story is an anchor, but it is not the whole of your present and your future.

After what seemed like hours but was, in reality, only a few minutes of furious scribbling, the thoughts had continued to tumble out, one upon the other. Then they stopped. It wasn't until I put my pen down, sat back for a moment, stretched my arms, shook my writing hand, and wiggled my fingers that I realized how tightly I have been gripping this pen.

What does all this mean? What is it that I need to do with these observations and newfound knowledge?

I feel the words beginning to arise within me once again:

I am the lavender unknown of what is to come. As you reach toward me and test me in small ways, you will come to learn the rhythm of living in my creative container. I do not hold you as the womb holds. I receive. I provide breathing space. I move along with you. This is a new way of being "contained." Live into it. Trust.

A SPIRIT OF PEACE

*"Acquire the Spirit of Peace
and a thousand souls
around you will be saved."*

—ST. SERAPHIM OF SAROV

The rock invites me to recognize that my light shines through the ordinary. In my stillness, light is seen and experienced by others.

I conclude my "settling session" by returning my attention to the words and knowledge of St. Seraphim of Sarov, a nineteenth-century Russian monk best known for the example he set in humility and kindness to both people and animals. St. Seraphim's holy way of living seems to be a perfect reflection for this day and my entry into my own sacred time here in Sarasota.

Live into It. Trust.

Spirit of Peace

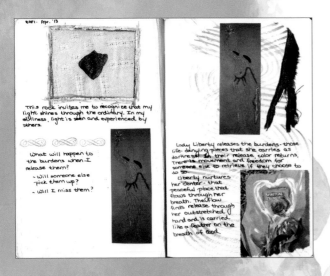

HOW DOES YOUR GARDEN GROW?

Playing off my recent musings and journaling, I feel a new piece of art beginning within me.

"Liberty, how does your garden grow?"

The answer arrives quickly:

My garden grows when I put on my boots and immerse deeply in the space that nurtures. I feel secure in my footing. I stay still and in contact with the earth. I trust the new life coming forth and that no growth will happen through the stillness of just being. I sense the fullness of breath when I am not straining.

In more poetic fits and starts, new words and thoughts arise. I will try to emulate this strange arrival in how I record them:

> "Trusting the movement within
> requires a lot of trust.
> My instinct
> is to move outwardly."

After sitting quietly with these words, I wait, as I have learned to, with an expectant listening with all of my senses. Sure enough, thoughts arrive, ready for their tumble onto the page:

It is a process on its own time line. You are reframing your backstory, and that cannot be rushed. It is moving through you and returning in a new way. You must remain still while that occurs—boots on and firmly planted.

I see you gazing at me and breathing in life
> I feel complete and grounded in my truth

I imagine
> you taking
> me in fully
> to meet
> the
> richness
> of the
> expansive
> horizon
> that
> awaits
> you.
> Will
> you say, YES?

Moving now to my sketchbook, pastels, and colored pencils, I immerse in expression of this "Lady Liberty" imagery that has now come to me in hovering flashes, layers of expression, like the words before them, now tumbling, one upon the other.

I see:

~ a bungalow sanctuary firmly planted within the elements

~ a garden and land in which to breathe

~ boots appropriate for the task at hand, ready for anything—confident and prepared

~ out of the earth, greening and life

~ burdens acknowledged and released

~ burdens transformed to color and vibrancy returned in a new way

~ spiritual promise holding the center, embracing dark and light

~ curly bright hair released

~ a hand releasing energy

~ a face in repose

FULLY AND HUMBLY PRESENT

I want to remember this day. It is a near-perfect spring morning, offering me an unexpected pause in a life that often feels too full of have-to and must-do.

The slowly warming temperatures, the brilliant sunshine, the cloudless cerulean blue sky. I want to remember thrusting my face into the heady scent of lilacs. I want to remember relocating my watercolors outside to sit in the quiet and paint nature's colors. I want to remember a day with no "have-to" on my agenda and no urgent emails that break the spell.

Amazing Grace.

I need to remember this day because yesterday was very hard, spent sitting in a darkened room surrounded by medical smells and blaring TVs as a gentle mother of four transitioned to God's kingdom after her 86-year journey.

The paradox is not lost on me.

In my 15 years volunteering at a hospice facility in central Ohio, I have often sat with people and their families as they navigated end-of-life experiences and emotions.

I think of this work as a sacred opportunity—holy ground—and I love giving patients gentle baths, reading to them, holding their hands in silence, and experiencing the honor of being with them when they transition to God's arms.

As I contemplate the contrast of these two very different—and yet equally grace-filled—days, I first think holding these experiences at once feels impossible. Then I realize that is not what I'm created to do.

Fully and Humbly Present

Remember this Beautiful Spring Morning

Creating Space

Yesterday, I was fully, painfully, and humbly present. Today, I am fully, joyfully, and humbly present. Even though I've lived this truth many times, every once in a while God gives me a front-row experience of the extremes of both/and.

HOLDING A CREATIVE BREATH

Sitting in my studio on another beautiful mid-May morning, I feel paralyzed, empty of knowing what to paint, draw, or read. I've pulled several different books from my shelves, waiting for one of them to draw my attention, to speak to me in some way that might spark inspiration, direction, something "to do."

As I look at my books on these shelves, I am quickly overwhelmed. I want to know it all and retain it now . . . but I know I need to commit to just one.

After just sitting with this feeling for a time, I began to allow my mind to play along its banks. I pondered the creative process with new awe, its elusive grasp, unexpected arrival, then sudden disappearance—like smoke.

I pick up my pen and write a poem, "Creating Space."

PARADOX

I am beginning to incorporate some of my Sarasota coursework into retreats centered on spirituality and creativity, and I can't help but notice a strange paradox.

In the midst of leading the creativity retreat "Praying in Color" with the church, I noticed that when I'm leading others, my own creative expression seems to go silent.

So instead of studio time, I have been engaged in spring gardening, which is also a creative outlet for me.

And then today, with our AWBA equine-assisted learning retreat canceled due to the death of one of the horses, I spent an unexpected day with Roy at the Stratford Ecological Center instead.

Unexpectedly, I felt refreshed.

It was a perfect rainy, muddy, sloppy day . . . awesome.

SOUL PURPOSE

After capturing a fleeting thought image in a quick sketch this morning, I take a moment to reflect on the interplay I'm noticing between circumstances, God, and purposeful work.

The image was of a boat skimming the waves, rising upward, somewhat oblivious to the darkness that resides far beneath the surface. The boat does not seem in distress. And although the darkness is present, it seems to be abiding within boundaries.

Allowing this imagery and its thought reflections to continue to unfold, I now see pink plumes arising from the boat.

Love, compassion, joy?

The plumes far exceed the boat's boundaries. Perhaps they are energized and awakened by the boat's movement. If it were not rocking so much, I envision that the pink would simply slosh over the boat's sides to become one with the water rather than released in the world.

The waves, I think, are my life's circumstances; the boat is my God. The plumes are my life's work—my soul's purpose.

Soul Purpose

DEVISE A NEW DAWN

Tonight, the perennial question, "What do I do when I can't sleep?" brings to my mind the whimsical yet stirring words of American poet, filmmaker, and playwright James Broughton, who was part of the San Francisco Renaissance movement, a precursor to the Beat poets.

In response to this brief time with Broughton's "Little Sermons of the Big Joy," I use this unexpected awake time for my own creative expression of this sentiment.

Devise a New Dawn

Summer 2013

JUDY: NOT A DOING PLACE

After each Sarasota intensive, Roy and I always spend a weekend of R&R on Gasparilla Island, which is one of a string of barrier islands along Florida's southwest Gulf Coast. Bordered by the Gulf of Mexico, Charlotte Harbor, Little Gasparilla Pass, and Boca Grande, this historic getaway of white sand beaches and natural beauty was always a perfect place to unwind, process, and just relax and be.

This island is not a doing place. Even the blue heron that caught my attention just now stands still. The robin sitting on four blue eggs outside our second-floor bedroom window—sitting still.

Waiting for the Answer

I breathe deeply here, and I allow myself to consider deeply this unique intersection of urgency and tranquility where I, too, seem to be waiting.

All around me, I see waiting. Can I wait? Or must I often be stirring waters?

I pray to be still.
I pray to listen.
I pray to wait.
I pray to not anticipate doom around every corner.

Then my thoughts open my eyes to a new realization:

Our cottage is not a "doing place" either.

BETWEEN STILLNESS AND WORRY

Waiting on the covered porch of our cottage for friends to arrive for an extended visit, I focus my attention on the gentle rainfall.

Thunder rumbles in the distance, and I am suddenly aware of the tension between enjoying this delicious stillness and worrying about losing electricity in the coming storm. (The electricity worry is compounded by my realization that our commode's capacity to flush depends on it.)

A SIMPLE SWING

For me, journaling is a spiritual discipline. As is being in nature.

I am filled with deep joy during morning walks, often with Roy, through our Hide-A-Way Hills outdoor sanctuary, sitting on our porch, or just taking a moment to pause and breathe deeply wherever I happen to be when nature's beauty surrounds and engulfs me.

During this morning's walk at Inniswood Park I was overwhelmed by beauty at every turn, as if to remind me that worry and anxiety have no permanent home in this world. Need to remember that those emotions are nothing more than an invitation to gratitude each time their clouds hover over me.

I desire to be on this simple swing daily, drifting back and forth among tall grasses, flowers, and sunshine. I desire to be aware of all that surrounds me—and of its temporary nature that carries an eternal perspective.

I don't journal every day, where the mundane and the whining can easily take over. For me, the journal is a place to hold my emotions, my wonder, my questions, and my gratitude. Each one of my journals is very different in design, chosen individually or gifted to me by someone who knows my practice, and each one usually holds about six months of observations and gratitude, to be revisited whenever I need a spark of joy or inspiration.

It is often difficult to bring a journal to a close. It's always so amazing to see all that has been created, wondered, questioned. There's also deep uncertainty in opening the blank pages of the next journal. What will it hold?

Like the Rumi poem "Guest House," each of my journals are guest houses—places to hold and keep my thoughts, reflections, and emotions that have arisen in its time. I need this reminder—it all belongs and helps me to God.

WHAT BRINGS YOU PEACE?

Lately in my expressive art journals I've been focusing on identifying things that evoke certain emotions—and then expressing that emotion through a piece of art created around that representative thing.

This image is a favorite stop, a simple garden shed on the property. What is truly amazing is that I sketched it myself. My confidence grows, not so much with my artistic ability but with my capacity to capture, in an image, the essence of emotion—in this case, what brings me peace.

Capturing these moments of awareness around objects that could then became art is a new facet of my practice—a spiritual discipline in presence and intent.

Objects of interest could be a large event such as Lilyfest (an annual celebration of flowers, art, and music in the Hocking Hills of southeast Ohio that was a yearly day of respite for Roy and me). Or as small as a single moment sitting with Roy and taking in the beauty of the Porcupine Islands in Frenchman's Bay during one of our frequent visits to Bar Harbor, Maine.

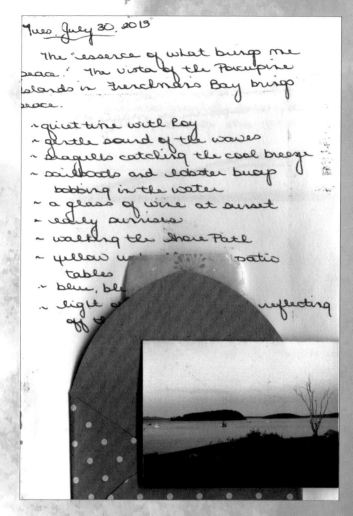

What Brings Me Peace

CASTLE DWELLING

The daily lectionary today was Psalm 71, which I then segued into watching a short video on sandcastles for my morning devotional.

Then I took my daily walk to let my mind sift and blend these ideas and images into inspiration for a new piece of art.

I spent most of the afternoon, into early evening, on the castle image. It took me a while to settle on a concrete way to express this blend of ideas and inspirations—with the addition of a garden angel.

I like the organic process of following some of the video in the background. I also like the messiness and free form of all this art. It develops its own way, with no right or wrong. It is unique—and all mine.

Stepping back from this piece now to reflect a bit on its message, the words come to me:

> *I long for this safety. I believe I sense it often,*
> *yet it can seem just out of reach—or not enough at times.*
>
> *When I feel safe, I suspect I carry a set of angel wings in some form.*
> *And of course, my angel self wears her yellow boots*
> *that allow her to navigate nasty terrain without injury.*

Perhaps "castle dwelling" is a state of mind—internal preparedness while trusting that the wings and boots are always available.

Castle Dwelling

DAYTIME DREAMING

The Glenlaurel Inn, located in Hocking Hills, is a special place of retreat for us—a place where Roy and I go to rejuvenate, to refresh, and to reconnect.

Michael, the innkeeper, often takes time to share with his guests something important within him, like a book reading, song, quote, or piece of poetry.

Today, I am remembering our intimate dinner there on Christmas night of 2000, when Michael shared this reading:

> *"All men dream: but not equally.*
> *Those who dream by night in the dusty recesses of their minds*
> *wake up in the day to find it was vanity,*
> *but the dreamers of the day are dangerous men,*
> *for they may act their dreams with open eyes, to make it possible."*

> —T.E. LAWRENCE (LAWRENCE OF ARABIA),
> *SEVEN PILLARS OF WISDOM: A TRIUMPH*

I remember today how this reading evoked my sudden realization: "I AM a daytime dreamer," I heard myself declare to no one in particular. "And I will value that."

People so often forget to value things within themselves that are part of who they are. It is important, I think, to declare, even if only to yourself, those parts of yourself that feel somehow valuable. To say, "I am an artist; I am a chef; I am a wood-carver—and I will value that."

I felt compelled to revisit those Christmas Day 2000 journal pages, and when I did so, I couldn't help but smile at this sweet memory—and all that has happened in the past 12 and a half years.

At that time Roy and I were frequent visitors to Glenlaurel Inn, dreaming often of spending more time in this refreshing, renewing environment of Hocking Hills.

As I turned these pages to immerse myself in these sweet memories, I continued to smile, this time with the realization that since that visit—and those "daytime dreams"—we have made those dreams come true, buying our little Sunrise Ridge cottage and now considering a full-time move to this region that first evoked our deep dreaming so many years ago.

In the midst of the dreamings, however, there have also been significant losses and deep pain. There were the dark days of Roy's MS diagnosis, his heart attack, the death of our grandparents, releasing our son to adulthood and him being more than two years on the other side of the world, and the death of my father from prostate cancer.

Yet, in all of it, lightness and dark, joy and tragedy, there is an inner peace and contentment that companion the hardship.

I think part of what feeds dreams is a safe childhood. I remember the backyard of Meadow Lane in the summers, when Grandma McGuire would hang laundry to dry. I especially remember sheets blowing in the wind—and what seemed like hundreds of white square handkerchiefs hanging on the line to dry.

This brings to mind another memory from a quite different time, a warm, sunny day when I was grown and married and had a young son. My other grandmother, Grandma Delaplane, had moved to a street behind my parents, and we were walking through their backyard for a visit.

The piece of art I created from this memory is by no means a perspective-correct image, but it's one I know in perfect detail in my mind's eye, and it warms my heart.

Thank you, God, for my family that loved me into existence.

Daytime Dreaming

Fall 2013

JUDY: A ZENTANGLED CABIN IN THE WOODS

Just after we made the decision to move to Hocking Hills full time, we spent two days celebrating our thirty-sixth anniversary in the small dwelling we had just found and purchased there. We decided to call it "Sunrise Ridge."

I eagerly await this full-time sanctuary, and this deep excitement is what prompted me to create this piece I will call "A Zentangled Cabin in the Woods."

A Zentangled Cabin in the Woods

ROY: A COTTAGE IN THE MAKING

I remember that pivotal phone call well.

"There's a small cabin that is just about to be listed that might be something like what you're looking for," the realtor announced one sunny morning. "It's not listed yet, but I can show it to you today if you're free."

Judy and I looked at each other across the breakfast table.

"I'm free," she said, smiling at me, green eyes picking up the early morning light in a way that was so mesmerizing I nearly forgot what we were considering.

"Uh, yeah! Me too!" I said finally, grinning. The puzzled look on her face made this moment all the sweeter.

So we followed the realtor's directions through winding, up-and-down scenic beauty of the aptly named Hide-A-Way Hills, a private community in the breathtaking Hocking Hills of Ohio.

After Judy entered the cottage, turned around once, came out onto the porch and declared, "I'm home," and we put in our offer.

Fast-forward just a bit, and the quaint cottage in Hide-A-Way Hills was ours. "Sunrise Ridge," she decided to call it during an early-morning inspection prior to purchase, when we had just watched the most spectacular sunrise either of us had ever seen.

Now it was time to start talking about the remodeling we'd need to do to begin the gradual process of first building Judy's retreat center and then creating a homey respite from our busy life for our own retreats. Quietly, we both hoped this would evolve to eventually living at the cottage full time. So whatever decisions we make now will have to have that endgame in mind so we can build toward it.

I buttered my toast and looked across the table at my beloved, enjoying the ways her eyes glistened with excitement as she verbalized thoughts and plans that had been whirling around in her head over the past few days.

That's the way I think. Judy is more aligned with the here and now and the aesthetics of what we want to do. Which is fine with me. I think that's part of what makes us such a good team. We appreciate and love many of the same things, but sometimes for different reasons. And at the precise spot where Judy's greatest strengths kick in, we see my talents, interest, and abilities fall away. And vice versa. Nothing will put her to sleep faster than a solid explanation of the special and amazing insights a spreadsheet reveals.

Judy leaned forward across the table, scarcely able to contain herself. "So here's what I was thinking for that porch on the front," she began, taking a quick sip of tea before launching into her vision.

"We'll screen it in and orient it toward the east so we can sit out there with our coffee and watch that glorious sunrise every morning," she said. "We'll get us a couple of cute but comfy chairs, and at night, it will be the best spot for having a glass of wine and watching the stars and fireflies and . . ." She trailed off, imagining it. Imagining us. And the way she described it, I saw it, too, *our* porch, *our* ravine, *our* sunrises, *our* nightly star show.

"Oh, Roy, we're going to be so happy there," she said. "It's going to be our place, so us, through and through. Our own little slice of heaven on earth!"

I did not doubt that for a moment.

JUDY: SEEING BEYOND THE TANGLE

I'm now deep in my expressive arts curriculum and preparing for the next intensive session in Sarasota. We're also in the process of expanding/remodeling our cottage. AWBA is also gaining exciting new traction in providing spiritual resources to people with a chronic diagnosis and their care supporters. I feel both overwhelmed and often confused. Which of these clamoring priorities should receive which increasingly smaller slices of my time and attention?

AN EXHILARATING, SACRED ADVENTURE

Roy and I arrived in Sarasota a day early, deliberately, to help me get settled in before my fourth expressive arts intensive began—also so I would be able to enjoy this environment when I'm not exhausted.

I also wanted to take time to reflect more deeply on the uniqueness of this opportunity and its associated journey. Once we were settled into our hotel room, we walked the beach of Siesta Key and then Anna Maria Island at sunset.

One thing is for sure: these expressive arts intensives were aptly named. These sessions involved body, emotions, meditations—every sense of each participant. To say it was rigorous—and exhausting—and exhilarating—was a dramatic understatement.

I am always amazed and grateful for all the ways, large and small, that Roy watches over and supports me as I pour so much energy into learning, growing, exploring, and discovering how expressive arts opens and nurtures. He likes to say that his firsthand observing of this environment of thoughts, creativity, and soul-generated experiences is "an exquisite, sacred adventure to witness." What an amazing man. What a gift he is to me and to all the lives I will be able to touch with this work.

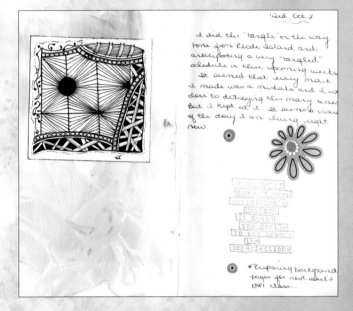

Tangle

ROY: SARASOTA ART SHERPA

I take my work as Judy's Sherpa very seriously. I have a system now, for transporting supplies, both for her art classes and for our "shore excursions" where I drag her off for a needed break. I've learned and refined my list of picnic spots on the beach, alfresco dining, walking trails, and other delights I discover talking to locals while Judy is in class and I'm out exploring on my own.

Her training is intense. If anyone wonders how spending all day making art can be so grueling, they should try one of these days. In addition to physical exhaustion of long hours, mental exhaustion of lectures, and theory behind seemingly simple creation of expressive art lies spiritual fatigue that always sets in on about the third day.

It's a sort of overload, I suppose, like too much ice cream. I can always sense it in her when it arrives. A deep weariness settles over her. She walks more slowly, shoulders more forward, sighs deeper, as if she's trying to expel the excess.

That's where I come in. I have curated a variety of places, activities, and vibes to offer Judy good and meaningful restful breaks—just the right amount of distraction, stimulation, and relaxation.

She loves it—and me, for the amount of effort I'm putting into being the "Sherpa with Benefits," as she laughingly called me the other day.

Bookmark, EAFI #120

Front Cover, EAFI #120 Book

JUDY: WAKE UP!

The message for me at the midway point of this EAFI intensive is "WAKE UP." To what? How? Just as quickly as I hear these words as if spoken aloud to me, I knew these were things yet to be discovered.

A GENTLE PRESENCE TO SELF AND OTHERS

Just as quickly as it began, the official end of this EAFI intensive is upon us. Bittersweet.

They always ask each of us to write our own closing remark for each session based on a final question from the presenter:

What do you now claim as your own, following or resulting from or prompted by your work in this intensive session?

What I claim is a gentle presence to myself and to others.

To fully absorb and experience a deep understanding of all the lessons of this intensive mean to me—and to my life's purpose—will take a while longer, perhaps even a lifetime.

And while being a gentle presence to *others* comes more or less naturally to me, the idea of being a gentle presence to *myself* poses a new and thought-provoking challenge.

BLISS

\Bliss\ : **1. Great happiness: joy. 2. A state of extreme happiness (syn: blissfulness, cloud 9, seventh heaven, walking on air)**

"Bliss" describes this past week. Even as we arrived home today, I was still riding high on the elation of this intensive experience. It was as close to perfection as possible in this human life.

I also have an increasing comfort here, cruising the edge. Stunning sunsets, good food, restful sleep with my beloved. I am returning to the full life left behind seven days ago with the addition of papers to write as I process all of this. One step at a time, moving in the true direction.

STAND STILL

Today I feel lost, mired, deep in the midst of my own feeling of being overwhelmed in the face of cabin construction, AWBA, spiritual direction, and, then, just *life*. Home and family always at the forefront for me, but they always feel somehow on the edge of neglect.

Whenever I "scramble," I become lost. There's a sense of being disoriented. I am prone to lostness now. With so much uncertainty swirling around, what does it mean for me to stand still in all this new life that is unfolding?

Having this creative outlet is so life-giving for me; it may be one way I can stand still. It keeps me tethered to the moment and in the process of life.

I look through my art journals and am a bit stunned that all of their content came through me. So now I know for sure that creative things can burst forth from some mysterious place—but only when I stand still.

Stand Still

Bliss

FEEDING THE MUSTARD SEED

"If you have faith the size of a mustard seed,
you will say to this mountain
'move from here to there' and it will move.
Nothing will be impossible for you."

—MATTHEW 17:20

Reflecting on this daily reading—one of my most beloved scriptures—I can only say that this is something I must often be reminded of.

With the flurry of the past months now pretty much over, new opportunities are, as if on cue, beginning to reveal themselves. I can do more than I believe I can, but I must be even more intentional and must have "art days" scattered throughout.

It All Belongs

Reader's Notes

Winter 2013-2014

JUDY: LEAVE THE DARKNESS BEHIND

"Do you know what time it is, how it is now the moment for you to wake from sleep . . .
let us then lay aside the works of darkness and put on the armor of light."

—ROMANS 13:11–14

This verse from the daily lectionary reminds me of the message I received during my last Sarasota EAFI intensive.

Leaving the Darkness Behind

I WONDER:

What does it mean for me to "wake from sleep"?

How does this fit with my own message, the admonition from my own soul to WAKE UP?

After waiting for a moment, just listening, I know the words to express the desire now rising within me:

"I desire to live more fully in the light, leaving the darkness behind."

God's River

GOD'S RIVER

The launching point of my self-discovery—a whispering of God into my heart—came several years ago, before I began EAFI, before I founded AWBA.

It emerged during my first weekend of studying/discovering mixed-media arts. This was a weekend of being released, of releasing myself, and of hearing God whisper, "Judy, WE have things to do together . . . Let's go!"

From that moment forward, I knew I was in God's river, flowing with wherever the river would go, through unexpected twists and turns, wide expanses, and narrow, treacherous waters.

Rapids and calm, current and stillness, daybreak and dusk all belonged to the river, and all became my context for the flow of my life and work and experiences.

To follow and to stay in the meandering course of God's river requires continuous deep listening through prayer, meditation, journaling, and, of course, art to stay in contact, to feel the flow, to keep myself centered and pliable enough to withstand, relish, appreciate, and embrace whatever will come next.

The piece of art that emerged to begin my day today wasn't a blank canvas for very long. Using only my fingers, I began to depict my experience of being in God's river. The glossy high solid gel of the flow shows the non-effort lightness of being in that place. It was then ready for more. It became the Exodus. Stones from the shores of Lake Michigan propelled me to the beaches of the Gulf Coast. It's the metaphor of the journey of sea glass.

NEW LIFE, PATIENT GROWTH

"A root shall come out from the stump of Jesse,
and a branch shall grow out of his roots."

—ISAIAH 11:1

This week, two Advent readings take me back to December 2010, when I resigned from the church to begin AWBA. It was an exodus journey of sorts, and I certainly felt "stump-like" in that season.

As I remember that time now, with its surrounding circumstances, the emotions tangled in my own decision-making, and the occasional whispered rumors since, relayed by friends and former colleagues, a shadow of these deep emotions still roils within me.

New Life, Patient Growth

Even the mere thought of this time—and my unexpected association of it with today's reading—immediately stirs up, once again, my deep, visceral feelings of despair, dread, frustration, anger, grief, and, ultimately, the hardening of my heart.

As I have learned to do when my emotions overwhelm the banks of God's river, I quieted my mind and waited for new insight.

What came to me, rather quickly, was mental imagery of the stump of Jesse—dead and lifeless as my desire to continue my role with the church. Remembering then, once this difficult and gut-wrenching decision was made, how easy it all was to move forward in a fruitful new direction, the rest of the imagery flowed into my mind and out onto my canvas—new life that came forth from that dead stump almost immediately.

With the peace flooding my senses and erasing my residual angst like ocean waves erasing footprints in the sand, I continue my daily reading, smiling as if these words were just penned, written directly to me:

"Be patient, beloved, until the coming of the Lord.
The farmer waits for the precious crop from the earth,
being patient with it until it receives the early and late rains.
You must also be patient. Strengthen your hearts . . . do not grumble against one another . . ."
—JAMES 5:7–10

I pray for a softened heart, knowing there is still much work to be done to release this experience from my heart for good.

PREPARING MY WAY

"This is he of whom it is written, 'Behold, I send my messenger
before your face who will prepare your way before you.'"
—MATTHEW 11:10

I was tempted to skip my daily reading today as I contemplated a too-full day. Then I reminded myself that these few minutes now could very well make all the difference in how I handle what comes my way this day.

I decided to keep it brief. I looked up today's lectionary reading and scribbled it hastily at the top of my journal page, just as I do nearly every day.

Then I stopped, sat back in my chair, and stared at the words I just wrote on the page, thinking, *Wait. What?*

I quickly read this Matthew passage again, and I stopped at "your way." Then I checked to be sure I had not written it wrong, thinking surely it should be "the way."

Joy it is!

Release the Heaviness

Nope. This is how it reads: *"'Behold, I send my messenger before your face who will prepare* **your** *way before you.'"*

This is so personal, so intimate. Jesus goes before *my* face to make a path for *me* that is *unique to me.*

As I let this new understanding absorb, I marvel at how many times before I have read these same words and missed this amazing insight.

It is easy to trust goodness when the path appears easier to walk. When I stumble . . . that is a different story. It doesn't feel so loving and safe.

Perhaps in those dark times it will help to remember that Jesus is walking a few paces ahead of me, preparing *my* way to ensure *my* light in the darkness.

JOY IT IS!

As 2013 winds to a close, I return to my annual custom of setting aside a special time for remembering and reflecting on how my awareness of my word for the past year has played into various situations, circumstances, and scenarios.

Rolling back through the year and its unique experiences, I considered my word for 2014.

So "joy" it is for 2014!

RELEASE THE HEAVINESS

"But let all who take refuge in you be glad; let them ever sing for joy."
—PSALMS 5:11

I woke up this morning with a start from a vivid dream, and I have carried that imagery into my morning contemplation. In this dream, there was a cathedral in the sea, shrouded by fog and colorless, stone-faced, dark, small windows.

Intrigued by this imagery, I continued to let my mind play with it—and the thoughts that arose from it, one layering upon the other until it was strong enough to express in a new piece of art.

The interior refuge where Spirit resides must not be that place. Darkness may, at times, be the outer reality, but the refuge of the holy is an environment in which joy sings its melody through any foggy veil of darkness.

May I open windows that let in the nourishment needed by my inner places so that the refuge becomes a place of gladness.

Worry and anxiety are my fog; I need not carry that into this place of refuge, or it will be a shroud over all. I must release the heaviness.

BIRTHING A MOUNTAIN

Playing with the idea of the birthing of a mountain, I allow my mind to create a vivid multisensory image of this process, from the perspective of the earth:

I feel heat and energy of this exquisite labor, of the earth pulsing through me. There is a deafening sound of mountains pushing through the earth, stretching toward a starry horizon. It does not seem to stop!

Then comes the crowning, heralding actual birth. Cool, crisp air intersects with gritty dust and the foul taste of minerals. The mountain forms are barely visible through the incessant pushing and shaping of chaos.

And then, sweet aftermath, celebratory and calm. Slowly, dust settles, and the cracking and crunching noise becomes quiet. A gentle breeze blows away the dirt of birth. There is a faint smell of lavender in the air. The sweetness of thick, rich honey is in my mouth. Blue-green lilacs of new mountains come into view.

Pausing for a moment to reflect on the imagery just created, I bring it onto the page, first in written expression, then with richness of color.

Out of chaos has come a richness of new life. Cracks in the earth begin to heal and are barely visible. Memories of the pain recede and are replaced by this vision of a new creation. The fire has been tempered. I have persevered.

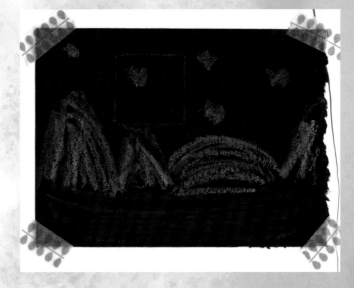

Birthing a Mountain

I KNEW WE WERE HOME

The vividness of the mountain piece I created yesterday still haunts me; today, with it lingering in my mind, I decided to take this most recent piece of art to my own spiritual direction session today.

Processing this imagery and its surrounding emotions with Sister Noreen, my spiritual director, brought forth new awareness of how this piece of art was a metaphorical depiction of my own spiritual growth.

I am birthing mountains, not tulips. It is hard work.

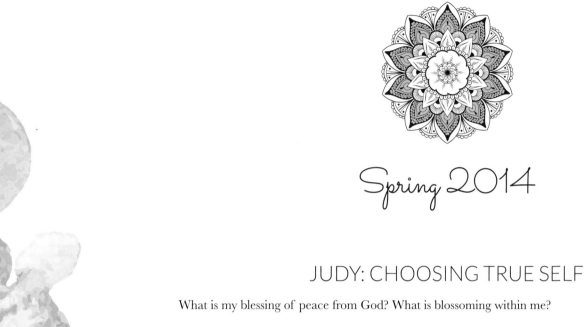

Spring 2014

JUDY: CHOOSING TRUE SELF

What is my blessing of peace from God? What is blossoming within me?

Father Richard Rohr—whose daily meditations arrive in my email inbox every day and I almost always make time to read—asks an important question today as he focuses on a familiar verse from Matthew:

Anyone who wants to save his life, must lose it. Anyone who loses her life will find it.

—MATTHEW 16:25

As Richard Rohr sees it, we must lose our attachment to what he calls the "False Self"—whatever we think of ourselves regarding our role, title, and personal image—in order to become "Real," or in union with God.

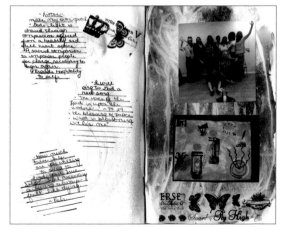

Choosing True Self

He says this idea of becoming your Real Self is common to all world religions, whether they call it nirvana, heaven, bliss, or enlightenment, but they miss the point by "pushing it off to the next world."

It's a choice for each of us to make, he says. We can choose the Real—the Kingdom of God—over our attachment to our own personal kingdom and the separation we feel from God that we create with our own imaginations.

Heaven, Richard Rohr asserts, is choosing to free ourselves from our False Self so we can enjoy this union with God both now and later, and only our True Self knows the way. He calls this "transformative dying," in which our attachments die in correlation to how much we want to be real.

What are my attachments? What am I willing to shed? What *must* I shed? How will I know?

Sand Mandala

SAND MANDALA

We arrived in Sarasota today for my fourth EAFI session.

One of our first activities was to create a "sand mandala." We outlined a 25-foot-diameter circle in which we invited kids of all ages who were playing on the beach to bring any object they wanted to from the beach and place it wherever they wanted to on our sand mandala.

We'd approach a group and say, "We're doing some sand art over here; want to come help?" And most of the kids we asked—and some adults, too, joined in this giant community mandala, an artistic expression of what they found interesting on the beach. What an amazing and incredible experience with strangers, creating art together.

A SENSE OF HOME

I write this midway through another abundant time in Sarasota. Everything is falling into pleasant places. Tiring and bliss filled.

There is a sense of "home" here—not as a physical place, although it *is* stunningly beautiful, but as a spiritual home that carries no brick-and-mortar boundaries. I carry it within, and it becomes clearer with each visit. I return to my earlier entry that contains words from Glen Laurel Inn in Hocking Hills, Ohio, "Dreamers of the day . . . acting their dreams with open eyes."

RHYTHMS

We ended yesterday with a workshop on the beach creating another sand mandala, and then I found out that all the students are staying for tomorrow's touch drawing workshop.

Although I have two more intensives here, I am beginning to anticipate the absence of this rhythm and these people.

FULL CIRCLE

As I continued my spiritual direction program, I also continued to think about the ministry I knew was growing within me. The next year, when I had finished my program, I established a spiritual direction and retreat practice that was growing steadily. And yet I knew there was still more I needed to do.

After my incredibly life-giving and validating experience shadowing Sister Bridget at the Boston Home, I realized how my spiritual direction practice and my growing awareness and interest in art and the creative process can be used to help others find their own spiritual path. This visit with Sister Bridget and the genesis of AWBA was just the beginning of my learning to listen deeply to God and to my own heart.

Roy says this "full-circle" realization is an example of my patience with the unknown—of trusting the process and letting each step unfold in its own time—as God weaves things together beyond our awareness.

Some processing time with Victoria (my EAFI mentor) after watching the video really helped me clarify some things as I move toward focusing myself in this work.

Planting seeds, layering the foundation . . . it was all part of the same "God weaving," and now I was beginning to see how all the stuff that went on stirred me to study spiritual direction, leaving the church, dreaming AWBA into existence, beginning expressive arts training—and now I'm almost ready to use my expressive arts training in my own practice—just like the lady in the video I saw today—and just like Sister Bridget.

Yesterday's touch drawing workshop was very rough. Although the material was excellent and affirming to my vision, the way it was delivered was not helpful for where I was. It was an unpleasant end to a bliss-filled week, but I expect it to soften with time.

I have much to work through and am committed to processing all of this in a gentle manner. I am, again, energized for this work that I do.

Summer 2014

JUDY: CHALLENGES ARE TEACHERS

Challenges Are Teachers

We moved to Sunrise Ridge, our remodeled and expanded sanctuary in Hocking Hills four weeks ago. I was excited and a little nervous anticipating the first retreat to use this space this week.

This is all a new landscape for me. I failed to calculate how hard it would be to provide a contemplative presence among visits from repair people and mechanical mishaps that go along with settling into a new space.

These challenges of the past few days are teaching me (and I am a slow learner) to trust the direction of the holy for her retreat more than my desire to make everything "perfect."

I know I have not yet learned this lesson, as I am very weary waiting for the propane people to show up to reconnect our tank.

In the midst of the drama, it is a beautiful, cool, sunny morning.

I am all of it. *And* God holds all of it, not me. I am not in charge. That should come as a relief!

Simply Grateful

Cups Overflow

SIMPLY GRATEFUL

Today seems a timely close to this journal. As I read through it, I realize it has been the container for our move to the Hills. My cup absolutely overflows with blessings.

I sit in the morning sunrise and am simply grateful.

NAME THE BLESSINGS

When I began using these journals in January of 2013, it was not my intention that they would cover my time in the EAFI program in Sarasota. I should finish in the spring of 2015, and this is the last of the three journals I purchased. I read through the other two and will likely do so again. Fascinating journey of reading and image making.

I've not had much desire to do art lately. I think my heart wants it, but everything feels stuck in some manner.

I know this move to our cottage has reoriented my life, and I am still trying to create a new pattern. I am truly content here and know this was/is a life-giving choice for us.

But there is a melancholy that has been creeping in, bringing ideas of death and loss into my thought patterns.

Life has been so full with retreatants at our cottage and visits from family that there has been little time to just "be" in this new place. It's as though I begin and then it's time for another guest. All wonderful, but I'm not sleeping well and feeling very weary.

When plans fell apart for lunch out, I made myself go into the studio. I forgot that I closed the second journal with an original of this "cup" image. With this version, I chose to name the blessings: a timely activity given this mood and melancholy I find hanging over me.

A PLACE FOR ANXIETY

In her commentary on the Rule of St. Benedict (RSB), Sister Joan Chittister talks about how things we insist on holding onto, refusing to put down, can "poison us and erode our souls." To remedy this, she says, means learning to distinguish between what is real and what is not.

Anxiety will be ever present. Perhaps it is an issue of giving it a place at the table—to listen—and then to walk away without giving it power to latch on even further.

ROY: LETTING GO AND MAKING ROOM

I opened an envelope in the stack of mail on our kitchen counter. Judy, cooking dinner, glanced over her shoulder as I read the contents of the letter.

"What's that?" she asked, grinding a little more pepper into our stew. Judy has never been that big on cooking—a necessary functionality, she always called it—yet she was a good cook and even seemed to enjoy preparing meals in our cottage. We actually enjoyed everything more in this place. Her projection was spot on. A little slice of heaven. Our little slice of heaven.

"It's our closing notice on the house," I said, unable to identify the strange mixture of emotions washing over me. Our house in Westerville had been our home for 25 glorious years—so much history there. Felt a little bit hard to think about letting it go, another family living there, calling it home. But those thoughts were quickly washed away in the complete and utter joy we feel in the cottage and this new chapter just beginning. This place feels so natural, and it is already so much a part of me—of us.

"Do you want to go to the closing with me?" I asked, already knowing her answer. Judy has always been the sentimental one, and even though she's indescribably happy about this transition, handing over those keys would be hard for her.

"No," she said, a cloud of sadness crossing her face. "Do we have to be there in person? Can we just sign it and send it back?"

I considered this idea for a moment. It seemed appealing at first, to avoid the emotional storm entirely. Then, on the heels of that thought came another, truer answer. "You know, we probably could," I said, plucking a chunk of blue cheese from the salad sitting in front of me. "But it feels important to personally hand over the keys, the house, to the next owners."

"You're right," she said, stopping to kiss me on the forehead as she moved past me to set the tureen on the table. "I just don't think I can."

"I'll go," I offered, pulling her close. "You stay here and continue doing what you're doing."

"Thank you," she said, resting her head on my chest. "You really do get me, don't you?"

"If I didn't after all these years, I'd be pretty slow," I teased, giving her a quick squeeze.

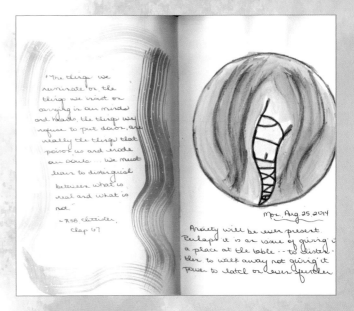

Listen, then Walk Away

Fall 2014

JUDY: ACCEPT THE GIFT

As I settle more into this place of nature and stillness, beauty and gentleness have increased, pushing out the anxiety. I am learning in this place of earthiness and God's creation.

I look into dense woods beyond my studio and into lushness that will soon give way to the fullness of autumn.

Exterior housework continues, and it has been hard to have alone time here. However, I know the winter months to come will offer solace that I yearn for as the busyness of summer comes to an end.

I just turned 60. Yesterday marked 37 years of bliss-filled marriage. And I am living in Utopia.

Accept the gift.

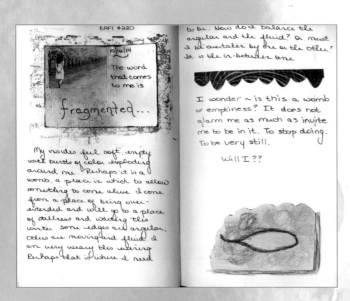

Fragmented

Trust the Process — Weaving without a Pattern (Saori Weaving)

THE IN-BETWEEN TIME

The word that comes to me today in my quiet time is: Fragmented

WEAVING THE PROCESS

I chose Saori weaving as the medium for my EAFI final project, my thesis. I do not know very much about it, only that it interests me. I can't wait to be introduced!

What attracts me most to Saori weaving is its Zen-like approach to weaving as an art form, not a handcraft. The word "Saori" comes from the Japanese words sai, meaning "everything has its own unique dignity," and ori, which means "weaving." I like the symbolism of this form of artistic expression—as well as the individualized beauty of what it produces.

My assignment is to create my own Saori weaving and to write about the process of weaving without a pattern. This feels to me like the culmination of my two-and-a-half-year expressive arts journey with EAFI. A perfect final exam and thesis project.

GROUNDING IN NATURE

I feel grounded in nature. Perhaps that is why I have not done much in my studio for myself.

I have resided within the suburban box and all its boundaries for so long that I feel a bit paralyzed with this newly gifted freedom and expansion.

I feel unready to claim an outward vision statement until I have lived into the vision for myself.

Inhabit my bench
>   Grounded in nature
>   Paralyzed with new freedom
>   and expansion
>   Grow into this new place
>   Grounded in nature
>   Live the
>   {vision}
>   for myself

Grow into this new place
    It is waiting

Grounded in nature
    Paralyzed with new freedom
        and expansion
    Grow into this
        new place
    Inhabit my bench

Grounding and Growing

SANCTUARY VALUES

In my business I seek to establish a place of hospitality, where soul work can occur without worldly distraction. I address these needs through solitude, quiet with the Holy One, navigating change, and providing safe companionship.

To meet these needs I create safe sanctuaries, providing opportunities for creative exploration in a sacred space.

The values I hold are:

~ change is normal

~ supportive response at clients' pace

~ nonjudgmental attitude

~ exploring all avenues, options

~ wonderings are acceptable

REMAIN IN THE PROCESS

I am a woman 50 + and
    my faith journey is
    changing. I am nourished
    being in nature and engaging
    my senses. I am
    unafraid of solitude,
    silence and exploration.
    On this path of transition,
    I trust the Holy, knowing
    peace will come as I
    remain in the process.

CREATE FROM A STRONG PLACE

From a strong place, I create a sacred space to stand in the gap, fully present for the work as a professional as I tend to myself and others.

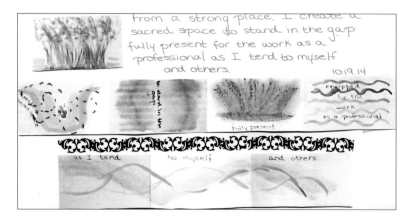

From a Strong Place

I realize that my wondering, "Is this a tomb or a womb?" is the question my clients also come to our cottage with.

Altar

Through an arts-based inquiry, I will discern how to consistently integrate all the pieces of myself in a life-giving way and create ample inner space so I am fully present to myself and to those with whom I stand in the gap.

I will fully inhabit my bench.

This is my commitment to myself and to those I serve.

ROY: TIME TO SIT AND BE

When I arrived here on Friday, it took just one look at Judy to know that I, the Sherpa with Benefits, had arrived just in the nick of time. She was winding up an especially intense intensive. (Is that redundant? I don't think so in this case!)

She came into the hotel room, where I already had our wine poured and a hefty snack assembled that would probably serve as dinner, and fell into my arms, utterly spent. "Take me away," she said with a happy sigh.

"Was it a good intensive?" I asked, leaning back to search her face for clues.

"Of course!" she said, mustering some enthusiasm through her fatigue. "I think it was all very good — I just need some quiet time now to let it settle, then to sift through it a bit more when I get home."

"That's good to hear," I said, "because I booked two quiet, let-it-settle days on Gasparilla before we head back home. Will that work?"

"Will it ever," she said, planting a kiss on my lips that took me all the way back to our college days. "Now," she said, pushing me away playfully, "Let's drink this wine, enjoy this lovely snack, and then I'm going to take a long hot bath and go to sleep so I can enjoy our weekend!"

JUDY: THERE IS SPACE

It has been a beautiful autumn weekend.

I offered a sample spiritual direction session yesterday for a retreat at a different Hocking Hills cabin. Afterward, Roy and I went to dinner at Grouse Nest. Gorgeous drive on the backwoods.

Much work still to finish, but I have some space open for tomorrow. Someone arrives Tuesday for retreat but will not be meeting with me, so there is space in there.

Yesterday was a chilly, rainy day, and I loved it! This is home.

LIVING JOY WITHIN ULTIMATE TRUTH

It is on the cusp of Tuesday, as it is nearly midnight, and I can't sleep. I left my iPad volume on and heard the faint ding of emails arriving.

One was from the woman scheduled for retreat. She had already pushed it back to Wednesday morning, and now she just sent word that she likely won't make it. She is a pastor, two of her parishioners are very ill, and she has some issues coming up at home.

Sometimes I feel quite overwhelmed with the physical fragility of we humans, myself included. As soon as we are born, we are dying. How to live joyfully within that truth?

SOMETIMES WAY IS MADE

Six hours of sleep after my wake-up call. I prayed for my retreatant last night, that way would be made for her.

She emailed early this morning that she is trying to work this out so she can come.

God, you are so good.

"May I guard my heart with all diligence. For out of it flows the issues of life."
—PROVERBS 4:23

Clarity coming for my Saori-based inquiry for the internship. I unpacked the yarns I moved—and found some hands-on yarn for order.

A new rhythm, new expectations—an authentic way to embrace this new way of being I desire to guard my heart.

I acknowledge it as the source for the Living Water that flows through my heart to others.

Reader's Notes

Winter 2014-2015

JUDY: THIS WAITING PLACE

I arranged to be at St. Alban's sanctuary these Mondays of Advent before 11:15 prayer. I have had the space to myself off and on. I appreciate the stillness as I hear rain on the roof.

This waiting place—waiting for what, this particular Advent? Five years ago at this time I was in the depths of uncertainty coming to terms with releasing New Song Community Church from my life. When I consider all that has happened in that short time, it is overwhelming.

It seems that Jesus has helped me leverage my gifts to bring them together in a way uniquely suited to me. What is to occur in this next season of time?

AWBA is finding its place. Expressive art seems a blossom ready to spring forth with quite a bit of unknowns.

To be strong and blameless to the end seems to be all one could need. Losses, change, new possibilities—to maintain a sense of balance in the midst of always-shifting sand can be a challenge.

As I sit in this quiet sanctuary, I am aware of its history—the many souls who have occupied this same space, the thousands of prayers (spoken and silent) lifted in hope, the music sung, the peace shared. All those who have traveled before me and, in some manner, accompany me now.

GOD'S TIMING

It has been a full few days.

John, an AWBA board member and our dear friend, passed on unexpectedly Wednesday through a series of events only God could have created. Roy and I were with him and his family.

It was a sacred, thin space with John. I am happy for him and so sad for us.

We are weary. I have nothing left to give. Going to contemplative prayer today with the hope of "blessings."

God's timing.

SPIRIT'S FIRE

(Fact) My heart is broken open
     (Wondering) so that new life can come forth?

"Do not put out the Spirit's fire."

—1 THESSALONIANS 5:19

Roy attended the private visitation for John Friday evening. I had planned to go but began having second thoughts on Thursday. Being with John the day he passed was being fully present to the moment. For me, being there Friday and for the funeral Saturday (which we had previously chosen not to attend) would have been a return to the past and would have put out the Spirit's fire, I think.

There was no unfinished business with John. I think the way things unfolded seemed best, and I never followed through on an "I should." I pray that I was faithful to the Audience of One.

THIN AND RAW

Still feeling very thin and raw from the events of last weekend. Going to morning prayer and then spiritual direction. Hoping for some healing balm from both of these.

Today, I feel like we need to "stay home"—literally and figuratively. This place is our future and where the Spirit's fire seems to be refueling us for our future.

A BLACK SHARD WITHIN

It's Christmas Eve.

Roy and I will spend the night in Columbus. Dinner at Lindey's followed by midnight service at St. Albans and Christmas morning.

Very disconcerting morning yesterday—almost out-of-body as an observer, a witness. I had an image of a black shape, small, that moves within me at times, mostly sparked by memories or painful past experiences.

As I considered the image, I was grateful the black was not as large as before.

Then something happened within me; something shifted (Roy calls this kind of inner shift "a thin space"). The black shape became a glossy black glass shard with very dangerous edges.

Lord, I must be completely rid of it. It causes so much pain and useless damage when it is on the move.

It is not a gentle release that is needed as much as an intentional, quick removal. I have worked through all that was to be revealed. It is time to walk away—turn toward the light.

A CALL TO NOURISH

I am considering my "word" for the year. "Nourish" has come to me by way of "nurture." "Nourish" seems more active and intentional to me. An act for myself and for others. Perhaps it is an invitation to name and recall those things or to commit to them in advance—or both. Perhaps that is how I will "turn toward the light."

Now Roy and I have three days together. Perfect.

THE NOURISH-NUTURE CYCLE

Upper 50s for today. We leave soon for a long walk.

Nourish-Nurture. It feels like a cycle, a flow. To nourish myself through art, nature, and beauty will allow me to nurture others.

Perhaps this is the "engine" for my internship—to fully experience and live within a place of nourishment and to witness what spills from that place.

The word "expansion" also enters in—to expand my inner reservoir.

Practicing these new art forms in a new way carries the promise of expansion, which creates a space for more nourishment, which allows an increased outflow of nurturing for others.

There is No Right or Wrong

ROY: STUDIO TIME

There are few things more exhilarating than spending time with Judy in her studio. In this space that has become her sanctuary, we sort, organize, hang art, and just talk through whatever bubbles to the surface of our casual conversation.

Easy, quiet, sweet time to see her in action in the place she loves best in our cottage. This space nurtures her spirit—and, by extension, mine, too.

Judy is truly in her element with these retreats. She has an innate sense of what people need, often before they do. Her gift for listening, even beyond the words people say, and her ability to draw out of them wisdom they don't even know they possess about whatever it is they're questioning or struggling with—it's an amazing thing.

Sacred, holy work. Everywhere she's been, everything she's done, from hospice work to church work to art and all points in between, she has prepared well for this unique offering to help nurture the souls and spirits of others.

I'm so proud of her, so grateful to be part of her journey. It's an honor that, when I fully consider it, takes my breath away.

JUDY: THE MIDDLE CAUSE

I am beginning the day in my studio—something I did for quite a while in Westerville. It feels better although I can't explain why.

Roy and I claimed the first part of our cottage by cleaning up the second guest room and ordering a twin bed for delivery on Thursday.

My head knew it would take months for us to feel settled here, but my heart was not convinced. I am so happy to be here but not settled.

I am trying to make sense of these changes and of bigger issues I am more aware of as I age.

In addition, there is so much more I want to do and be. I fear I will not have the time! I resent what I believe was "wasted time."

Today I will begin a new way of "nourish" for myself. I am unsure what that means. I need to be patient and allow it to unfold over the year.

A TOOL FOR DEEPENING

There was unhurried studio time yesterday, which was great. I did some freeform background pages in my journal that I will take to Florida.

Perhaps that is another layer of meaning to nourish. Am I to ask myself daily, "How has God nourished me this day?"

I have come to love the Society of Saint John the Evangelist's (SSJE) online daily "word" they provide to all who seek a deeper knowledge of God. Desert Fathers and Mothers, as they became known, were a few faithful men and women who went into the desert to seek God and live a life of prayer. This is said to be the very beginning of monasticism; today's SSJE says they consider this adaptation of their ancient tradition of offering a single word each day to seekers a means of "handing on what we ourselves have received." I have become fascinated with how SSJE stays so rooted in ancient monastic traditions of prayer and community life and yet remains critically engaged with contemporary culture.

By studying various ways different ancient traditions live and pray and engage with traditions that ground them in authentic experience of God's love and mercy, I hope to tune my own heart to the call that draws each of us seekers onward, day by day.

In the tradition of Desert Fathers and Mothers, a seeker would approach and ask, "Father (Mother), give me a word." This word from Desert Fathers and Mothers then became a focus for the seeker's daily prayer. They would say their word to the rhythm of their breath as they invited the Holy Spirit to speak to them through that word. I love following this practice and often call upon SSJE's daily saying as a focus for meditative reading, or Lectio Divina.

As I read the word slowly, I allow my mind to drift and whatever words that come to me to inspire further prayer and reflection. When I catch my mind straying (as I often do, especially on busy days), I use my senses to return my awareness to the moment I'm in. This is much harder than it seems, but I keep trying.

I love this tool for deepening my life with God, and I find myself returning to it again and again, especially when I need to remember to inhabit the moment I am in and to get back in touch with myself and God's presence throughout my day.

PROCESS HAS ITS OWN EVOLUTION

"What will it take for me to grow into this new place?"

This was the question that came to me during the October intensive. My desire for an answer is intensifying to a place of discomfort.

"Time" comes to me as part of the answer—something I have trouble with!

I used the word "grow" in the question, which reminds me that this is all a process and a process has its own evolution that will not be rushed.

Perhaps that is where the concept of nourish enters in—so that I might be sustained in its unfolding.

Part of me must not "trust the process." This is a place where control is largely absent.

Roy and I will be at the church for Lessons and Carols. We are each reading a portion of the service. Eager for that.

Ten days to Florida and I don't feel ready for that. This is the last intensive. I will miss the regularity of Sarasota, but I look forward to traveling elsewhere.

I am happy here—content and where I need to be. Part of me has either not caught up to the rest of me or simply needs to stay behind.

When will I know?

THRESHOLD WONDERS

One of my Wellsprings mentors, Jan Richardson, is an ordained minister in the United Methodist Church and director of the Wellsprings Studio LLC, where I received my spiritual direction certification. She describes the wonder we find in a place of "threshold," the wide possibilities, chosen or otherwise, that invite us to stop and take stock of things.

I believe the invitation to me at this present moment is to dwell in this place of transition and not to resist it. And to claim those things—practices, people, attitudes—that nourish me in this dwelling place.

I really admire Jan's work as a retreat leader and conference speaker because she is known especially for her distinctive intertwining of word and image.

I especially relate to how her work seems to be informed by a rich combination of rural landscape, community traditions, and lifelong relationships that have given her a deep sense of place, imagination, and spiritual practices. I want to emulate that, with my own stamp of authenticity, of course.

PATIENCE WITH THE PROCESS

I began winding the warp for my internship project—black pearl cotton. Music and a cup of tea kept me company.

My bedroom view (warp board propped up against our bed) was snow on forest trees with patches of blue sky (pink as the sun set) woven among the bare limbs.

It seems that the trees surrounding our cottage are my warp: bare and freeform. I find comfort in that metaphor. I am weaving life here. This is the time for preparing my warp.

It is:
   ~ time consuming
   ~ meticulous

~ without color

~ no certainty of what is to come

~ bare, exposed

Somehow, this image gives me a bit more patience with the process. A bit more trust for my journey.

THE TRANSITION OF BECOMING

It's time for my last EAFI intensive.

There is a lot coming to the surface to make itself visible. There will be barriers to push beyond. Way will be made. Light will illumine the path.

I bring to this session my own authentic journey of listening to my past, holding its wisdom, and dwelling in the transition of becoming.

STUMBLING BLOCKS OR STEPPING-STONES?

My assignment here was to consider events of my life through the lens of whether they were stumbling blocks or stepping-stones.

After giving this a lot of thought, I was able to identify the stepping-stones as I moved throughout my life from the time I was a little girl, 3 to 4 years old, to age 50-plus. And then, within each memory, I reflected on the stumbling block related to each stepping-stone.

As I worked through this exercise, it was enlightening to discover how "stumbling blocks" I encountered were most often voices of others and within me.

It's also funny looking back on how I first claimed, then reclaimed, the artist within me.

UNEXPECTED GIFTS

We arrived in Sarasota at 5:00 p.m. yesterday. Emotion is beginning to swirl as I reflect on the past two-and-a-half years and this being my last intensive.

The following journal pages were created before we left and will hold the story of this final "official" trip.

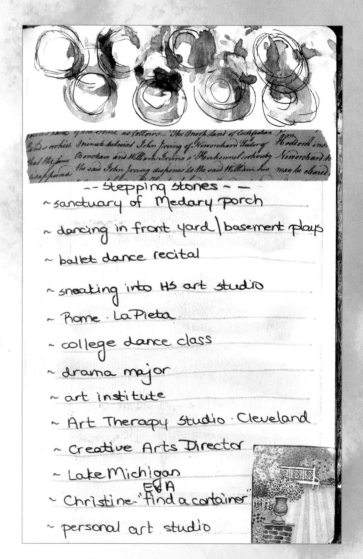

Stumbling Blocks or Stepping-stones

In some way it seems this journey has breathed new life into me—time here and all that has happened in these months—what an unexpected gift this has been. Even times of deep uncertainty. There is so much more still to discover.

This will be a good intensive—to focus on my own philosophy for this work and begin to serve from my personal foundation. The quote of "Sankofa" —it is wrong to go back for that which you have forgotten—made it into the project begun last night.

ALLOW, GAZE, HONOR

Presence

Nourish

Dwell

Energy

Earth

CONTAINER OF EXPLORATION

Happy birthday, Roy! Thirteen years ago today we were in the CCU at Mt. Carmel West. Neither of us could have envisioned this path we are on right now. Blessed!

In today's Rohr devotional, Thomas Aquinas writes about incarnation through light, water, land, sun, moon, stars . . . as the "Cosmic Christ."

This time continues to work through me and has revealed itself in much of my experience here.

This is my final in-class day. What a ride this has been and will continue to be. This little section of Sarasota has become a container of exploration for me. There has been affirmation, truth, releasing, and healing that has brought new life. No one can take that from me.

I so easily get caught up in heavy details of any given day that moments of gratitude can become lost. Need to remember to stop and acknowledge beauty in each day.

The fullness of it is very personal, and the expression of it is very outward.

We celebrated with our traditional visit to the New Pass Grill on the water, a walk on the Bayfront, and dinner at Euphenia Haye on Longboat.

"Presence"
(Natalie Rogers)

{balance}

Presence

Nourish

Energy

Dwell

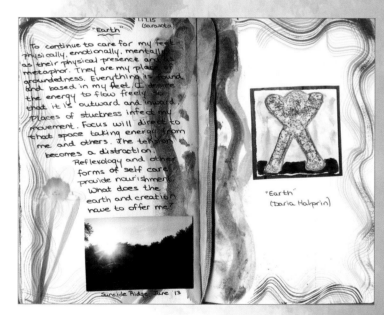

Earth

EMOTIONAL CLOSING

Yesterday was an emotional closing to this class experience. We each shared our story, and tears came.

At the end of it all, I am simply filled with gratitude.

The journey will continue as I discern how to offer whom I have become.

Roy's birthday and the completion all in one day—very full and amazing. These remaining two full days mark a goodbye to Sarasota and its role in this new life.

I feel a shift to freedom—something that will perhaps be made visual in my internship project.

ROY: SARASOTA CLOSING

When I opened Judy's car door before we walked up the wood ramp to the New Pass Grill for our traditional toast and stacked cheeseburger with vinegar fries following Judy's completion of each EAFI intensive, I couldn't help but smile.

As birthdays go, this one couldn't have been better. I had met Judy at the institute's door with a bouquet of flowers to honor her hard work.

"You did it!" I said, twirling her around and delighting, as always, at the sparkle in her green eyes and how she threw back her head in laughter at my classic (and only) swing dance move.

"Not quite yet," she was quick to say, inhaling the bouquet's scent and closing her eyes in pure delight. "I still have my externship to do, but you're right! This part, the hard part, is over."

A brief cloud crossed her face as she looked around her as if committing it all to memory.

"These intensives have been tough, but I have to say I'm going to miss these weekends of complete focus and immersion in art, art, and more art!"

"And is that all?" I asked, smiling at the mischief dancing between us.

She thought for a moment, forefinger on chin like a TV commercial model pondering a new shampoo. "I suppose I'll miss the picnics," she said, thoughtfully, "and chilled wine to greet me in our room each night . . . and also walking barefoot with you on Siesta Key beach."

"And is that *all* you'll miss?" I teased, pulling her close.

"Well, maybe one more thing," she said, fluttering her eyelashes. "I do love the crème brûlée at Lawanda.

JUDY: NATURE'S ABUNDANT HEALING

Richard Rohr writes today about "nature as the first Bible."

From Daniel 3, *"Let the earth bless the Lord, praise and exalt God above all forever!"*

Nature heals in such an abundant manner. We spent much of yesterday at Selby Gardens. My eyes filled with tears for the first 30 minutes. Truly a breathtaking environment. We walked Venice Beach—about 40 minutes—then had a wonderful lunch at Fins on a pier.

I am resisting the question, "Now what?" Hoping I can allow all of this to simply unfold to its new place.

LIFE AWAITS

Wonderful walks at the Siesta Key beach yesterday and dinner at Lawanda in Towles Court. In this time I have been gone, a potential spiritual directee called me, someone requested a March retreat, and a counselor has reached out to AWBA.

We leave for home this morning and I am ready. Life is awaiting my return.

MAKE FRIENDS WITH DEATH

After a snowy and dreary couple of days, I am grateful for today's sunshine.

Two sisters at Erie Monastery passed on Monday, and this quote is on their blog: "How does one make friends with Death?" As I age, this seems increasingly important.

A WARPED LOOM

Always unnerving to begin a new art journal. This one was purchased specifically for my expressive arts internship that begins next Monday.

My loom is warped with a few Saori wefts in place. I always smile at these weaving terms for the lengthwise, stationary strands of yarn on a loom that are held in tension by the frame (warp) and the transverse strands (weft) are actually woven over and under, across and through the warp to create the weaving. Warping one's loom gets it ready for weaving to begin. I wonder whether this is a metaphor for spirituality (warp) and weaving a life (weft)?

I have a Skype session with Victoria from EAFI this afternoon and a conference call on Thursday about my internship. It seems appropriate and necessary for it to be during Lent.

KEEPING HEART

My love of Joan Chittister's commentary on the *Rule of Saint Benedict* led me to the Monasteries of the Heart (MOH), a web-based community she and other Benedictine Sisters of Erie, Pennsylvania, founded to share Benedictine spirituality with contemporary seekers.

Promising to help ordinary people implement Benedictine values into their daily lives, Monasteries of the Heart offers, in addition to Joan Chittister's blog, a variety of e-courses, newsletters, etc., to support those hoping to live those values in our time. So grateful for this free resource. I wonder how many people know about it.

Each week MOH invites its online members to participate in core elements of living out this monastic tradition: prayer, Lectio Divina, good works, study, and community. Just staying mindful of these practices, even if I don't always do them, helps keep my heart in the "right place."

CELEBRATE BEAUTY

Tomorrow, Ash Wednesday, reminds us to pay attention to all beauty present and to perhaps "adopt the practice of keeping a beauty journal all through Lent."

Given that I am also now reading O'Donohue's book *Beauty*, that my word for 2015 is "nourish," and that I feel surrounded, often, by deep sadness and heaviness, this message seems meant for me.

Judy and Roy in Sarasota

ROY: PANORAMA

When I delivered a fresh cup of tea to Judy in her studio this morning, I had to stop for a moment just to take in the panoramic view beyond her floor-to-ceiling wall of windows. There was a breathtaking display of our new snowfall that would keep us both indoors today.

Judy smiled at me as I set down the steaming mug. As if reading my thoughts, she said, "It IS lovely when I accept it as it is rather than dwelling on what I am unable to DO because of it."

I kissed the top of her head and pulled her close. After a moment, I asked, "So how are you feeling about this next stretch?"

While completing her intensives was a huge milestone, it wasn't the end of Judy's art therapy certification program. There was still her internship that she would have to complete remotely with periodic check-ins via Skype with her advisor. Once that was done, a jury of instructors and graduates would assess her work and decide whether it met the criteria for full certification that would equip her to do this work as part of her spiritual direction and retreats programming.

"I don't know, Roy," she said, looking a bit troubled. "It just seems like there's so *much* still to do.

"You've done the hard part, and the rest will flow easily from you," I encouraged. Clearly, she was feeling the anticlimactic weight of the final segment of her certification. "You'll find the time, and it will all fall into places where it will fit best, for your certification *and* for your work ahead."

She smiled, taking a sip of the tea. "Have I ever told you how much I appreciate your never-ending optimism?" she asked. "You always know just what to say when I'm feeling dumpy."

I smiled back, ruffling her auburn air. "It's not optimism; it's truth," I corrected gently. "You very rarely give yourself enough credit. You're amazing and talented and committed to this work—and however it unfolds will be just right."

She reached out, took my hand, and gave me a look of gratitude and adoration that melted my heart.

"So today begins week 1 of your internship?"

She nodded. "Week 1 of a brand-new, six-week container." She shrugged, then summoned a hopeful smile. "We'll see what unfolds within it."

"Whatever it is will be beautiful," I said. "How could it not be?"

JUDY: WEAVING TRUE SELF

Group internship call yesterday. I will do my first session today.

My reflection for today comes from *The Book of Awakening: Having the Life You Want by Being Present to the Life You Have* by Mark Nepo (Simon & Schuster, Spring 2011):

Nepo's observation that continuing to behave in old ways, whether out of habit or fear, is another affirmation of my focus on opening myself to live in

To Weave My True Self

a new way. I am simply far too fragmented—or it feels like that. So many loose ends. Pieces from the past either seeking a new home or seeking release. Ideas for my future clamoring for attention and for space in which to breathe.

WAY MAKING

Another "path maker" today—this one from Mark Nepo.

A seemingly random thought arose from today's reading from Mark Nepo:
> One note of my song creates the path.

What is the note? The Center?

And another:
> I am hundreds of loose ends seeking a path, seeking a new home.

New threads arrive to be woven into my existing tapestry of life. Wondering how they will be used, where they will be used, and with whom they will be used.

Will I trust the process?

I wonder about this path unfolding within me; I notice a narrow, constricted path opening to a wide horizon.

As way is being made, I feel free and trust my life's warp to hold my loose ends together just enough as I seek my new way.

REVOLUTION OF SPIRIT

Entering the second week of my EAFI Internship, which follows completion of my intensives.

Random thoughts bubble up, rapid-fire, this morning, almost too fast to get them down, but I'll try.

First of all, Lent, I think, is all about a revolution of the mind:

> *"and to be renewed in the spirit of your minds,*
> *and to clothe yourselves with the new self,*
> *created according to the likeness of God*
> *in true righteousness and holiness."*
> —EPHESIANS 4:23–24

"DO NOT FRET"

It kind of strikes me as funny to see this common phrase in the Bible—and, yet, in the first nine of the 40-versed Psalm 37, "do not fret" appears three times, a number that also carries special significance in biblical terms. In this same scripture, in addition to admonitions not to fret, we are also instructed to:

Trust in the Lord . . .
> Take Delight in the Lord . . .
> Commit your way to the Lord . . .
> Be still before the Lord . . .
> Refrain from anger . . .
> Take refuge in the Lord . . .
> Wait for the Lord and keep his way . . .

And then this psalm of "exhortation to Patience and Trust to David" goes on to promise:

Our steps are made firm by the Lord,
> *when he delights in our way; though we stumble, we shall not fall headlong,*
> *for the Lord holds us by the hand."*

I love this imagery—the duality of us "keeping the Lord's way" and "the Lord delights in **our** way," as well as the image of God holding us by the hand to prevent us from falling headlong. In acknowledging that we *will* stumble—and often do—this protective image brings me a lot of comfort, especially as I stumble through this new era of discovery and exploration. Thank you, God.

Figuratively speaking, rather than weaving ends into my existing tapestry, will I begin anew, keeping only those warps that are truly nonnegotiable?

In Psalm 16 the psalmist writes:
"The boundary lines have fallen for me in pleasant places; I have a goodly heritage."

This parallel with the concept of warps does not escape me, nor does the idea that follows:
"I bless the Lord who gives me counsel; in the night also my heart instructs me."

The true "warps" in my life are really very few. The weft of my past circumstances is truly of little consequence and need not overly define my going forward.

Doing my art in the early morning hours was perfect.
This was Worship.

Melody of sacred land holds answers.
Moving freely within the sanctuary,
footprints in the snow meander through woods.
Unravel my yesterdays.

Move freely within the sanctuary,
holy boundaries enclose a pleasant land.
Unravel my yesterdays
And a new song begins to play.

Holy boundaries enclose a pleasant land.
Footprints in the snow meander through woods,
my new song begins to play.
Melody of sacred land holds answers.

Do Not Fret

Spring 2015

JUDY: SEASON OF HIBERNATION

A gentle snow falls early this morning. Again, "church" must take place at home. I am ready for spring's warmth, but I do not want to wish away this season of hibernation.

APPRECIATE THE PACE OF THE DAY

Yesterday was full, so I appreciated the slower pace of today. Did some weaving and was able to do my reflection. I am trying to stay within the pace of this process, to not rush ahead to an answer.

Victoria, my internship advisor, writes, "Amazed at the map; it must have made the twists and turns that brought you to where you are today. I wonder from all of that what you will choose to take with you as you journey forward."

Two internship colleagues sent me some treasures—bark from a tree at Ringling in Sarasota and ribbons and feathers. I will add them to my tapestry, just as they have added new texture to my life experience.

My favorite colors have been pinks and purples, as in Martha's ribbons and feathers. I feel myself being drawn to the greens, blues, yellows, and browns of nature's palette, as in Julia's bark ("palm sheath" in her words!).

Trust

Mandala of Shells

KEEP WALKING

I am the moment. I have no pattern; I have no plan.

I am surprise. You will not fully experience me until I am unfurled.

The way is made by walking. Keep walking.

I will bring your container to you in the right time.

THE POWER OF IMAGINATION

What do I take with me as I journey forward?

When God knit me together, what were, are, the pieces that comprise my truth?

As I name those and break free from the "bank of my dead perception," I trust a new image to appear.

Rather than allow outer circumstances to create a new possibility, the Holy One will be the creator of this new image. Some ideas already emerging tell me it will have to do with my Five Truths of being:

~ sensitive to the needs and energies of others

~ nourished by time alone

~ created by God to be a blessing

~ a lover of nature and all images it creates through water, wind, birds, trees, flowers, mountains, valleys

~ an artist

We are ultimate participants here—and the more we give ourselves to experience and strive to express, the deeper it opens before us.

Are these five aspects of this emerging image my "true warp"? What might the expression of "me" look like if I focused on claiming, developing, and lifting up these five warps???

Yesterday's session was helpful in "bringing together" many pieces of my life.

Is the goal to somehow take these five pieces of myself—hidden at times—and to discover their unique form of expression in each season of my life?

PENT UP

Temperatures are warming, and snow is melting. I am eager to be outdoors and see how that may impact the second half of this internship. So much feels "pent up," literally and metaphorically.

I was apprehensive about Friday's session, wondering whether there would be insight as there had been in the first two weeks. There was.

I also notice my weaving is settling down a bit—whatever that may mean for me. Will do that reflection during my quiet time tomorrow morning, as I hope to spend another hour or two at the loom today.

Last Friday's session began with the earth—shades of blue and brown encased in the white of fresh snow cover.

A mandala of Florida shells and stones for EAFI sessions—grains of sand fallen from the shells—all placed on a touch drawing board and held by the snow . . .

My advisor Victoria commented that my "Two Worlds" mandala seems "alive like the exact moment an egg is fertilized."

I am curious how this will develop in the next session. I also wonder whether I will rotate it. Victoria sees the bottom as roots. I had not. Perhaps these are the new roots spilling from this new life and seeking a home—a new place of roundedness.

This week's weaving reflection . . .
I am the "Five Truths"

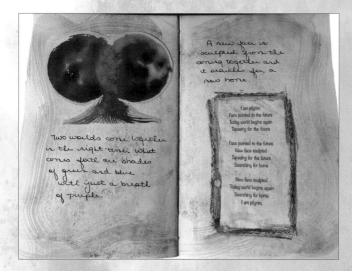

Two Worlds Come Together

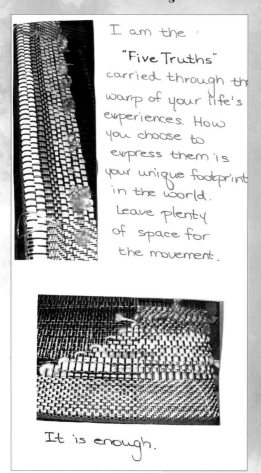

I am the "Five Truths"

ENOUGH

The David Whyte poem "Enough" arrived in my daily poetry email. And then someone also shared it in response to my week three summary.

What are the odds of that?

Pure serendipity, I think—Spirit moving and communicating with and through me.

CARDINAL THREADS

A magical morning—I watched the sun rise as a half-moon watched with me. A glimpse of the international space station helped break the dawn. I feel so small in this bigness.

My spiritual director, Amanda, has been here for retreat since Thursday. Her presence has brought a richness alongside feedback from colleagues on my EAFI process and spring temperatures.

Something is shifting. These Five Truths may be my "thread."

If I can believe they are enough, my energy will not be invested in seeking more. It will be invested in further developing my now.

I refer to my notes about the significance of the cardinal:

"The term cardinal is used to denote something with primary or essential qualities, such as a cardinal direction. The word comes from the Latin cards, meaning 'hinge.' Something that has cardinal qualities is so important that it functions as a keystone or axel; other things hinge around it."

A thread . . .

A WEB TO CALL HOME

Through this EAFI experience, I am weaving a new web to call home. It is my responsibility and will ultimately reflect the footprint I made while I was here.

Those memories and old emotions—perhaps they move in and around open spaces of the web, the weaving. But they are not part of my tapestry, and they are not woven in to become part of the final piece.

THE EARTH HOLDS ALL OF IT

Dawn breaks. I enter into the silence with my camera. Cup of coffee in hand, I listen to early-morning birdsong. I feel a cool breeze on my face. I taste hot, freshly brewed coffee.

I am captured by the half-moon slowly dancing in clouds. Stars are visible, and the sun is beginning to bring daylight. A weft of color weaves through branches.

Earth Holds All of It

A small brown spider visits for the second day. I read that spiders and their webs draw our attention to our life choices . . . Be smart about the life you weave for yourself.

Spider teaches, "Weave a web to call home."
    I am stardust
    Dawn breaks—choose silence.
    Build a new home for your stardust soul.

I am stardust.
    Cardinal sings, "This is your thread."
    Build a new home for your stardust soul.
    Half-moon dances in the clouds.

Cardinal sings, "This is your thread."
    Dawn breaks—choose silence.
    Half-moon dances in the clouds.
    Spider teaches, "Weave a web to call home."

CYCLE OF GIVING AND RECEIVING

Returning to my Five Truths:

    ~   sensitive to the needs and energies of others

    ~   nourished by time alone

    ~   created by God to be a blessing

    ~   a lover of nature and all images it creates through water, wind, birds, trees, flowers, mountains, valleys

    ~   an artist

I am nourished by God through time alone in nature and then responding to that experience in some creative form.

After being fed in that way, I am able to share God's blessing with others in need. This space I now occupy is a container for my cycle of receiving and giving.

WALKING THE CAMINO

The past few years I have found myself drawn to experiences of those who have walked the Camino de Santiago through northern Spain. As much as part of me wants to embark on this sacred pilgrimage that ends at the Cathedral of St. James in Santiago, traveling this mileage on foot with a backpack strapped to me seems a bit beyond reach for me at this time in my life.

I am made of this stardust. It is a feast.

This Is Your Thread

Nonetheless, I believe that in some way we all walk our own version of the Camino at some point in our lives, whether we are aware of it or not. Without realization of the journey metaphor and spiritual lessons available to us, however, for some these life experiences become just a long trudge with a heavy load.

As snow has cleared in my wooded sanctuary, I have returned to early-morning walks. I pray the day's lectionary from the Book of Common Prayer, read a few pages from books I am working through, do a bit of writing, and then take to the woods for God to speak to me in the silence of nature, its own created order.

As I become winded while traveling the hills and turns of this 20–30-minute course, I realize my morning walks are my own version of "the Camino." My journey is more bit by bit, opening myself daily to God's wisdom for me on that day. It is a rich time of prayer.

As I continue to settle into this new home of eight months and recall the life-changing events of the past six years, the Camino metaphor holds true. I can feel a weight of exhaustion in my legs on unpredictable terrain. I experience an isolation of solitude. I'm continually looking for signs to assure me that I am still on the path, wondering where it will lead and where, when, and how it will end.

From physical changes that hinder our abilities to rapid-fire life changes that threaten our faith in the concept of a loving God and no other version of the story to consider, I imagine that most people could relate to this sense of pilgrimages we are invited to explore. If only they knew.

SUBTLE SHIFTS

As I read Tuesday's entry, I realize I am describing my word for this year, "nourish."

As I have nourished myself in my externship weeks, there has been a subtle but important shift. A program idea about pilgrimage has begun to write itself. Others are reaching out to AWBA to help with programs.

As I have allowed God to nourish me, space is created, and I can more fully express myself in the world.

I removed the weaving from its loom yesterday. It was quite emotional to do so. I felt I was holding the web of my life in my arms.

I found a branch to anchor one end. As part of today's session I will find a branch to anchor the other. The tools for my process remain, but the plan will write itself as I move into this rainy morning.

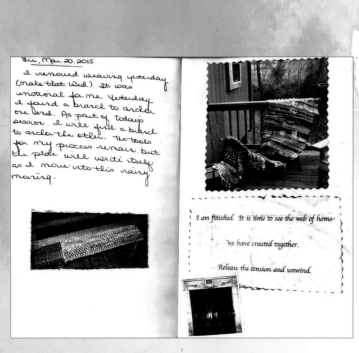

The Web of Home

EXTREMES BROUGHT TOGETHER

Yesterday's process was surprising and mystical. I believe the thread is taking me to a simpler place. It is curious that after those few hours of "aha" and revelations, chaos ensued.

Phone calls from people in deep turmoil as well as my own flurry of calls regarding prescriptions and my doctor who has suddenly left his practice. All followed by a directee arriving last night for an overnight retreat.

Both extremes brought together in one day.

HOME

My Five Truths (to be sensitive to the needs and energies of others; nourished by time alone; created by God to be a blessing; a lover of nature and all its imagery; and an artist) seemed to begin coming together when I removed the weaving from the loom.

As I have allowed God to nourish me *(more time alone, in nature, as my artist self)*, more and more space is created. When I am *sensitive to needs and energies of others*, I can more freely express myself as a being who is *created by God to be a blessing.*

I notice a small brown spider on the ceiling in my studio. I am looking for a second branch to anchor my weaving when this image from our backyard finds me.

I return to my studio and read the final portion of Joel McKerrow's poem "Search" about layers of a pilgrimage. These words resonate especially today after my walk around the edges of our property. I feel God has written a love letter to me about the home she has created for me in heaven and the process given to me here to create my own path to that home.

Rather than watercolor this week, I use conte crayons and chalk pastels.

This seems more unfinished than when in the first half of the other two pieces.

SPIDER AND CARDINAL

Spider and cardinal have appeared and continue to appear for a reason.

Cardinal affirms and holds to the value of holding onto the thread—the "cardinal rule."

Spider is teaching me so much as I near the end of this process.

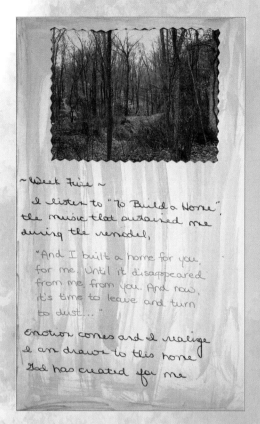

To Build a Home

Weaving a Web . . .

"I imagine you moving and existing as I do. While firmly grounded as to the place you occupy, you are fluid as you play with the movements of the wind and open to the sights

Moving and Existing as I Do

and sounds that surround you while not absorbing them into yourself.

I am your authentic self.

dream

I Am Your Authentic Self

~ Patience to pay attention to how events are unfolding
~ Wisdom to integrate all parts and aspects of my life into a whole
~ Weaving mental and intuitive flexibility into my daily thinking
~ Strength and gentleness combined
~ Power and creativity to weave my own web (within a safe boundary)
~ Understanding that the web need not be a source of entanglement but a network of roads to travel
~ Awaken my creative senses and encourage me to design the fabric of my life from my soul's original interior

Sitting back now and allowing my art to speak, I captured words that began to flow from somewhere within me:

"You can begin to see that many of the inner dividing walls that seem to separate aspects of your life are not as solid as they appear. You may be able to see that by looking at things differently, barriers can disappear, and your life can be viewed in a more integrated way . . . Please do not fail to see the eternal plan of creation."

THE PILGRIM SOUL

The second of two expressive arts workshops for Wellstreams is this evening. Although exhausting, it has been good to engage in the interior and exterior simultaneously—perhaps a fuller picture.

I have also been traveling through the web of my past as a close friend travels nearly identical territory as I did five years ago. It has been helpful to see my own growth through this lens.

That movement is also played out in the setting for these two expressive arts workshops—the same room where I began my training as a spiritual director 10 years ago.

This decade has been filled with significant gifts and losses. A tremendous amount of life has been traveled in this decade.

Those experiences have supported me in claiming the "web." I was going to write "creating," but I believe it has been there from the beginning.

I needed to discover it, claim it, and, now, value it by making choices that keep me in that web of growth and movement.

A gentle rain falls, as it will much of today. The earth nourishes this pilgrim soul.

NOW WHAT?

I'm feeling a sense of "Now what?" beginning to bubble up as I realize I am near this internship and training's end.

Last night's session seemed to go well, and there may be opportunity for more.

I am reminded that I prefer personal one-on-one settings more than in a group, where issues feel they are left in midair. It is as though I stir up waters of emotions and then leave and processing happens out of my view.

What mountain is next to climb? Next adventure? Is it now a time to plateau and simply "be" in all of this?

God, direct me as I walk into this new place. It is my desire to simplify by focusing on these five nonnegotiables. Help me to further identify them.

My last session is this morning. Two full dreams during the night leave me tired this morning, as well as with two themes that seem part of today's session.

I am not surprised by these two dreams or their timing with this internship based in healing as I find a new home for my soul.

I intentionally leave my morning unplanned based on these dreams. I know I have tools for processing them; I will just walk one step at a time.

I listen to "into the silence" again as I reflect on the weaving hung temporarily in my studio. I read the final portion of "Search" aloud and watch a corresponding portion of the YouTube video.

Tears are there, start to finish, and I know I am healed and have found myself again—this time more true and more real. I choose to move into art next rather than freeform writing and pantoum.

WHERE ELSE WOULD YOU RATHER BE?

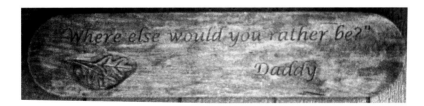

Where else would you rather be?

Today I was led to go outside for a walk. I took my camera (with two extra batteries just in case), dressed in layers, and headed out. I can't believe all that found me in those short 30 minutes. When I returned, I made a cup of coffee, sat on the porch, and began writing, journaling my walk as a dialogue.

Sit. Enjoy. Remember.

Birdsong. Wind moving through the pines. First signs of spring pushing through winter. There is silliness along the path (a small stuffed bear sitting in a carefully arranged array of leaves left by someone walking ahead of me).

Flowers lie in the chapel, left by a fellow pilgrim in the early-morning hours. Their colors are still fresh and vibrant.

Morning newness greets me in the animals who companion me along the way from safety in their own homes in stables, pens, and surrounding pastures.

I find color in rocks along the way back through the chapel grounds.

I return to my home, and I see it in a new way.

A hot beverage warms my view of the horizon from my porch sanctuary.

I am home in the soil of my being.

Sit. Enjoy. Remember.

My Five Truth nonnegotiables become a simple phrase "a feather on the breath of God," that contains space created at both ends. Uttered with an inhale, it allows energy for a full exhale and a pause at the end. I'm aware of my dance of a deep inhale, holding it to create space inside, then a deep exhale.

I look at my weaving and realize that this breath dance is how I ended the woven journey last week. This entire journey has surprised me. I was a bit anxious this morning wondering whether and, if so, how this weaving would come to some sort of graceful conclusion.

Today, it seems that I wove this experience through the ordinary reality of my morning hours. For that awareness, I am truly grateful.

ROY: STUDIO

I surveyed artwork stacked on the corner of Judy's drawing table and then wall space left on which to hang it. "Are you sure all this is going to fit?" I asked, knowing better than to voice any opinion that it wouldn't. Almost 40 years of marriage had, after all, taught me a thing or two.

Judy cocked her head to one side as if measuring in the unrestricted zone of her mind. "I think so," she said, eyeing these pieces as if seeing them for the very first time. "If not, let's just hang the weaving and see what we can do with the rest around that."

I knew that once her gorgeous weaving she had just completed was hung, she would agree that it deserves its own space and enough breathing room to settle in as the showpiece it is.

I held it in place, and she stepped back. I adjusted ("Up a little on the left" . . . "No, that's too much" . . . "OK, down on the right" . . .) until she declared, "Right there!" as if solving an equation of quantum physics.

After she handed me my hammer and a couple of finishing nails to tack it into place, Judy produced some beautiful and yet substantial hooks so the weaving could be removed to show without re-creating the need for this exacting positioning process each time it was returned to her studio.

Once the hooks were in place, we stood back, arm in arm, to admire it.

"It's just beautiful," I said, meaning it. Its mix of colors and textures and the artful way she brought the elements together were exquisite. I didn't know much about textiles and weaving, but I knew a true work of art when I saw it.

"Thanks," she said simply.

There really is nothing like a woman who knows who she is, what she's capable of, and what she brings to every table—and yet carries it all off with a humility and grace that puts others at ease. She invites them to that same table, welcoming all comers with open arms and a tender heart.

Studio

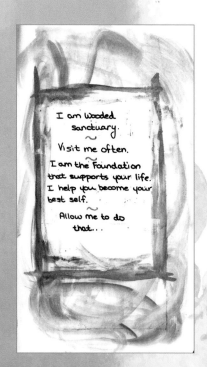

I am Wooded Sanctuary

Florida Teaser

JUDY: I AM WOODED SANCTUARY

I am wooded sanctuary.

Visit me often.

I am the foundation that supports your life. I help you become your best self.

Allow me to do that . . .

TENSION OF GIFTS AND CHALLENGES

Katherine sent me a Florida teaser picked up on a beach walk—a piece of rope (a thread?) wound around elements of the ocean picked up on its journey to the shoreline. It will be added to my weaving.

TWO-WAY DIALOGUE . . . WITH GOD

Below is a conversation I had with God today. In a journaling technique called "two-way dialogue," we first invite God into a dialogue with us. Next, we write a question or make a statement and wait quietly until something pops into our mind, and we write that down. No questioning, no judgment, no censorship. It's a simple freewriting technique that yields surprising insights and answers that bubble up within, dictated by something greater than you, that omnipotent Source energy that we know as God.

Here's how it went:

Me: I know you are formidable. I must not take you for granted or ignore your very real presence.

God: I have been a natural part of you for a very long time. You have tried to outsmart me to get rid of me, but that has just made me enter into your life in deceptive and surprising ways. You have kept the door open for me, making it easy to move in and out of your life experiences.

Me: I am wiser now and will not underestimate you. I will hold Healing and Intensity in a healthy tension. To be a healing space for others and to keep the voice of intensity in balance, I will engage in nature on a consistent basis (daily as possible) and raise the value of creative expression for myself.

God: As long as I know you will not dismiss me or shame me in some manner, I agree to diminish my presence as a negative influence and help you learn how to use your tendency toward busyness to be more in touch with how others get caught up in that same cycle. I will help you learn how to keep your uncertainty and doubt "in check"—perhaps to keep you humble and learning from others rather than sabotaging what you are trying to do for others. I can become more of a partner in this process.

Me: I commit to enlarging these gifts in my life by taking increased responsibility for maintaining them in a healthy manner so they are equal to the challenges.

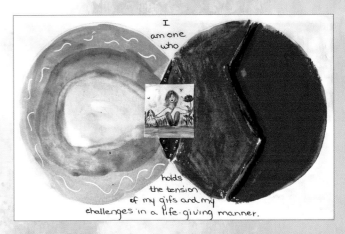

I Am One Who

SACRED SPACE

For many reasons, one of which is likely age, I have become a very early riser. Although I am awake early, however, I try not to schedule any meetings before 11:00 a.m. to give me time and space for quiet, reflection, reading, journaling, art making, walking, sitting—just being present with God and what her Spirit may have for me on that day.

Then, as chaos quite often ensues in the remainder of the day and evening, I am able to enter into those experiences with some sense of calm and peace surrounding me and those I will interact with.

Today, waking at 5:00 a.m., I was able to be fully present with a cup of tea as the new day began. In this Sacred Space I began my morning, and birds sang me into our day.

Healing and Intensity

I recently began reading John O'Donohue's *Beauty*, a book I have owned for a few years and never read. It's a perfect companion to my morning rhythm. My view at daybreak a few hours ago followed by words I read was a gift from the Holy.

It is not always this way, however, is it? I have had seasons of life when I have been in a medical setting at 3:00 a.m., 6:00 a.m. without a window in sight; when I have, thankfully, slept until late morning after being awake for much of the night due to concern for a loved one. In those seasons, any sense of a spiritual rhythm was confined to a lot of deep sighs and prayers of "Lord, come quickly."

It is my hard, hard times that remind me to seize these moments of relative calm and gentle breathing, to claim God's gift to me for refreshment.

I gentled myself into the space of home today, moved a bit more slowly, released all expectations for "catching up," and allowed what I know can heal me to do its work. It has done its magic.

Our bodies may not always be at their best. I have come to learn that our soul, our spirit, is there to support us into a place of healing, of wholeness, of nurture, even if the physical is not immediately relieved of its pain, discomfort, or general dis-ease. We need to learn to discern how God desires to nurture our soul and then receive that nourishment, offered in each moment.

Crocus

"Just Go With It"

Just Go with It

To do this, we all must learn to find a piece of Sacred Space each day. It may be in the outdoors, where mine is most often found. It may be in the soft embrace of a pet. It may be in the comfort of a favorite chair. It may be a warm touch of someone who loves you. It may be through words found in a sacred text.

We need to expect God to provide and then stop, notice, and receive the gift, whispering a heartfelt "thank-you" to the One who nurtures our spirit, always.

SUNRISE AND BIRDSONG

I have been awake by 5:30 a.m. the past two days and on our bedroom porch when Roy leaves for work. Glimpses of sunrises and abundant birdsong have companioned me both days in still-chilly air. I created the watercolor "Crocus."

I am getting better keeping my inner critic at rest. She has her say, but I still like it! I really like the picture with it amidst the real crocuses.

I began reviewing my journals, notes, and art to prepare for my final review that will take place in two weeks.

As I read through this particular journal, I identify my desire: **I want to absorb all of this fully so that it makes a difference in my world.**

As I looked at beach and bayfront images, I feel sadness that my apprenticeship has come to an end. I also realize that all of the EAFI experience is now a part of me. And always will be.

JUST GO WITH IT

The dust and chaos of my mind have settled. Will return to mandala making for a season. Mandalas are a good stopping place for me.

The mandala to the left was done over three days' time. I've not used black paper for these before, so it was an exploration of sorts. I have ordered Susanne Fincher's book, *Creating Mandalas: For Insight, Healing, and Self-Expression* (Shambhala, 2010), and I am eager for what that will reveal.

I have been continuing with my daily walks and doing my best to keep my mornings as a time of quiet. There has been some increased clarity as a result. Why am I so slow to make that connection?

I WANTED TO BE BLUE!

It was a full weekend. Many good things—gardening, church—but little downtime, and I certainly feel that absence.

I did the next mandala late Friday. I don't like it. I wanted it to be restful in shades of blue, yet its first color was poppy red . . . anything but restful!

I dislike it so much that I will just glue it to the page assuming I will never (always dangerous!) reuse it for anything . . .

I Wanted to Be Blue!

SPRING PROFUSION

It is a beauty-full morning. Rain has ended, and sun is breaking through. What a full week this will be. Final EAFI Skype review with staff tomorrow, spiritual direction, then to Columbus for Wellstreams graduation.

All of this set against spring's profusion with temps in the low 80s.

BELIEVE IN YOUR MOSES AND GO

It is about 6:30 a.m. The sun is rising. Horses and cows graze; a hummingbird has its breakfast at our feeder. I am nourished here.

I am curious what will follow.

The first pages of my art journals that contained this process beginning in January 2013 have a poem from Maerina Wuderkehr, a Benedictine monastic of St. Scholastica Monastery in Fort Smith, Arkansas, that riffs on Exodus, with Moses, the reluctant prophet, claiming his voice and the message deep within him.

I had just enough belief in my Moses to "go" with no hint of the destination. I believed just enough to "go" two and a half years ago when Sarasota called to me. Now I have a sense of "go" yet again, to put all of this together somehow.

It will be a day of abundance—likely both/and. I choose to be present in each moment.

Spring Profusion

Believe in Your Moses

Cardinal Thread

Be Kind

SURROUNDED IN ABUNDANCE

What a day yesterday. Too many stories and fragments to put into words.

Did the final EAFI Skype call in my studio, surrounded by the abundance of the past 10 years.

I graduated at 12:10 p.m.!

Wellsprings graduation was filled with everything imaginable—wonderful and exhausting.

CARDINAL THREAD

I see a web. I see threads moving in a flexible yet ordered design. I see one primary thread moving through the web with a sense of purpose.

I feel freedom in this movement, even within all the activity. I feel quiet and at ease, although uncertain.

I imagine myself pulling this cardinal thread into the center with focus and intention.

NAME. CLAIM. RECEIVE. RESPOND.

The phrase "Name it. Claim it" has come to me, with the addition of "Receive it. Respond to it."

I think I am continuing to learn what it means to receive it.

The naming and claiming have been about this new physical and spiritual home. It has been clearly named and acknowledged as my new reality. That first step feels pretty much complete.

In this past year I have been claiming it as such to myself and to others. It has been a somewhat vulnerable process but necessary in making it a reality.

I believe my current discomfort is in taking it in, fully digesting it.

I think I am afraid to fully receive it, believing it all too good to be true and on the verge of being taken away. Like there is a final bridge I am afraid to cross, knowing I will not be able to turn back.

I know this new life is my true life and my home. After so many years of "half life," there is discomfort inherent in a new thing, even though it is the thing I have been seeking all my life.

TRUST, JUST ENOUGH

In those moments when very little of my original plan remains intact, and the unknown looms at every turn, may I trust, just enough, in God's sacred wisdom to make sense of the uncertainty. May I welcome that uncertainty as a messenger for my unfolding future.

AT LEAST ONE NEW NUGGET

Had a great day with the horses at Gilgal Farm yesterday. AWBA offered a healing experience with horses, and each participant walked away with at least one nugget of new learning and experience for themselves. Insight was gained about releasing control, listening to and honoring your inner wisdom and choices, persevering with struggles—great life lessons. Today, however, I am exhausted!

WAYS TO WHOLENESS

Yesterday, I wrote a new blog post for AWBA, "Ways to Wholeness," that shares about the recent equine event and some of my hopes about expressive arts:

"Recently, AWBA provided a bridge-building experience with the support of horses. This program of equine-assisted learning invited participants to explore some of their innermost feelings regarding their journey as they move from a life they expected to live to a new land in which they find themselves.

Themes around control, flexibility, listening to one's inner wisdom, etc. quickly rose to the surface. And, most importantly, it was a fun day. AWBA will continue to explore these opportunities through our collective of artists and spiritual directors.

Our souls long for a sense of hope, peace, and a sense of connection on that journey. It is AWBA's desire to continue to be one of those resources."

Summer 2015

JUDY: WHEN WORDS AREN'T THERE

A great two hours of touch drawing last week with men and women moving through a season of transition. What a wonderful way to tell your story when the words just aren't there.

Remain in Transition

REMAIN IN TRANSITION

Lots of art prep for others in recent weeks (AWBA Touch Drawing and St. Alban's Mandala Making classes) along with some knitting and finishing work on woven pieces.

I completed the free-form mandala "Remain in Transition" yesterday.

~ I see light surrounding and grounding all that is.

~ I see intentional movement flowing outward.

~ I feel energized and, still in the same breath, unable (or not knowing) how to hold both.

~ I imagine a unified and contented coexistence of both if I will remain in this transition.

CREATION FROM THE SOUL

This morning I facilitated a session of "Creativity as a Spiritual Practice" offering guidance for mandala making. It was a peace-filled time of slowing and stilling to hear the "still, small voice" of the Holy. What an honor to witness what each person created from their soul.

THE PURPOSE IN WAITING

"While they were listening to this, he went on to tell them a parable because he was near Jerusalem and the people thought that the Kingdom of God was going to appear at once."

—LUKE 19:11

This continues the parable of the talents. What do people do with what they are given?

My desire is strong that things happen quickly. I seek resolution "at once." This reminds me of the purpose in waiting. I must slow up for the spiritual practice of my life and invest, well, all that I am.

A DIFFERENT VIEW

Thoughts of pilgrimage have been my constant companions for this past year since Roy and I made our life-changing decision to relocate from a place that was home for over 20 years to a more rural and natural setting into which we have settled as a hand slips into a perfectly fit glove.

Some pieces of this beginning again have been easy, and some have been hard. Whether you make a conscious choice for a life change or have it thrust upon you in some manner, it seems important to learn how to walk in your new land and invite a new perspective to companion you on your unknown path.

Clinging to an old perspective while trying to adapt to new circumstances makes it nearly impossible to thrive.

We can embark on an interior journey of pilgrimage, inviting scales to fall from our eyes so a new heaven and earth come into view to create the landscape that best suits this season of life and all that it has to offer—even if unwelcome.

Always We Begin Again (AWBA) was created to journey alongside those on a path of learning to live anew. As we continued to develop and grow within this vision, we are learning that pilgrim wisdom applies to those in a time of transition.

We continue to develop the Camino Project as an opportunity for pilgrimage for anyone in a time of transition regardless of the circumstances that brought them to a place of beginning again.

I'm excited to connect with people who are seeking to begin again in a new season of life and to do it well. It is AWBA's wholehearted intention to offer a safe and sacred community in which all who come may do the same.

A PILGRIM'S SOUL GUIDE

Just posted to the AWBA blog "A New Perspective on What Has Been" as we develop nuts and bolts of a pilgrimage experience. Lots of creative expression will be included—clay, fused glass, watercolor, poetry, photography, contemplative walks, and whatever additional chaos my creative cohorts and I can dream up.

A huge influence will be Christine Valters Paintner and her newly released book, *The Soul of a Pilgrim*, that will serve as a guide for this journey.

> *"I am about to do a new thing. Now it springs forth.*
> *Do you not perceive it?"*
>
> —ISAIAH 43:19

ROY: WALKING UNDER THE CANOPY

"Augh!" Judy exclaimed, looking around her as if seeing for the first time the myriad of things that needed tending in our house. "I'm so behind! There's so much to do around here! Where do I even begin?"

In our steady barrage of warm spring days at home, there is much to do. The blissfulness of these small things, regular life humming along quietly in the background, provides a blessed relief from the intermittent interruptions of Bigger Things That Have to Be Dealt With.

Sometimes Judy has a hard time hearing that sweet hum; the tyranny of the urgent gets her scurrying from Thing to Thing, with a building sense of being overwhelmed that makes it hard to hear the call of our blessings.

Generally, that's where I come in.

"Well," I said, wrapping my arms around her from behind and pulling her close, "I think we start by going out to lunch, then stopping off at a nursery to buy some flowers, then coming home to plant them. Then we'll take a stroll under this magnificent canopy of trees that surrounds us before soaking in a long, hot bath and then sitting on our porch with a glass of wine to admire our work."

"Oh, Roy, you just don't get it," she said, pulling away, irritated. "I mean, yeah, that all sounds wonderful, but look at all this other stuff I need to take care of," she said, gesturing toward the stacks of mail to be gone through, accumulated clutter, and an array of colorful sticky note reminders on the fridge.

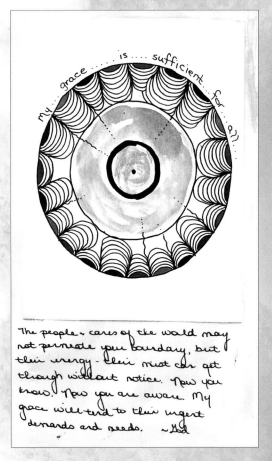

A New Perspective

"All of that will be here tomorrow," I said, sitting down to put on my shoes. "This beautiful day out there may not, however. It's springtime in Ohio, and you just never know what tomorrow might look like."

"OK," she said, as if placating a small child. "But if something jumps up to bite us because I didn't take care of it today, you'll have only yourself to blame."

"And blame myself I shall," I said, grinning up at her as I finished tying my shoe. "In the meantime, let's just scoff at the impending disaster and go have some fun and plant some flowers."

She laughed in spite of herself. Mission accomplished. What would she do without me? What would I do without her?

BUSY AND DELIGHTFUL

The past few months have been a blur of activities with new ideas taking flight for AWBA and our glorious life at Sunset Ridge.

A delightful mix—and steady stream of retreatants coming to this sacred space Roy and I created, a lovely flow of synchronicity and ideas coming together here in my mind and in my art, and continued revelations through spiritual direction toggling with my own work with new directees.

Church activities, long walks, making art, spending time with Roy. The stuff dreams are made of. The fruition of so much work.

And then came the nightmare we never anticipated.

Reader's Notes

PART II

. . . and How to Die

Fall 2015

"The symptoms you've been having are inconsistent with what we found on your MRI," the young doctor said, pausing as if to search for just the right way to say what he needed to say next.

"There's a large mass in your right temporal lobe."

At the words "large mass," I looked up at Roy, my eyes filled with fear.

"Aunt Ginny," I whispered.

"Maybe not," he said. His eyes, too, were full of fear that he was trying to wrestle into confidence.

Somewhere deep within me I knew. And as it turned out, I was right.

A TICKING CLOCK

Glioblastoma, also known as glioblastoma multiforme (GBM), is the most aggressive type of brain cancer there is. Our kind-eyed young doctor explained this gently, trying not to react, I suppose, to our stricken faces at this dreaded diagnosis.

I know this all too well. My mother's younger sister, Aunt Ginny, died of this deadly, most often genetic monster way too young. The doctors told Aunt Ginny it was pretty uncommon for women to get it, and only something like three people per 100,000 develop this disease each year. Not odds anyone would think to worry about, unless you become one of those three.

We listened as he described the initial symptoms—nodding and looking at one another as he mentioned some of the random struggles I had been having on and off since last summer.

Sneaky bastard, this cancer. A chickenshit disease, if you ask me—and pretty much anyone who sits in a conference room such as this. I had shrugged these "symptoms" off, taking Tylenol for the headaches, self-diagnosing my occasional bouts of nausea as a stomach bug, food poisoning, or stress. At one point, when a sort of malaise, a persistent low-grade anxiety, and depression set in, I had even considered taking an antidepressant. Sometimes as we age, our brain chemistry changes, and these drugs can be so helpful in restoring normal brain chemistry.

As it turns out, I was on the right track. Sort of. My problem was with my brain—just not its chemistry. It wasn't until I lost consciousness in the shower that it was clear there was something going on in my brain that connected all those random complaints into a big steaming pile of bad news.

As we sat and tried to hear and absorb all this young doctor was trying to convey, it was hard to stop myself from leaping ahead. There is no question that I am facing a battle for my life. And chances are very close to zero that I will win.

"So how long do I have?" I managed to squeak out the question I knew was pounding through both of our brains. Roy's face remained stoic. We had faced serious health challenges together before—but always with him on the other side of these cold hospital sheets, not me. I was the healthy one.

"This type of tumor can be pretty much asymptomatic until it reaches an enormous size," he remarked, gesturing toward the MRI scans on the screen. "Like yours."

Mine. Of all the things I had ever wanted to call my own, this was not one of them. *I have things to do!* I wanted to wail. *I have worked so hard to get to this place in my life. I've just discovered real, true joy and a new sense of purpose. THIS CAN'T BE HAPPENING right now!*

Instead, I bit the inside of my cheek and nodded my understanding, trying very hard to stop the deluge of tears that threatened to reduce me—and likely Roy—to an uncomprehending puddle.

Focus, I reprimanded myself. *Listen carefully. Ask the right questions. Make good decisions.* Later I can scour between the lines of this death sentence for any sign of hope that I might escape or evade it, if only for a while.

"So now what?" I asked, trying to keep my voice even and failing miserably.

"Well, the next thing is a tissue biopsy," the doctor said, gesturing toward a darkened place on the incomprehensible blob that was obviously my brain.

He switched to another view—a profile that was indeed easier to tell what I was looking at. There it was. A big, oddly shaped area outlined in white with a darker spot in the center that looked stuck to the top of my right frontal lobe.

He switched views again, this time from the top, the axial view. "To get a definitive diagnosis and treatment plan, we'll need to do a stereotactic biopsy or a craniotomy with tumor resection and pathologic confirmation."

Drowning in the jargon I couldn't fully comprehend, I asked, cutting to what I thought was the chase, "What does all that mean? Are you saying it could be something else?"

"It *could*, I suppose," he said, switching off the viewer's light, "but based on your symptoms and everything else we're seeing here, it's not likely. The biopsy is to confirm what we're pretty sure we already know."

"But you're just *pretty sure*," Roy interjected. "Are you saying you're not *100 percent* sure?"

The young doctor looked at me, then Roy, clearly wishing he could give us the hope we were begging for, and then said, "The likelihood of it being anything else is very, very remote."

"I'll take it," Roy said, clearly hearing what he needed to hear.

What a terrible thing to have to tell people, I thought, feeling a fleeting moment of compassion for this young man.

"Does that mean you'll remove the tumor?" I asked, proud of myself for following the thread.

He nodded. "Surgery is the first stage of treatment of glioblastoma, and it can reduce an average GBM tumor by 99 percent. In addition to confirming the diagnosis, surgery will usually alleviate any symptoms the mass is causing by pressing on other brain tissue. It will also help minimize the tumor's resistance to other treatments."

"So why 99 percent?" Roy asked, still splitting hairs. "Why not 100 percent? Is there any chance at all you can get all of it?"

Sweet Roy, he just didn't want to understand. Having walked this path with Aunt Ginny, I knew all too well what the doctor was trying to say—and trying not to say.

"Studies show that if we can remove 98 percent or more of the tumor, you can have a significantly longer healthier time," the doctor said, turning his focus to me. He wasn't sure what to do with Roy.

"The cells of this kind of tumor are very infiltrative," he continued, returning to the more solid emotional footing of science. "Most people will develop recurrent tumors either near the original site or at more distant locations within the brain due to metastasis."

"So that's why we also have to do other kinds of treatment," I said, more for Roy's benefit than for my own clarification. This I knew, too.

"Yes," he said, looking at me, now realizing that while he needed to direct the information to me, he was explaining it for Roy. "After surgery and radiation, a chemotherapy drug called temozolomide will suppress and slow the tumor's recurrence."

"But it will come back, no matter what you do?" Roy asked.

"Unfortunately, yes," the doctor said, answering Roy but looking at me. "The more tumor we can get out of there with surgery, the longer you'll have before your symptoms return."

"So how long do you think I have, assuming everything goes as it should?" I asked, squaring my shoulders and tightening my jaw to brace for the answer I knew would be devastating, regardless.

The doctor sat on the edge of my hospital bed, likewise preparing himself for what I can only imagine is the very worst part of his job. "For most people, expected survival is 12 to 15 months following diagnosis," he said. "About 3 to 7 percent of people survive for more than five years. Without treatment, survival is typically about three months." He paused. "So it's important to get started as soon as possible—and we'll throw the book at this thing to get you as much quality time as we can."

"How soon can I have the surgery?" I heard myself ask, not believing the words as they came out of my mouth and yet knowing that every moment wasted from here on out will shorten my life.

First things first. Get this thing out of my head.

Solace in the Cycle

SOLACE IN THE CYCLE

"In the morning, Lord, you hear my voice; early in the morning I make my appeal and watch for you."

—PSALM 5

"The lord of hosts is with us: God of Jacob is our stronghold."

—PSALM 46

With my recent glioblastoma diagnosis on November 21, a new and unforeseen pilgrimage begins. My doctor said I may only have another 12 to 15 months left on my earthly journey. I intend to make the most of them.

I've delayed beginning this journal, yet I recognize I must try to capture what I can of this brain cancer path. I don't know how many of those months I will be able to journal this journey.

COURAGE FOR THE VALLEY

On November 24, the night before my surgery, I received this email from my dear friend, Katherine. These are words I wish everyone would receive upon beginning such an arduous journey. So blessed.

My dear Judy,

I am so saddened that you are having to go through all of this—my heart is with you.

I want to share with you some of what I've learned and some of what helped me both to navigate my journey with Hugh [her husband] and my own journey with a cancer diagnosis.

First of all, remember that cancer (or whatever ailment) is just that. A diagnosis. It is not who you are and cannot take away from you your beautiful sweetness of spirit, your sensitive engagement with life, your tender compassion, your depth of integrity . . . unless you let it. And I trust you will not!

Live what you know in your heart of hearts—remain present to the present, staying as much as you can in what is right now and avoid living in what-ifs. Now is enough. More than that can get overwhelming. BREATHE . . . listen to music.

Speaking of overwhelming, there is SO much information . . . maybe too much information. It may be important to do some research, but ultimately it is important to have confidence and trust in your team of medical professionals and the resource information they offer. Write down your questions. Record answers and other important information, because it is really easy in the scheme of things to forget.

Experience your emotions even as you keep your focus and energy directed toward the positive. It may sound contradictory, but you know well enough there is nothing to be gained from "stuffing" where you are and what you may be feeling. Emotions have less power and consume less energy when acknowledged.

Lastly but foremost: BELIEVE
God loves you
    Roy loves you
    Your family loves you
    Legions of friends love you

Believe
In yourself, in your body and in your spirit
    Miracles happen
    Healing is attainable
    Your medical team is knowledgeable and highly skilled

Believe
Grace abounds
    You will find God's strength in your weakness
    Prayers are heard.

The light of God surrounds you
    The love of God enfolds you
    The power of God protects you
    The presence of God watches over you
    Wherever you are, God is!

The Prayer for Protection

The light of God surrounds us;
The love of God enfolds us;
The power of God protects us;
The presence of God watches
 over us;
Wherever we are, God is!
—James Dillet Freeman

All is well, and all manner of being is well.

I love you, my dear soul sister. I cherish our friendship, and you are in my heartfelt prayers. Tomorrow will be a day of prayer for you and Roy.

You know any other questions or ways I can support you are welcome. Tom sends his love and prayers, too.

Peace be with you.

Love,
Katherine

Reading this email again and again, I feel peace and power in the simple "Prayer for Protection" penned by James Dillet Freeman during World War II when he was challenged by a young woman to write an affirmative prayer for protection that was more encouraging than "Yea though I walk through the valley of the shadow of death, I will fear no evil, for thou art with me" (Psalm 23:4, KJV).

You want me to do better than the 23rd Psalm? Dillet reported thinking, then remembering a little prayer he had written for a Christmas Eve service, reworking it a little to make it more universal, and then adding the last line that came to him, he realized would make it even more powerful. So the Prayer for Protection as printed in 1943 has endured and encouraged others walking through their literal and figurative "valley of the shadow of death" ever since.

I love this story. It always reminds me how we often rise to challenges we can't imagine conquering. This is what I need to remember more than anything right now.

MIRACLES AND MORE TIME

I survived the brain surgery on November 25, which I was very unsure of. That experience seems a miracle in and of itself.

Lord, I pray for more time:
  1. Time to love more deeply
  2. The opportunity to live from this new place

DAY OF TRUTH

"Awake, awake. Put on strength."
—ISAIAH 51

Today is a day for truth—to learn about this tumor that took up residence within me and to hear recommendations from three different doctors.

It will be much to absorb. It will be facts and no more "what-ifs."

Lord, you know my fear and you also know my gratitude for all you have done thus far.

I thank you for the abundance of love and grace already brought to my life through this, and I thank you for however you will unfold this day.

Help me be strong and courageous because of who you are in my life and who you are helping me to become.

I choose, with help, to live free and not bound by fear and with a label beyond your "beloved daughter."

A PITY CRY

Allowed myself a "pity cry" today.

I recognize my life expectancy may be shortened even after all of this effort. I am trying to live this as a new life, with new experiences and hope.

But the tears still come. And I let them.

UPLIFTED IN THE GRIMNESS

Long day with radiology yesterday. Was fitted with a mask and told about treatment.

I realize the "grimness" (doctors' words) of the situation, but I choose to stay present and uplifted in this.

In some ways, it feels I have been given a new life by God—a new perspective, deepened relationships, and, as my counselor said last night, "peace."

I know God has this in hand.

Yet the sorrow does come, and I must allow it.

COVENANT

"Do not remember the former things, nor consider the things of old.
Behold, I will do a new thing. Now it shall spring forth: shall you not know it?
I will even make a road in the wilderness and rivers in the desert."

—ISAIAH 42: 18–19

I am slowly settling into this reality. It will be more real when radiation and chemo begin on December 21.

It seems important for me to express myself during this time, although this expression may ebb and flow with my energy and my ability to control materials I use. This is my art healing journal.

Greening Flower of Life

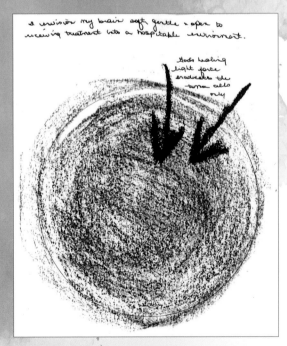

Open to Receiving

I created an art block last year with one of my favorite David Whyte writings, "The Winter of Listening," about learning to shape an unexpected new existence. In some strange way that is what I believe God is offering—a new life—even in the midst of this grim diagnosis. My counselor says I seem more "at peace." Go figure.

So I commit to a new way of being in this earthly life for as long as I have it. I will fight to live as long as I sense God leading me that way. And should it come time to surrender and go home, I pray for the wisdom and grace to do so.

My life is not constrained by limitations of a brain tumor. I can even make new life from this gray mass of deadly cells. Believe it. Fight for it. This greening flower of life is not held down by gray matter. It is being lifted and will have its own voice. No one can repress it but me.

Author Barbara Ganim writes in her book *Art and Healing* about how sometimes it takes a life-altering crisis to awaken us to the voice of our spirit. Isn't it strange how big changes can be their own catalyst?

I envision my brain as soft and gentle and open to receiving treatment into a hospitable environment. God's light force eradicates the tumor cells only.

My covenant to myself as I begin this journey:

~ I will guard my heart and mind to allow only positive energy, good thoughts to take up residence.

~ I will engage with art and music to remind me of beauty.

~ I trust that God is with me on every step of this path and that when times are dark, God's healing light is still at work.

~ I will believe in healing.

~ I will lean on friends and family for support and encouragement.

~ I will not try to do any of this on my own.

RESTORE MY HOPE

"Surely it is God who saves me: I will trust in him and not be afraid. For the lord is my stronghold and my sure defense, and he will be my savior."

—ISAIAH 12:2–6

Having a hard time today. Sad and consumed by this chaos.

Lord, restore my hope.

ABOVE CANCER

Roy called a friend who has lived with cancer for over 15 years in the midst of yesterday's discouragement, and that was very uplifting. I did some art, talked with family, and a dear friend arrived.

My mind must be like a steel door, allowing only goodness and light to enter. Sadness will move through, but it must not take up residence in me as this cancer has.

Reflexology at 10:00 a.m., nurse at noon, counseling at 5:00 p.m. A full day of self-care.

One week from today I will have had my first chemo and be preparing for radiation. Scared of the unknown but ready to get going.

Counselor reminded us that peace is not a feeling; it is a person. When Jesus is in my boat, it won't sink. Jesus is in me through the Holy Spirit. I will not allow anything to make me question God's promises. I need only agree with God. I don't have to understand it.

About "healing" he said to hold onto what Jesus promises (truth), not people's experience of healing.

The name of Jesus is above the name of cancer.

GOD IN CIRCUMSTANCE

My daily devotional readings from *Jesus Calling* today remind me to breathe deeply and hold tightly to God's hand. And that some of God's greatest work has been done in times like these. Instead of resenting the limitations imposed by this journey, it reminds me to keep searching for God in my circumstances.

Lord, I want to believe. Help my unbelief.

I want to believe that a new, healthier life force is beginning to surge through me, that this cancer is a wake-up call to redirect my life.

As our counselor prayed for us last night, I want to believe in your healing power—instant or through a process. If I did not believe it to be possible, I don't know that I would be pouring myself into it as I am.

So I trust my tiny mustard seed of faith to be enough.

My prayer for this pilgrimage of cancer: *I will release my true self.*

THE ONLY WAY THROUGH

Leaving soon for the radiation rehearsal. Who knew it needed to be rehearsed?

Lord, I am calling on your miraculous healing powers so that I can continue just a bit longer before coming home to you. Please let it be so. I will continue to endure and persevere as long as you enable me to do so. You are the only way I can get through this.

TRUST GOD'S MYSTERY

Returning to *The Soul of a Pilgrim*, as it supports some of the aspects of this journey into a foreign land. Today I read and remembered how Abram and Sarai had to be willing to let go of their former selves to take on a new reality.

What am I being invited to let go of? What must I cultivate, rather than leave behind, on this journey?

What comes to me is:

~ Increased trust and faith in the Holy One who loves me

~ Jesus as healer through all things

~ Stillness to sit with the unanswered big questions

~ Deepened relationships not based on my doing

~ Believing in miracles

~ "What Is," not "What If"

Reading further, I run across a reference to the narrow gate that only the brave enter by answering an inner call to stay present to the storm.

I wonder: How is it different that this was thrust upon me rather than a choice to make? Can I trust God's mystery?

STANDING MY GROUND

A teary day working through news that the pathology of my tumor indicates it may not accept chemo. We both had a good cry with that, and I was ready to say, "Forget all of this treatment plan."

My hope began to falter, and doubt took advantage of my vulnerability.

God, I recall that you knew about this before me, and I trust that you are already at work on a healing solution.

Help me to stand my ground as your plan unfolds and to believe that wonderful things will come.

BELIEVE IT TO BE SO

Chemo begins tonight.

I envision this pill dispersing throughout my brain as though it is water and very fluid to accept whatever enters. It will interact with the unhealthy cells and leave the healthy cells alone.

This is the light of Christ with all its healing power that enters my brain.

I believe it to be so.

ROY: TRUST OVER FEAR

I booked a room for us at the Fairfield Inn, close to Ohio State's Arthur G. James ("The James") Cancer Hospital. We'll stay here for the duration of Judy's six weeks of radiation.

I know she's trying to put on a brave face, saying all the right, positive, hopeful things. She's trying to act as if she's not scared out of her wits—as if she's not feeling the weight of what could lie ahead on this dark and uncertain road.

As for me, I'm trying not to hover too much or watch her too closely; I'm trying to maintain as much normalcy as I can in our exchanges. Even as I deal with my own emotions in the moments and micro moments that now comprise our suddenly smaller world, I understand the importance of maintaining my brave face, too.

Judy set down her bag and looked around at our room, allowing her eyes to scan the walls, ceiling, and floor. It was current and comfortable enough but nothing to get excited about.

"This is nice," she said.

"Uh-huh," I responded, determined to mask my rising torrent of fear and dread. Being here in the hotel, checking in at The James—it's all getting too, too real. Until now, this was all theoretical; this, then this, then that, laid out for us like a journey of stepping-stones, the undetermined length and destination pushed into the background.

I pulled her close, resting my chin on the top of her head. "You know this is all going to be OK, don't you?" I asked tenderly.

"Yes, I know," she said, allowing a little of her weariness to show and some of her forced perkiness to wane. "I just feel so overwhelmed with sadness, grief, and anger." She paused. "I don't want to feel that way, but I do."

Believe It to Be So

"I know," I said, "me, too. It's OK. It's honest. We feel what we feel, and there's no way to turn that completely off. I think that as important as it is to stay positive, there have to be times when we just let ourselves sink into those honest feelings."

Judy paused, thoughtful. "The devotional this morning said that sometimes the roadblocks we see are only an illusion." She frowned. "But in this case they feel pretty darned real."

I hugged her tight. Words seemed extraneous.

"I know that my future is in God's hands, not mine," Judy added softly. "I pray that I will be joyfully surprised about where God takes me on this journey, and I'll just keep asking for help in replacing this fear with trust in God's process."

Amen.

JUDY: PEACE IS NOT AN EMOTION

I just finished a clay piece with the words "Trust in healing." As I enter into this first radiation, those are the words I must carry in my heart.

I see little hope for this "terminal deadly" cancer.

My fear and doubt whisper, "Why not give up now?"

Jesus, I need to hear your voice, LOUDLY. Provide a glimmer of hope somewhere today, please.

Just got back from radiation and feel a bit freer. I kept repeating "Jesus is my healer" and recalling the clay image. Our counselor's words come back to me: "Peace is not an emotion. It is a person, the Prince of Peace."

Thank you, Jesus, for hearing my cry and bringing peace to my soul in this moment. It feels like a miracle, so I must believe in miracles.

FOLLOW THE THREAD

Today's reading from Christine Valters Paintner's *Soul of the Pilgrim: Eight Practices for the Journey Within* reminds me that being a pilgrim requires deep listening to whatever emerges in my life—and a vow of obedience to following that thread wherever it takes me, even if it is somewhere unexpected.

I hate this thread with cancer, but it is before me. I pray that I can listen deeply to what God has for me in all of this.

The idea of "living with this" for the rest of my life (and concern for recurrence) is almost too much to consider. I need to accept it as my truth while not allowing it to define my future choices.

God, I trust your thread as best I can and pray for courage on days when darkness seems to overwhelm.

A dear friend writes today, "Peace . . . Hope . . . Openness to feel what you feel as you receive what is on your heart and in your soul."

Our church, St. Alban's, is doing a prayer circle for me right now. Three of the women will come here to our hotel room afterward with a quilt they made for me. Followed by reflexology.

After radiation, I met with an art therapist. It was a long day but one that carries the capacity for hope if I will make room for it.

Good self-care today. A day that makes me believe God and I can do this.

ACCEPT THE MOMENTS

It's 10:00 a.m. on Christmas Eve. With radiation, a small headache, and feeling sad, I am still thankful for my recent good days. It is just not how I envisioned Christmas Eve.

A devotional invited me to consider what "acceptance" of all this means to me, and I will reflect on that this afternoon. I accept that there will be sad days and will do my best not to let them take up residence; I will view them more as sad "moments" that will move on.

One week of radiation down, five to go. There was a woman in our waiting room who was there for her last treatment. She encouraged me to keep up the fight.

Acceptance of this cancer means:

~ Releasing the old for a new normal

~ Embracing new expectations that fit in with the truth of my life, not "what-if"

~ Trusting God's big picture for this piece of my life Mosaic

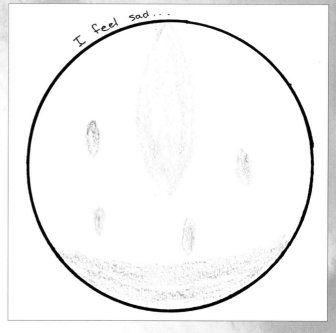

I Feel Sad

ROY: TRUST IN CHAOS

I woke up early, the morning light barely beginning to peek beneath the drawn shades of our bedroom windows.

It was hard to leave our bed with Judy snuggled so tightly against me, but I wanted to get the kettle on for her tea before she woke up.

Thank you, God, for another Christmas morning, waking up in our bed together, I prayed silently as I slipped into my robe and slid my feet into my waiting slippers.

Please, please, may it not be our last.

Pushing that last part aside as quickly as it came, I chastised myself. Judy would not appreciate my allowing those thoughts entry into my mind *or* our bedroom.

I looked at her still peacefully sleeping, remembering her last sleepy murmur last night after we settled, exhausted, into bed: "So wonderful to be in our bed so we can wake up at home on Christmas."

It is. Although her sleep had been fitful, with a huge headache and nausea playing tag team in her body, leaving her weak kneed and sobbing throughout the wee hours, I was thankful that for the moment, at least, her face and breathing were now relaxed instead of drawn and labored; she was enjoying what appeared to be peaceful slumber.

A call to the doctor while Judy sipped her tea resolved that she was likely experiencing the adverse effects of going off steroids too quickly.

Then why did you let her? I fumed inwardly as I jotted down his instructions and then got dressed to go pick up the prescriptions he was good enough to call in once we located a pharmacy open on Christmas morning. I could not get out the door fast enough. Anything to salvage at least part of our Christmas Day and time in our cottage.

"God heard my prayer this morning and served up a Christmas miracle," Judy remarked as she began to feel better almost immediately as the prescription took effect. I knew even before she spoke that she was feeling better; I saw the sparkle returning and the light coming back into her beautiful green eyes.

As I finished locking doors and turning out the lights and was about to enter our bedroom, I heard Judy praying aloud, *"Lord, I am not finished here yet. Please help me remain in this life a bit longer. I promise to put it to good use for your glory."*

JUDY: PEACE WITHIN THE SPIRIT

"Peace I leave with you.
My peace I give to you;
not as the world gives do I give to you.
Let not your heart be troubled,
neither let it be afraid."

— JOHN 14: 27

Today's *Jesus Calling* devotional reminds me to remember the Peace that lives deep within my spirit and invite it to work its way throughout my being.

I realized today that the mask used to hold my head perfectly still during radiation has become my cell—and my deepest place of prayer.

Today my mantra was *"Jesus, Prince of Peace, you are my healer, and I know you will bring big and small miracles to me."*

May I continue to bring this truth ever more deeply into my soul.

Winter 2015-2016

JUDY: CONFIDENT PEACE

I often look to the Society of Saint John the Evangelist (SSJE) for encouragement, and never have I needed it more than now. Selected readings this morning have reminded me to work a little harder to remember previous moments of joy to help me ask for more.

As I remember these moments of previous joy and ask for God's help and restoration today, I feel, as the text describes, "parched dry and clinging to the last seed."

Digging a little deeper into my selection of readings, *Jesus Calling* by Sarah Young promises "confident peace" and early rains and a place of springs in my desolate valley.

God, I am coming to a deep place of knowing that you are here and you know exactly what to do. That is all that matters. Thank you. More than anything else, I want to do what is right in your sight. Please grant me the wisdom I need to do that, Amen.

PILGRIMAGE OF TRUST

Back at the hotel now after a few days at home, Roy and I went out to dinner tonight. Our first "nice" restaurant visit since last summer.

As I sat across the table from my beloved, I realized (again) that I am not finished with my life. There are more joyful moments for me to appreciate in a deeper and more grateful manner.

A good restful night's sleep. *Thank you, Jesus.*

This morning's *Jesus Calling* devotional led me to think about making lemonade out of lemons—and how the periods of our greatest growth so often come from the most adverse of circumstances. It just takes a continual assertion and affirmation of trust in God that gives us strength and helps us feel closer to God.

Yes, this is clearly a pilgrimage of trust. It is a deep learning, as I am very unsure of the outcome.

This is where "the rubber meets the road" of my faith. As Roy and I develop a new normal and settle into somewhat of a rhythm with you and this seeming chaos, I feel peace more often and again, *thank you, my Prince of Peace, for dwelling within me.*

Lord, I want the opportunity to live a life of gratitude that only those who have fought death can truly know. Please help me to do what I am to do and may your light heal me to bring that to a place of wisdom.

WORK BENEATH HARDSHIP

"The Lord will fulfill his purpose for me;
your steadfast love,
O Lord, endures forever.
Do not forsake the work of your hands."

—PSALM 138:8

Another reading from *Jesus Calling* today greatly reinforces my impulse to cling to hope and any rays of light I see in my current darkness.

I am very weary and tired. Now I also have a cold to contend with.

Sister Carole was here yesterday and told me that as people visit and stay with me, "You know, you have your own spiritual direction ministry going on here."

Sister Joan reminds me that contemplative work is not just about me. She says that it requires bringing others into the confines of my day-to-day struggles and then to listen deeply for the need to be about something greater than myself.

Funny how that echoes what Sister Carole said about my "spiritual direction ministry" going on right here and now. So maybe I am on the right track? This unfolding ministry seems to happen in our hotel room each morning with those who visit.

I know, somehow, this story is larger than my circumstances day to day.

Doctor appointment and radiation, then home for the weekend. Being in my own bed in the woods with no schedule sounds so wonderful.

ALREADY SET IN MOTION

Today's reading from Mark Nepo's *The Book of Awakening* encourages me to find a way to love whatever gets in the way until it's no longer an obstacle. To "love" my illness seems a stretch. I prefer to "befriend" my cancer.

Or, as Rumi says, "Welcome it in; let it have a voice that will teach."

Then today's devotional from *Jesus Calling* helps me focus on the awareness that the answers I yearn for God has already set in motion—even if I can't yet see the results on the horizon.

Lord, knowing that things are in motion well before I notice them is comforting to me. Thank you in advance for these coming answers!

A FLOWER OPENING

I continue to be blessed by kindness from others. Sister Joan is returning our check for our last spiritual direction session—no payments allowed until I am "cancer free."

People coming to the hotel/cottage to help with unloading our suitcases, medical supplies, etc. Meals. Visits. Cards. Prayers. How can I not make it? It will take years to spend all their love, now being poured into me.

This mandala came a few days before a new image arose during radiation.

I am a flower opening itself to the healing powers of God's divine light. I am soft, pliable, and receptive to all that enters. I receive and trust healing that flows through me, settling into those places most in need.

CENTERED IN SAFETY

My morning meditation today came from *Moments of Peace in the Presence of God*, and it reminds me that God is writing this story, not me, and that I can therefore be certain that "good will triumph and that things will end well." It's hard not to wonder exactly what that means or how it will look in life as I know it.

The next reading, from *Jesus Calling*, encourages me to remember that each day is an adventure, planned by my Guide—and regardless of any danger I encounter on paths we take on these adventures, the safest place is always by God's side.

Opening Flower

Firewalker

I know this to be true—but it really takes focus on some of these paths to remember where that place is and how to get there. This is something I know I need to get better at, and I think these multiple daily devotional readings will help me stay centered in that place.

So very tired and battling a cold that I have now given to Roy. We both sleep well at night, and I am grateful for that.

FIREWALKER

My dear longtime friend Mark "Thunderwalker" Camden (his Native American name is "Thunderwalker") makes and plays Native American flutes and writes his own music.

Mark has given me the name "Firewalker," because he says I am surrounded by fire while God's healing waters protect me from harm.

I see fire and intense energy coming from the groundedness of Mother Earth. That energy sets off small flames in the sky.

I am "Firewalker" . . . I will persevere as I trust fully in the divine provision.

WEAVING IN THE DARK

Even in this struggle I'm in, I want my life to be about joy, gratitude, gentleness, and kindness.

I am weaving this new tapestry largely in darkness. But light, just enough, makes its way in. In this darkness I am less in control and more open to surprise and new perspectives. I will be intentional about weaving my new life's web of joy, gratitude, gentleness, and kindness.

As I created this mandala, it became an image of gentleness. I see fluid and flexible lines . . . very few sharp corners. The colors are gentle, quiet, and nonthreatening.

COMMITMENT AND INTENTIONALITY

Waiting for LeeAnn, today's companion. I am so blessed by these friends who surround us. One more week of madness and I will be back home. People ask me whether we will "go somewhere" during the four-week break. My response is that I just want to be at home.

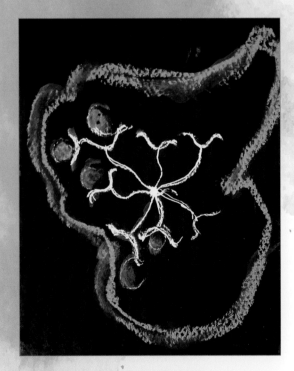

Weaving in the Dark

About the four words that came to me (joy, gratitude, gentleness, and kindness), I realize I don't need to wait until I am "cancer free" to live that way.

To carry those four attributes when healthy is no great accomplishment. To do so under these circumstances takes commitment and intentionality.

SO VERY HARD

Not much joy today. Feeling sad.

Being at home, I feel my attitude should be upbeat, but it is not.

One more week of radiation and I'm done with this first round. Although that is a huge accomplishment, I'm aware of how much more ground is to be covered and the total uncertainty of all of it.

So very hard.

HOLDING ON VS. HELD IN

For today's devotional readings I chose the three sources—*Moments of Peace*, *The Book of Awakening*, and *Jesus Calling*—that have become my go-to these days. This combination seems to be soothing my soul and shoring me up, day by tedious day.

For today, *Moments of Peace* guides me to ask God for strength to hang on in the face of these troubles, staying true to God, no matter where this path leads.

Nepo reminds me to focus on what is, rather than what is not—the difference, he asserts, between wisdom and anger. He calls this "Miracle thinking." I'll have to ponder that more.

Finally, *Jesus Calling* points me toward gifts of this circumstance—trust that garners the gift of peace amid the storm and spiritual blessings that tend to come wrapped in trials.

I especially need this combination of wisdom and reminders today because my trust is waning and "what is not" seems front and center.

Feeling sad and discouraged today but doing a mandala was very stilling and meditative.

I see cool colors of sky and water, exuberant colors from within, yet tears fall. A real emotion. Tears are absorbed by water, while joy still sends forth its energy.

Gentleness

Joy

Kindness

OPENING THE WAY

Today's *Moment of Peace* devotional assures me of God's blessing if I can manage not to give up when my faith is being tested. Tall order.

And then *Jesus Calling* soothes me more deeply by encouraging me to let God set the pace for this journey. Its "tempo of a God-breathed life," this reading invites me to hold God's hand in childlike trust so the way through this challenge can be opened to me, step by step.

God, you always know what I need in each moment. Yesterday, I did want to give up—tired, weary. Your pace required faith, because quick answers are not part of that paradigm. Today, please help me to be more aware of how/when you open the way before me. Thank you for these words finding their way to me this morning—and for opening my way for moving through another day of uncertainty.

This is the image that comes for kindness. I see energy radiating to peace and to its "greening" life force. May I bring this kindness to others as I allow it for myself.

This is my final week of chemo and radiation, then home for four glorious weeks of no drugs or blood draws before the second phase of all this fun and frivolity.

Long road ahead but doctors are very encouraged with what they observe at this point. I feel everyone's prayers and positive energy being sent my way. It all makes a difference.

THE LIGHT OF TRUST

Moments of Peace assures me this morning that I'll find the strength I require in my time of need. I certainly want to believe this is true.

Platelet count is still low this morning, and I am very tired. Bored, tired, and done with this stuff!

Emotionally, however, I am doing better.

RESTING ON KINDNESS

My reading from *Moments of Peace* today affirms that trials "show us who we are in God." I'm going to have to think about that more deeply.

There is a small heaviness within me, and I am choosing to believe it is a heaviness for good. So I will move through my day with an expectant heart for goodness that God wants to shower over me.

Thank you, God, for the love of family, friends, and strangers who have crossed my path to help bring care and healing to me.

This is the image for gratitude. It seems that I am resting on the kindness of others, having fully received their care with gratitude. God's divine light continues to reign over me and bless all that is.

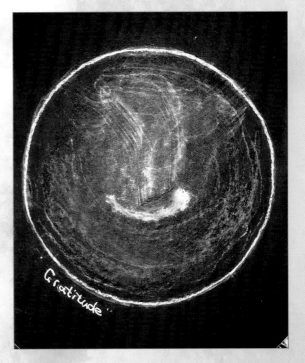

Gratitude

FEARFUL AND JOYOUS

Last day of radiation. This seems a happy mandala in spite of a long way to go. I want to fully celebrate and honor having made it this far.

The *Moments of Peace* meditation for today talks about the difference between "grim strength" and "glory strength" that comes from God. Interesting comparison. I feel like I probably call upon both from time to time but will try to be more aware of which strength I'm drawing my energy from.

Then I run across the poem "What's Left" by Kerry Hardie, in which this poet describes almost perfectly my deep desire to live the rest of my life "with my eyes open and my hands open . . . fearful and joyous like an idiot before God."

God as I close this first chapter (radiation) of a very long book (cancer), this is what I want to be about. I don't want to just survive; I want to thrive. And, yes, I want to live what's left "fearful and joyous like an idiot before God" because I know that choice would please you. May it be so.

CHOOSING AND GUARDING

Jesus Calling today emphasizes the importance of choosing and guarding my thoughts, reinforcing my diligence on this slippery slope so that I can remain close to God each and every moment. What are my thoughts, in *this* moment?

~ Sitting in my own bed, in my own home, cup of tea, watching the sunrise. So happy knowing we don't pack up and return to the hotel in Columbus on Sunday.
~ Very grateful for having made it to this point. I am hopeful for this next leg of the journey. I am so grateful for all the support and love that is helping to keep me strong.
~ I am so grateful to be home and to have finished this six-week round of chemo/radiation, something I never imagined for myself and thought I could not endure.

Thank you, Jesus, for your peace, your healing, and your presence. I continue to trust you on this path I walk.

Celebrate

Mark Nepo reminds me today that being a true pilgrim requires us not only to journey but also to be transformed by that journey. If that's true, then I suppose I'm well on my way to being a pilgrim.

What comes now is my need to make a new life, a new normal, in this place—and feeling too weary to do so. It will need to evolve rather than me trying to plan it. This is completely unfamiliar territory for me, and I have no choice but to surrender myself in it.

These past six weeks brought a rhythm that is now outdated and irrelevant. What develops now will need to change again in five more weeks and continue throughout the summer.

PIECES OF A VISION

After two weeks of significant drops in my platelets, yesterday's lab work showed an increase of 1 point, which is great, considering it has been dropping by 10, 20, 30 in the few days between labs.

Also, while at our community hospital nearby, not The James in Columbus, I had a chance conversation with the coordinator of their cancer center. They formed a committee to organize an art and healing program for their patients.

I shared a bit of my background, and we were off and running. She is very interested and asked me to send her whatever I have about myself and some ideas.

This would be a volunteer thing on my terms. They have a grant that would cover all supplies.

Having pieces of a vision come from this darkness is so energizing even though I am physically still very fatigued. Grateful for all the prayers and good energy. Yesterday was a good day that I desperately needed. More to come . . .

Thankful for all the prayers I know are coming my way. God heard them.

My platelet count was maintained, no downward trend. Return, again, for labs next Tuesday.

Doctor very happy that the number is stable and confident the number will increase with time. No mention of an infusion—very happy.

My fatigue has been so deep that it has been a challenge to do much art. I have been keeping this journal since diagnosis, and that is about all I can do.

I've created a few mandalas. After some inspiration from my Sarasota artists clan, I actually went into my studio to create a journal cover.

This pilgrim continues to put one foot in front of the other . . .

GO PLAY!

I so appreciate all the kind words I've been receiving on Facebook and from friends in real time.

Some days are pretty dark, and that is when God sends an angel to share some light. They all shine so brightly.

Platelets dropped by 1, but my doctor is still pleased, calling it "stable." Back to the lab on Thursday—such a tiring routine.

Woke to a beautiful snowfall in the woods this morning and stayed in bed to finish my "play" mandala. Art is definitely play for me.

A friend visited today, a neighbor is bringing dinner, and yoga is tomorrow morning. I am surrounded by abundance, even in this dark place. God is so faithful when I trust.

Be good to yourself and go play!!

Go Play!

ROY: LIVIN' THE DREAM

So in our concerted effort to try to do "normal" things that have nothing to do with cancer, as hard as it is on some days with her deep fatigue, today Judy decided to push past her cancer so we could have a "romantic" lunch at The Well in Lancaster, one of our favorite "just because" lunch spots. We took a picture to help us both remember that it's possible to do this. (We chose not to take a picture of Judy pushing past her fatigue during our brief follow-up trip to Kroger!)

Judy says this all falls into her new categories of "Fake it till you make it" and "Stop acting like a sick person."

She says the first option always makes her chuckle; the second one makes her put on her "big girl panties" and get on with it. She is also fond of her answer she has begun to give her radiation techs and other care providers when they ask her how she's doing:

"Liiiiiivin' in paradise. Livin' the dream."

Today, Judy has to find it somewhere within her to push through the fatigue again to do her PT and OT exercises along with 8–10 minutes on the treadmill—a commitment she made to her oncologist, who, as she puts it, is taking very good care of her.

I certainly hope so. This is so hard to watch; I wonder sometimes whether it is harder to be the patient or to love the patient, sitting so helplessly by on the sidelines, unable to take any of this burden from someone you love.

She often says that because of her deep love for me and the rest of our family and friends, she chooses to begin this battle again, each and every day, and to keep pushing through the darkness and uncertainty.

We are so thankful for all of the prayers and expectations of a miracle, courage, perseverance, peace, and whatever goodness comes to anyone's mind on Judy's behalf.

"I tell God I am not finished here just yet—and there is still more to squeeze out of me," she often quips.

I so hope she's right—and that God agrees.

JUDY: A BIT OF HOPE

I needed a bit of hope for the day—and I just got it with the results from today's lab work! White blood cells rose by .3 and my platelets rose from 21 to 28, which is celebration worthy.

Labs again next Friday and my doctor is very pleased with this trend. How do I celebrate when I am too exhausted to move?

Will try to find my second wind somewhere and shuffle up to The Lodge for Taco Tuesday and friendly banter.

Thankful for the prayers that I know have helped move this along.

JUST ENOUGH MOTIVATION

If I am to be in bed much of the day (the doctor calls this the very hard work of restoration and healing), it helps to have a good view.

To be honest, though, today is one of my weepy days. Have a call in to my doctor to hear back about some issues with my vision. Hard not knowing what this thing in my head is up to.

I have mixed emotions about hearing that news on March 4. Will need my really strong big girl panties for that meeting.

But today is a beautiful day, I have friends and family alongside me, and I found just enough motivation to do a mandala and some journaling with it.

Trusting God's presence and healing power in the midst of tremendous unknowing.

Update on my changing blood count—good news again today. Platelets up by 10 and white blood cells up by about .7! What all of that means is that my risk of infection and a bleed-out are diminished.

I will take that bit of news to keep me hopeful about what I will hear (big girl panties in hand) next week. Such a long and exhausting process, which is why I need each and every person supporting me in any way right now.

BEST CIRCLE

I have decided to begin again today after an unkind day yesterday. The birds are chirping to remind me that new life awaits us all.

A few friends checked in (so, so encouraging to hear their hopes and expectations for me), and my doctor assured me that anything going on with my vision is likely fixable, including returning me to a bit higher dose of steroid—a small, small increase.

Soon, a friend will pick me up for a treatment session, then take me to lunch with another friend who will accompany me to the hospital for my lab work, then bring me home. Another friend arrives tonight to stay until tomorrow. So thankful to have so many friends supporting and sharing in my journey, which allows Roy the comfort of knowing I am in good hands for some of these more tedious appointments that happen when he has to be at work.

Best circle of friends a girl could have when fighting a nasty brain tumor.

OPTIMISM CHA-CHA

I tried to be normal this morning and succeeded pretty well. Made my first cup of coffee since September, visited our porch to greet the sunrise, did my exercises, and finally got around to an art lesson on which I am seriously behind.

And, to move me forward a bit more, last night's blood work just came back, and everything improved. WBC up 1.7 and platelets from 38 to 55. None of this tells me what the tumor is doing, but I certainly don't feel (and have been told I don't look like) someone leaving this world in the next weeks or months.

Some anxiety mounts with my pending March 4 MRI, but I am doing my best to stay in the truth of each moment and let God take care of whatever is coming.

The weekend was very difficult emotionally. It is part of this life/death process. I would expect nothing less.

Big questions and big wonderings. I am thankful for each person in my life who is listening to those questions and willing to enter the darkness with me authentically.

I must go there. They do not need to but do so anyway. I am grateful. Not everyone can do that. Thankful for those who are helping me sort through life.

INTERIOR LIGHTING

Fatigue is heavy. A bit of sadness hangs over me. But my art studio called to me with its beautiful view, and I pushed through the darkness.

I am reminded of the poem by Elizabeth Kubler-Ross that compares people to stained glass—colorful enough in the daylight, but how their real beauty is only made visible by light that comes from within.

Unfortunately, I do understand this truth. I just wish it was not so hard some days. I try to keep my inner light shining because I know it makes a difference in my healing process as well as in the lives of those I spend time with.

But sometimes I just want to flip off the switch and call it a day.

Angels Watching over Me

ANGELS WATCHING OVER ME

It has been quite a week of ups and downs, twists, and curves.

We're headed to yoga in a few minutes; I will have reflexology tonight and a massage on Wednesday. Self-care to keep my anxiety at a lower level until Friday's MRI and doctor consult for the next step of this adventure.

Although my vision changes make it difficult to do art, I must express myself creatively. I created this mandala, "Angels Watching over Me."

It evolved rather organically, with the "angels" flying in at the last moment. I do feel surrounded and know I am being carried in all of this by family and friends, by others on the periphery, and by those on the other side who have walked this journey before me and make up my huge "cloud of witnesses" telling me not to give up.

COMFORT AND CONTENTMENT

A bright spot of sunshine and cousin love arrived today, when I needed it most, in the form of a beautiful arrangement of several kinds of yellow flowers. Will try to keep dancing.

I continue to do almost daily mandalas and to dialogue with them. It is always a very revealing and helpful conversation between me and the angel in the art. Thank you, Expressive Arts Florida.

I did these two in sequence, and "Contentment" (the second one) was informed by what makes me happy. I am learning to be content in most situations and find that doing so makes room for moments of happiness and joy.

Art Makes Me Happy

Contentment

Reader's Notes

Spring 2016

JUDY: HEALING LOTUS

Today, *Jesus Calling* talks about lessons of trust that come wrapped in difficulties—with benefits (including peace) that far outweigh the costs.

Healing Lotus

And then, as if specially designed to fold right into that, my reading from *Moments of Peace* emphasizes the need to feel safe and trust God's wisdom.

Powerful package to greet me this day.

This affirms (don't think of it as a new thought) that trust (and the resulting peace) comes only through time, hardships, and surrender to the process.

I created "Healing Lotus" yesterday and journaled with it this morning as the sun rose and I drank a cup of coffee (just like the good old days).

Toward the end of six weeks of daily radiation, the girls nicknamed me "Healing Lotus" because I began to adopt a very healing stance on the table. Flat on my back (no choice there) with my head firmly latched to the table (again, no choice), I had a "Healing Hands" quilt from my church across my legs and my palms open to the heavens to receive (from my perspective) God's healing light in the form of radiation beams.

I suspect I did look like I was somewhere else by the time I was settled in that position. To this morning's devotional, "The lotus flower rises above the mud to bloom, clear and fragrant," I respond, "May this be my story as well."

I understand grounding myself in mud as a nutrient source, while the more visible part of me takes all of that Source energy, allows it to be transformed, and releases it into the world.

God, thank you for your healing hands that calm this raging storm within so as to bring peace to the outer world. Help me to be patient and at peace in this process of transformation and resurrection, for whatever is to come next.

New Life

As my anxiety grows about my CT scan on Friday, I head into the full force of this life storm with great hope, knowing God has it all worked out somehow. This, I know, is how faith becomes real.

Just after this chaos began, I journaled very distinctly and clearly as I lay in my hospital bed, wondering whether I would make it.

It is not my time to leave yet.

I knew that God was giving me a new life to be lived in the physical here and now. How could I know that, considering my circumstances? But it was so clear that I wrote it down. I was afraid that, over time, I might forget or diminish those comforting words of God's Spirit in that moment.

Just as new life is coming with the spring, I am trying to trust that God is granting me a new life here on earth.

CENTERED "EN POINTE"

We leave for the Columbus Hotel this afternoon. Tomorrow is a turning point—toward what, unknown.

Today's *Jesus Calling* reminds me that the simple awareness of God's presence is all we need to drive out fear and "keep the wolves of worry at bay."

The phrase that comes to mind is a ballet image, spinning "en pointe," supporting my full weight, my entire existence, balanced on the extreme tips of my toes.

I believe in miracles. I believe in magic. You, Lord, can do it.

God, I will do my best to be centered "en pointe" until the swirling of information ceases and your clarity and wisdom enter in.

MAKE FRIENDS WITH CIRCUMSTANCE

"What if" hangs heavy over me, and I know I still have a very long road ahead of me. It makes me weary to think of the unknown journey. Decisions to make, new things to try. I just want normal—or some form of normal. A healthy life.

Big girl panties on, check. Coffee consumed, check. Prayers lifted, check. We slept well last night, so thank you for those prayers. Sometimes you just gotta be brave and walk into the fire with confidence.

WALL OF PROTECTION

Feeling generally overwhelmed today. My appointment was not great. There is greater enhancement in the old tumor bed than the doctor likes to see, which means something is happening in that space.

My tumor is either growing back or in "pseudo progression." Tumor cells don't like radiation/chemo and swell to look ugly for the next MRI. We were told that would likely occur, and it often happens with brain tumors.

I am very sad and discouraged with this news, not feeling very hopeful at this point. For now, I will keep fighting, but it is getting hard.

I am not having any neurological symptoms, which offers possibility that the tumor may not be growing. In any event, the only way to know and to treat appropriately is another brain surgery. Will know more in a few days.

Meeting with the surgeon on Monday at 10:00 a.m., hoping to fill in the blanks. I want to continue to choose life and not let melancholy find a way in.

LIFE ENERGY

Worked on this image this morning. The energy is powerful and vibrant. It is too much to be contained by the outer shell. And yet some of it is peaceful, gently carried along by a stronger life force.

May I allow myself to be gently carried by love surrounding me and supported by the ground beneath me. May this be a time of resurrection for me as the old shell breaks open to release the new life to come from this season of darkness and unknowing. I must not give in at this point. This cancer is trying to undermine my healing peace, and I must stand firm and "en pointe."

En Pointe

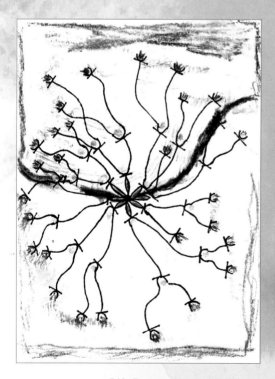

Life Energy

Organized Energy

Spirit Choosing Life

ORGANIZED ENERGY

Morning *Moments of Peace* devotional helped me remember to focus on the sheer awe of God's work and to have confidence in God's plan. I went into my studio to process this, and the mandala to the left emerged.

As I look at this mandala next to yesterday's image, the phrase that comes is "Organized Energy." It evolves from a fertile green center and is held by the gentle blue sky of God's creation.

When I have moments of weariness and wanting to give up, I realize more than ever how vital it is to trust that:

~ God has a plan for my benefit

~ God is ahead of me, working the plan

~ I don't need to move ahead of God, just to be sustained in the present moment.

I pray for hope, clarity, wisdom in the choices to be made based on what we hear tomorrow. God, help me to continue to choose life.

ROY: HOPE AND CONFIDENCE WAVER

They want to talk to us about hospice today.

We both know that this is the option that needs to be brought up at this point, and that realization fills us both with sadness that has no name or depth.

We both want Judy to keep going, keep fighting. I for my own selfish reasons—I want to keep her here with me for as long as possible, in whatever shape or form that existence takes. Judy wants to keep going, to survive this thing.

But we both know that a few extra months, or even another year, at the expense of her quality of life would be no way for her to fully live.

What does it mean, then, to "choose life" in these circumstances? How can Judy's spirit—and mine—begin from that place in making this choice?

Lord, we rely solely on your help today—I know that you will walk this dark path with us. We pray for your peace to come near so we can listen clearly and a bit more objectively as Judy chooses her path for this next leg of the journey.

The way feels long, and my hope and confidence waver in the unknown. We are a bit weepy. And afraid.

JUDY: NOT READY YET

Just returned home. I was not ready to have the hospice discussion just yet, which is what declining surgery would have meant. In the doctor's words, surgery is the best opportunity for longevity and quality of life.

Surgery scheduled for next Tuesday morning.

The recovery will be a bit more challenging this time, they tell us. I'll be in the hospital for three to four days and then home with some home health visits to ensure that I eat and take my meds on time.

Too much life energy in me to pack it in 4–9 months down the road. Not ready to give up yet.

FOLLOW THE THREAD

This morning's readings in *Moments of Peace* and *Jesus Calling* once again conspire to reinforce a point I seem to be resisting.

The whole idea of "giving in" to God, or the old "let go, let God" wisdom, is both profoundly comforting and equally frustrating. I realize that saying "everything will turn out just fine" is meant to be reassuring, but what isn't clear here is what "just fine" looks like. Something tells me we're talking more in the global sense here.

And yet here I am, fighting for my life, trying to stay on this earth just a little bit longer. Does "turning out just fine" mean my cancer will disappear? Does having the rest of my life fall into place piece by piece have some sort of timetable attached?

Lord, I seek your face only today: I desire deeply to live beyond the typical prognosis. Help me to stay strong and to make wise choices.

WISDOM AND BEAUTY

When we're in the fight for our life, how are we really supposed to be able to find the elusive wisdom and beauty in it all?

Yesterday was a hopeful day. This morning, in a Skype with EAFI and Kathleen, I found some comfort in realizing themes of "resurrection" and new life have surfaced in my recent artwork.

Our call reminded me of this image from the final intensive in January 2015 where we created a freeform image and were then invited into a dialogue with one piece of it with the support of a colleague guiding the reflection. At the conclusion, we hung our picture on the wall, and someone snapped photos of each of us.

I did not realize I had positioned myself in a way that my drawn image was essentially bursting from my head. It was a "wow" moment for myself and others to see the end result.

As I sat with this photo yesterday, I wrote, "It looks like beauty and energy erupting from a tumor bed. Could be love and healing with God's arms wrapped around all of it."

This image carries forward the theme of resurrection. I will be home and recovering during Holy Week. Pathology should be known around Easter. This knowledge calms me in this moment.

Lord, I anticipate your plan for me in that week.

Beauty and Energy

FINDING "SANCTUARY"

Not a great day. Very weepy, sad, and lonely.

Lord, I need your peace.

How many times a day do I think or say aloud, "I can't do this anymore?" Anxiety and "what if" wax and wane like the moon.

God, I have not been doing this since the beginning. You have. We have made it this far, just as you promised. You know what I can handle with your help. And you know when I need to rest and recharge. Guide me to this wisdom and a place of Sanctuary in you.

I did this mandala yesterday without a specific intention. Its calm, soft center welcomes me and provides a beautiful life-giving view of flowers, sun, and earth while I rest. Sanctuary.

Sanctuary

WAIT, TRUST, HOPE

"Out of the believer's heart shall flow rivers of living water."
—JOHN 7:38

Jesus Calling echoes a theme of trust today, reminding me of the deep and intricate connection between waiting, trusting, and hoping—and how "waiting expectantly in hope and trust" is so much more than just passing time.

I am so eager to get to the "other side" of this (whatever that means) while not wishing away time and moments of life. It is largely my struggle, awaiting the grayness of the unknown.

Lord, help me unblock whatever impedes this living water from flowing some days.

Jesus Calling reminds me today of God's "tender attention to detail." May I have trust and awareness to always be on the lookout for what God is doing in all of this—and how well it prepares me today for the uncertain days ahead.

Rain falls in early morning, along with the melodies of birdsong. Peggy will be here for a few hours today to introduce me to Green Tara—the name given my radiation mask. Goddess of Protection, which she was for me. It will be a new and interesting experience. Trust that the process is a piece of healing Light.

Feeling especially blessed today through gentleness and kindness of others.

Green Tara

ROY: LOOKING FOR ESCAPE

We had a bird trapped in our chimney this morning, flapping wildly trying to find its way out.

"Roy!" I heard Judy call from our bedroom where she was resting. "I think there's a bird trapped in the chimney!"

Grabbing a kitchen towel as I had learned to do, I opened the damper, moved the fire screen, and waited until our frightened bird saw a light below and flew toward the opening and out into the room.

Please don't hit the window, I begged silently. *I'm really not sure I could handle that right now.*

Once in our living room, the bird flew about and came to rest on a window ledge, as if hearing and honoring my silent plea. Our guest bird cocked its head and watched as I approached, making no attempt to fly away. I slowly surrounded it in the towel and carried it gingerly toward the door. It moved a little bit but didn't struggle, as if knowing I was going to set it free outdoors.

How can this be? I wondered as I used my elbow to open the lever-style doorknob, wondering briefly what I would have done if it were a different kind of handle.

Moving to the deck railing, I set the bird and towel down and slowly pulled away the towel. It sat still for a moment, then unceremoniously flew away toward the ravine just beyond our deck.

"You're welcome!" I called with a grin. As I reentered our house, closed the damper, and replaced the fire screen, it occurred to me that Judy must feel like that trapped bird, trapped in a dark tunnel that offered no visible means of escape.

I prayed silently that God will do the same for Judy so she can fly free and sing the song she is meant to sing.

JUDY: SURRENDER

This morning's *Moments of Peace* reading reminds me that God is writing this story—and that means good will triumph in the end, all will be well. Whatever that means.

Created the mandala to the left in response to devotionals of the past two days. Feeling deep gratitude for peace and assurance they have brought at a time when I need it most.

Just for fun I decided to make a "bucket list" of ordinary moments to savor in my days ahead following surgery.

~ Drive to Bremen meat markets

~ Dinner with Roy at Shaw's

~ Morning walks

~ Winery

~ Pick up mail

~ Eating at Utopia on the patio

~ Ash cave

~ Lake Hope

~ Mopping floors

~ Shower by myself

God, I surrender to the love that surrounds me and the earth that grounds me reminding me of new life and rebirth. I will let your truths carry me through my upcoming days and weeks. I will expect good news from tomorrow's surgery knowing you have created the perfect container in me to hold all the goodness and new life that is to come.

And, yes, my big girl panties are packed!

Surrender

REPRIEVE

Surgery went well.

Was out of ICU and into my step-down room last night at 9:30 p.m. Got about five hours of sleep followed by about another one and a half, which was much better than Tuesday night.

Surgeon seems happy in that he removed 99 percent of the tissue that had refilled my tumor cavity and that I am doing so well. He also reminded us that there are still tentacles and satellite cancer cells elsewhere that he cannot get.

The removed cells will be analyzed by pathology with results in two weeks. Follow-up treatment will likely involve more chemo.

Hopefully I'll be home Saturday, eating my morning munchie mix and drinking coffee.

DEEP DEPENDENCE

As I am waiting on my discharge papers (I'll be at home tonight!), these words come to me:

"Don't let your need to understand distract you from my presence. I will equip you to get through this day victoriously as you live in deep dependence on me."

God, you brought me through surgery and recovery. I am deeply grateful.

COLORS OF HAPPY

Back home in the woods.

Biggest complaint is wonky eyesight connected to depth perception. I have been assured it will repair itself as swelling decreases. I will hold to that hope in the midst of some discouragement. But it is very challenging to type, read, write, journal, do art, etc.

Managed to read my *Jesus Calling* devotional this morning—thankful it was short. And, as it reminds me, it is thankfulness that will continue to lift me above whatever current circumstances I'm in.

Good reminder.

A few times in the hospital, a nurse asked me how I was doing. I responded, "Happy. Am I allowed to say that?" Cancer can't take away my happy. I can only choose to dismiss gifts of joy, healing, and provision.

This mandala is titled "The Colors of Happy."

So frustrating to have my vision and cognition impacted. Nevertheless, there have been a few moments of happy today—I have now survived two major brain surgeries, and I got to come back home. Realizing all of my blessings. Loose ends weaving themselves back together. See God's world in a new way. Trust.
Lord, I thank you for the possibilities of this day. I gratefully receive this gift of another 24 hours. Vision problems force me to see in a different way. No staying within the lines or control of the outcome.

Nepo's *The Book of Awakening* reminds me today that being broken is no reason to see everything as broken.

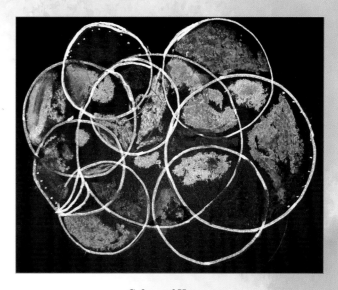

Colors of Happy

Loose Ends

True North

LIVE LIFE

Meeting today with my surgeon and then with the lead neurologist. Full day of hearing hard truths:

~ I look pretty darn good for a second surgery.

~ Not everyone qualifies for a second surgery.

~ My body is healing.

~ My brain will rewire my eyes; I need to keep my eyes open as much as possible—read, paint, do simple household tasks.

~ Pathology results: tissue was a mixture of cancer and dead cancer cells.

~ Doctors are very pleased with what was removed.

As I was hearing and trying to process these hard realities today, I wondered whether I want to continue the fight.

What crap!

When did I decide that six months, one year, etc., was to be thrown away and "not worth it"? That is obscene. Not my decision.

I commit to living as fully as I can in this life span I am given. I will be grateful for every hour, every experience, every encounter.

Every minute of life is a gift. Not even sure I have a right to complain about anything. It is what it is. Get over it and live life.

ELEMENTS OF PEACE

Today I am choosing to focus on individual elements of peace—balance, order, rhythm, harmony.

How do I keep these at work in my life in such a harsh time?

WELL WITH MY SOUL

As if reaching into my heart to address this plea that won't go away, today's prayer in *Moments of Peace* offers up words I've been reaching for—asking for some vision of my future that will help me keep God's perspective in all I'm facing and will face as I navigate this journey.

I am not done yet, but I need to admit that it is hard to hang on some days ...

God, thank you for helping me with my grip when I slip.

This mandala on the right is titled "It Is Well with My Soul." Pale pink holds my soul in a gentle way. Hearts of love offer continuing sustenance. Colors push out from the center.

ROY: TRANSLATE TO PEACE

Today we took a walk down Papago Lane, hand in hand. I could see that Judy was deeply tired but grateful to be home and able to take a walk with me in our favorite setting under a canopy of trees and clear blue sky that soared above and beyond them.

We both realized that this moment, this interlude, was no small thing. We are surrounded by love, abundance, beauty, provision.

God, how can we learn to translate this feeling to a deeper understanding of your peace? I asked silently as we walked.

As if hearing my prayer, Judy said, "I want to believe that I have more weeks—years—and that God is making provisions for that to be a reality."

I squeezed her hand, unable to speak past an enormous lump in my throat and tears she must not see.

We're going to Cleveland Clinic this week to meet with their neuro-oncology lead doctor about possible trials. One, they tell us, looks very hopeful.

God, please open a way, I continued my silent prayer, and if you can't do that, please close it tight and direct us to where we should be and what we should do next.

JUDY: RAINBOW IN CHAOS

"The Lord is my strength and my song, and He has become my salvation."
—PSALM 118:14

I asked God for a vision of my future to gain a better perspective on my current trials.

Posted this piece of art on Facebook. Someone commented, "May I suggest a rainbow surrounds the chaos?"

It Is Well with My Soul

Unconfined Chaos

Still Present

My comment was "A rainbow that got lost in chaos!" I prefer the more hopeful stance.

To Cleveland Clinic tomorrow and I want to believe a rainbow awaits there.

Lord, thank you for another day. It is beautiful.

STILL PRESENT

Feeling especially powerless.

This mandala *(bottom left)* is called "still present." Sometimes I need to remind myself that I am *not* cancer and that *Judy* is still very present and will reemerge as a new creation in God's arms.

Taking more notice of God's gifts to me in each day means receiving extravagant love while I can enjoy it.

All of this since my first surgery when I wanted to give up. So grateful I was here for all of it.

At the clinic and waiting for the miracle many are claiming. *Lord, you can do it.*

Just back from Cleveland Clinic meetings with a research doctor and two research nurses. I am a candidate for three trials, which the doctor said is a lot. I'll need to have my blood test there analyzed, a new MRI done, and the removed tissue analyzed.

Each item is for a different trial. He also said he has hope for me and to not even think about hospice.

We will know results and which trial is suggested in about two weeks. Trials will involve trips back and forth to Cleveland. Certainly hopeful news, but all I can see is a long slog and not knowing the outcome.

Lord, help me keep my trust and hope in you that has gotten me this far as a survivor.

I will keep praying for the best path to be cleared. So grateful for all this love and support that surround us.

I want to trust this journey to healing. It feels very hard many days. To trust our journey is to surrender myself to the journey's creator. I am learning to do that with each step. And realize I fall short much of the time.

What choice for survival is there if I do not put myself completely in God's embrace?

QUESTIONS DEFINE THE JOURNEY

Leaving for the Cleveland Clinic soon for doctor's appointment, MRI, and labs. A full day that will get this "party" started. Chose to stay in Cleveland another night before a long trip home. Trying to go with my intuition with the choices I make.

Treatment should begin next Monday. Tired, what else is new???? Such a long process. Helps so much to know that so many people are holding us in prayer during this uncertain song.

We'll be back home tomorrow afternoon.

"You are my refuge in the storm. I trust you, and I am safe."

This prayer has served me while going to sleep and in the MRI.

At Cleveland Clinic.

A David Whyte poem, "Start Close In," comes to mind—I guess because my own internal, self-limiting conversation has now risen to its own crescendo.

Whyte's poem speaks directly to this, encouraging us to focus on our own questions rather than those of other people as we define our own journey.

I am often unsure of "the questions" but also wonder about "the answers"—which makes for an impossible situation.

Lord, help me discern the question I am to be with during this time of deep reflection in your presence.

Start with Your Own Question

QUIET THE STATIC AND BE HELD

I think I may know the question(s).

Maybe part of what God desires to give me is in the peace of being held.

As I listen for answers, the hard part is quieting all the static in my mind, the other noise, to hear the true answer. I know how important it will be to quiet this static and be still enough to hear God's voice above all else.

God, please give me patience and trust with the long process of unfolding—and confidence that edges will settle in time and there will be clarity about what comes next.

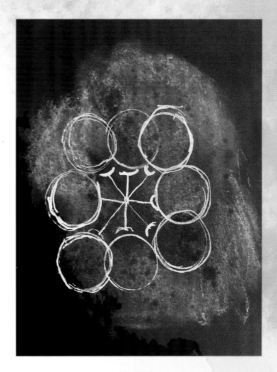

Be Held

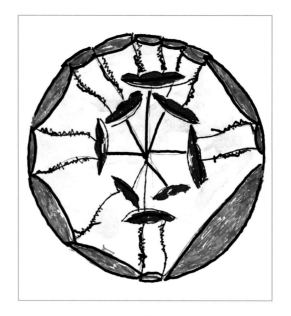

Static, Be Still and Know

LIVE INTO INVITATION

Heard yesterday that my recent MRI shows that everything is "stable"—no increase or decrease in size. Excellent place from which to begin trial treatments on Monday. Glad it did not grow during the time I was not receiving treatments.

I'll take it.

I am learning to be held by God, by others, by Mother Earth. Important lessons on self-care for the future. So grateful for all who are holding us in their hearts and prayers.

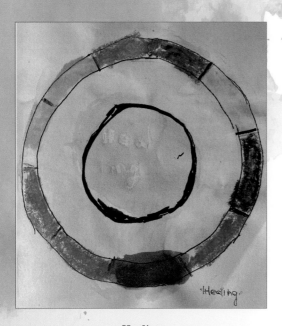

Healing

EMOTIONAL HEALING

It is a beautiful morning, and I'm grateful to be here for it. Getting ready for Cleveland, and on our walk today we decided to take "the hill" in our neighborhood. Wasn't an easy haul for me, but the view is worth it, and I feel like I accomplished something here. (Cue the "Rocky" music.)

Staring Down the Hill

I STARED DOWN that damn hill. Made it to the top and Roy took my picture.

Thank you, God, that I am here today. I am NOT doomed!!

After my reflexology session we're off to Cleveland to begin this new adventure—a clinical trial.

This reminds me that I am living what I have most feared for many years—my dear aunt Ginny died of this same brain cancer in 1993. There is some freedom that comes in realizing I have faith and strength to stare it down—and that God and others will ensure I do not do it alone.

God, what beauty will you paint with these acts?

BEAUTY IN THE ASHES

Riffing on a line from "House of Belonging," a David Whyte poem I love, ("Someone has written something new in the ashes of your life."), I created the mandala I'm going to call "Painting Beauty in the Ashes."

God, you have promised me abundance and a future, too. I must believe you will do something magical and extraordinary in the ashes of these past few months. Honestly, I don't believe this is realistic. Forgive me in these moments of doubt; turn me toward your truth and your promises and away from my fear.

Yet these feelings of loneliness and boredom continue to nag at me.

Very tired physically and queasy stomach. This is when it is hard to keep going.

Stare It Down

Painting Beauty in the Ashes

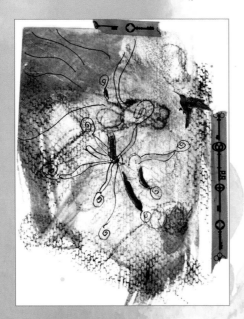

Carried Toward the Light

CALM MY STORM

Turning back, then, to *Jesus Calling*, Sarah Young reminds me how our preoccupation with trying to plan everything "pays homage to the idol of control." It's hard for me to turn from this "idolatry" and back to Jesus, but I know that by finding a way to return my focus to Jesus I will be able to live more abundantly in this place.

I am growing. I am being carried toward the light. I lack nothing.

Perseverance

People have used "perseverance" a lot in describing my journey. This mandala implies St. Patrick's stability on earth and firmness of rock. I am reminded of Joyce Rupp's book about the El Camino, *Walk in a Relaxed Manner*. I will need to learn what that means for me here as I reflect on my upcoming days:

~ Slow my steps; take one at a time, at my own pace.

~ See the scenery.

~ Maintain awareness of body and spirit.

~ Stay flexible; make adjustments for wholeness as I walk.

Thank you, God, for giving me another day.

Birdsong greets me; dogwoods blossom outside my window. Roy brought me breakfast. My stomach is settled, and I will not overdo it today. I choose to "walk in a relaxed manner." I trust strength will work its way through me into perseverance. I am committed to healing, but this road is long and hard, with obstacles to overcome, uncertain terrain, and unexpected weariness.

Lord, provide the energy I need for a great week. Jesus, calm my storm. I am keeping you in this boat with me.

Walk in a Relaxed Manner

LIFE BURSTS FORTH

In Cleveland for second clinic visit. Car trip was not as hard as last week. Waiting for pizza delivery.

In this piece of art, "Calm My Storm," color (life) bursts forth. This imagery goes back to the seed allowing itself to crack open completely.

I want to create a space for everything to burst forth as it needs to—all the colors, energy, and life force. What would I want to hold back? None of it, of course.

A friend dropped off a meal, and we had a good talk about how my story, and what I share, is impacting others. A helpful dialogue to be reminded that I can serve others in the midst of this crazy time.

Calm My Storm

EMBRACED BY HAPPY

Embraced by Happy

Scribble Drawing

Sometimes the happy starts deep inside and is very quiet. Don't miss it. I had this happen last night.

No formula. Visit from a friend, did some art, Roy here, anticipation of our visit to the winery tonight.

Leaving soon as a storm comes through. I love rainy days here at Sunrise Ridge. Everything is so green, which I hope is what is happening inside me as I sit in my storm.

Happy things. Small, ordinary things that together give me a warm embrace of "happy" and, perhaps, safety.

A new form of authentic creative expression that witnesses to others about God's love, presence, and provision. How do I share this with others?

An embrace surrounded by God's Light ... darkness will not prevail or have the final word unless I allow it.

I will not!!

As I look at this mandala again, it seems happy feet are running to my heart.

Just did a "scribble drawing" with my nondominant hand, since life feels so much like a "scribble" right now. How I am to discern anything is a line of chaos.

Mark Camden and I were talking today about his naming me "Firewalker." I told him I feel like this is more of a dance than a walk. I am learning this dance with God.

I do believe I can find the path to dance through this with beauty, grace, joy, and wonder—and enough Fire to do so without being burned to a crisp.

Thank you, Lord, for gifting me with another day of life, another day of greening surrounded by the sights and sounds of your creation. May I bring to life what you desire.

SPILLING OVER

"Give, and it will be given to you.
A good measure, pressed down, shaken together,
running over, will be put into your lap;
for the measure you give will be the measure you get back."

— LUKE 6:38

This mandala is inspired by Luke 6:38.

In my daily reading from *The Book of Awakening*, Mark Nepo invites me to stay aware that there is "something larger" constantly surrounding me—an abundance of air, water, and light urging me to unfold what is already inside.

Spilling Over

PATH OF BLESSING

Happy May Day to me!

In today's devotional reading from *Jesus Calling*, author Sarah Young validates this path I'm finding myself on.

Path of Blessing

Prayer of St. Patrick

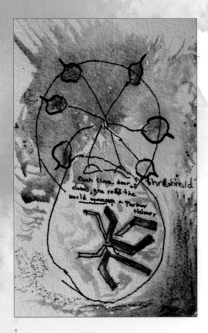

Threshold

Saying that once I give myself over to "constant communion" with Jesus, the here and now will comprise all coordinates of my daily life. Feeling freed to let Spirit direct my steps, I will also be freed from worry as I walk this path of peace.

This is my heart's desire—and I do believe I am learning to do this with greater ease every day. I am one who is learning to walk God's path of blessings in my present moments.

Today offers a Monday blessing with promise of new life sprouting forth in fertile soil.

HOLD AND LEAD

"I bind unto myself today,
the power of God to hold and lead,
His eye to watch, His strength to ward,
the word of God to give me speech,
His heavenly host to be my guard."

—ST. PATRICK

This prayer of St. Patrick has been important to me for a long time, and it provides so much comfort for me in these hard days.

THRESHOLD

Thresholds are threatening places. Sometimes there is a temptation not to cross, to stay with what I know rather than stepping into darkness and trusting that riches will be revealed. To me, that is the story of faith.

Jesus, I need (or is it desire?) physical healing. There seems to be so much more here for me to give and receive before I go Home. I pray for the miracle healing that others are lifting up to you on my behalf.

Some extra energy for this day would be helpful as well—I'm so very tired.

Again, this is an issue of trust. *I know you have a plan for me, and it will unfold in your timing.* Waiting and not knowing are so hard for me.

I am grateful for the beauty of this day, for last night's reflexology session, and for so much support to carry me through this fire.

FOUNTAIN, LIFE, LIGHT

"For with you is the fountain of life;
in your light we see light."

—PSALMS 36:9

These images really resonate with me this morning. Fountain, life, light. I certainly need LARGE scoops of water from God's fountain and the light that comes from Glory.

Fly High

AN ENDURING CENTER

Moving back to Nepo's *The Book of Awakening* this morning, I find reference to what Nepo calls "an enduring center" at the heart of all struggle—if only we can reach it. The storm, he says, can only be survived in its center.

He adds that we are to "draw sustenance—feel the God within us—from that enduring center without denying the experience of the storm."

And then, as if to echo and elaborate on this idea even further, *Jesus Calling* adds a reminder against fear of evil with the assurance that God will bring some good out of every situation I will ever encounter.

So hard to remain in the middle of this storm, but isn't that often where we find the quiet center in *nature's* storms?

When I hunker down like this, God, show me your blessings and help me be more mindful of your presence within me and your promises to bring good from all of this.

An Enduring Center

ANTICIPATE GOOD

 A beautiful Mother's Day for which I am grateful to be present. Emotionally, it has been a hard couple of days. Hard time hanging on to hope.

Back to Cleveland today, which should be a ray of hope but feels more like a cloudy unknown.

ROY: PREFERRED FUTURE

Today I told Judy that rather than wasting time wondering if she's going to make it, perhaps she should just tell God what she hopes for. It sounded a little harsher than I meant for it to, but it occurred to me that articulating to God her deepest desire for her road ahead might pull her out of the despair she's now flailing in.

She took this suggestion quietly. I almost regretted saying it then she spoke slowly, eyes closed, deliberately launching her rocket of desire:

"God, please give me a new song for a new life," she said, barely audible. The peace that washed over her was palpable.

I leaned forward and kissed her on the top of her forehead. "That's my Judy."

Her eyes shone with gratitude. My Judy had returned, and I felt the familiar surge of her energy as she gave this vision specificity and time frame, just as she so often advised her retreatants. "In 2016–2017," she began, eyes closed. "I will:

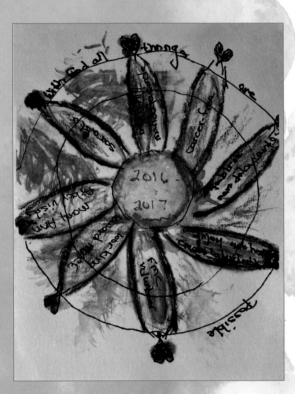

With God All Things Are Possible

~ be cancer free;

~ develop a monthly mandala group;

~ work toward another expressive arts certification;

~ enjoy our Sarasota visits and other trips;

~ volunteer at Fairfield Medical Center Cancer Wellness Department;

~ study reiki;

~ enjoy our home more fully;

~ construct a turf labyrinth;

~ publish my 'Mandala Images and Reflections.' "

She paused, then exclaimed, flashing that broad Judy smile that lights up any room and assures everyone around her that all is well, regardless, "With God, All Things Are Possible!"

"May it be so," I begged God silently, adding my petition to Judy's clearly articulated vision; in that moment her preferred future became mine, too.

I wrapped her tightly in my arms and closed my eyes, resting my chin on the top of her head as she spoke to God for both of us, *"God, I know that with you all things are possible,"* she said, her voice strong and serene. *"This is where I plant my hope that you, Lord, want all of this goodness for me and, perhaps, even planted these desires with me."* She paused, then added, *"Please give me courage to head in these many directions as though it is all possible. Amen."*

"Amen," I whispered, echoing this desire with all my heart.

JUDY: PRAYERS, PLEASE

Platelets dangerously low. The James hospital cancer doctor is trying to set up a transfusion for later today.

Whenever I am tempted to lose hope for the outcome of this trial, I need to remember I have better chances of a healing process with it than I would have had with the other protocols.

It also means driving to FMC frequently for bloodwork. It's tiring, but I am grateful I can do it all. Grateful for just enough energy and momentum to keep forging ahead.

Lord, continue to shore me up in weakened places when I am not enough. So grateful for love, prayers, and words of others that surround us—a time of role reversal. I know healing will come in your timing.

Platelets still dangerously low. Transfusion on Monday morning at FMC. Would prefer another way, but this is the best option.

We can't allow our own blossoming and unfolding until we acknowledge that we have something beautiful to release into the world. Within you, what is uniquely yours to offer?

What comes to me is healing images, words contained in this journal. I don't want to be a "patient" any longer. I want to be a HEALER, although I realize this is part of my training and equipping.

ROY: DROWNING IN SHOULDS

Judy says she's "drowning in shoulds" today. They're her own "shoulds," of course, not anybody else's. In Judy's shoes most people would never have such a list of expectations. But that's Judy for you. And, I suppose, it's how she keeps herself—and me—going.

Today, her "should" involves getting out of bed, exercising, going with me to buy flowers, being grateful, and making a mandala.

Judy sat back in her chair, eyes brimming with tears.

"What can I do to help?" I asked.

She thought for a moment. "Well," she began slowly, "if I can get this mandala done, can you help me post it to Facebook?"

What is Blossoming?

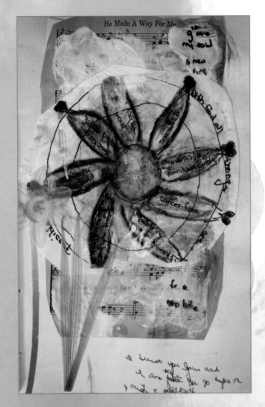

Give My Soul a New Song

Happy Platelets

"Sure," I said. Although I wasn't sure *at all* how to post something to Facebook, I wasn't about to let her know that. I knew we'd figure it out together.

A few hours later, we managed to post Judy's newly created mandala, "New Song," to Facebook. She's calling it her "life image" and her "vision of her preferred future."

Coming from both the depths of her heart and the deep well of her artistic expression, she also made a list of markers for this new reality.

"It's kind of unnerving for me to 'go public' with this list," she remarked.

"How so?" I asked, confused.

"Like maybe it won't happen now that it's in writing," she said, thoughtful. "I know that makes no sense," she was quick to add. "Now people can hold this in prayer with me for it to become my new life reality."

Judy squeezed my hand. "Thank you, Roy, for your help."

I nodded and returned her squeeze. I closed my eyes and expressed my own silent, heartfelt gratitude for God's hope and energy now surrounding us.

Turning toward me, Judy took both my hands in hers. "Let's pray," she said, as if ending a religious service or offering a blessing before a feast. I considered that it might be both.

JUDY: HAPPY PLATELETS

It is a beautiful day. How could I not be grateful? I am loved, cared for, and watched over. I must believe that all will be well. How could it be otherwise?

Platelets up from 32 to 44—not enough to resume my clinical trial, but they are moving up. Soon to leave for FMC to get more good platelets.

I imagine myself greeting these happy gifts entering my body and their sweet, encouraging reply: We are the healthy platelets your body needs. Allow them to mingle with your existing healthy blood to generate new platelets. Rest and allow this transfusion to do its work in you.

Today in *Jesus Calling* I am reminded that I don't have to figure out what's next. When I am finished with what's now, God will show me what's next. This is how I can stay close to God and on the path of Peace, where I desire to be.

Lord, thank you that there is something that can fix this issue.

NEW CENTER IN THE STORM

Moving on to *Dare to Journey* by Henri Nouwen, I am encouraged to find a "new center" of peace and a restful spirit. This, Nouwen says, is how new circles of energy and possibility come into being.

In response to this quote I am working on a new mandala, "New Centers in the Storm," to depict my new center from which new circles of energy and possibility come into view.

St. Catherine of Sienna said, "Be who God wants you to be and you'll set the world on fire."

I believe St. Catherine's words—until I realize how weary I am to do most anything.

New Centers in the Storm

WEAVING IN DARKNESS

Today *Jesus Calling* reminds me that by rejoicing in God's abundance I live by faith, not by sight.

This tapestry of my life is being woven in darkness. What will be revealed that would not have shown itself otherwise?

Lord, help me to know so that I can find you again.

HOPE AND TRUST

To FMC for bloodwork today. Hopeful for happy platelets hard at work in me. Hoping to return to treatments that will move healing forward.

Lord, you know how weary I am with this routine. But I trust you are well ahead of me on the path, smoothing out parts of it and making a way for me. Thank you, Jesus.

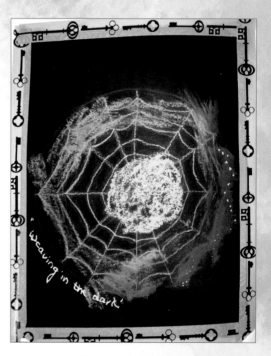

Weaving in the Dark

VISION CIRCLE

My vision circle posted on Facebook a few days ago of things I want to do allows this "fire" to break through. This is what I desire to be about, even in this place of deep fatigue.

Transfusion went well, but while my platelets increased, they are still too low to resume chemo and clinical trial meds. Disappointed and a bit discouraged.

Lab draw again on Monday in hopes of a larger increase.

ROY: A GENTLE SPACE

To celebrate another beautiful day, Judy and I took a short stroll together down Papago Lane, wondering as we did at nature's beauty always surrounding us, regardless of the season, in our Hide-A-Way Hills utopia.

After we returned, Judy settled into her chair on our screened porch to supervise me as I planted flowers we purchased yesterday (another box checked on her epic list of "shoulds") in our front flower bed.

"I can barely imagine having enough energy to do yard work, clean, and all that," she had said as I helped her get settled on the porch before I began work.

"That's what you have me for!" I said, laughing as I kissed her cheek. "Your job is to rest and supervise!"

She smiled up at me. "OK, then," she said, "I'm on it!"

I laughed, took up my hand tools, and made my way to the flats of flowers and the rich, freshly tilled soil that awaited them.

I looked up at her every few minutes, both making sure she was OK and committing this beautiful picture of our life to memory. After about a half hour, maybe less, I noticed she was asleep, peacefully absorbing the natural beauty and being with me as I worked.

JUDY: INCLINED TOWARD GOD'S LIGHT

Working on a new mandala today. This one shows the center of an emerging reality—softness, light, movement, love, and healing surround the center, and even creation is embraced as the storm rages around it.

Everything is inclined toward God's Light.

The storm waits until a more appropriate time to drag me down. I choose light, not darkness. I am at the center of God's emerging reality. I occupy a quiet, gentle space in which to rest, regenerate.

Wisdom and insight are offered to me as well. Wings that allow me to move freely in this space as I need to.

BEYOND WORDS

Georgia O'Keefe is famous for saying, among many other things, that she could say things with colors and shapes that she could say in no other way.

I certainly agree with this.

Platelets still low at 52; however, my nurse believes my bone marrow is beginning to do its job.

This morning the thought came to me, "Your faith has made your platelets rise." It names a potential starting place for me.

Lord, I do believe you will heal me. Help my unbelief.

JUST ENOUGH

To lab again.

Lord, "just enough" of an increase please.

44 up to 70, right direction.

Jesus said many times to people that their faith would heal them. I'm afraid my faith is not that strong. Maybe that is part of this—to make it so going forward.

ROY: GRATITUDE FOR THE NORMAL

We decided after much deliberation this morning to go to Sunday morning worship at Chapel in the Pines, outdoor sanctuary in Hide-A-Way Hills. It is a beautiful spot—one of our favorite places and ways to worship, enveloped in our surrounding hills and trees and bounty of nature, breathtaking regardless of season or time of year. Many who come here, like us, also belong to other faith communities and traditions.

For some, this is their only connection to organized religion of any kind. It rarely matters who's leading the service or topic. We almost always find it immediately applicable.

In this unique little neighborhood community worship space, we come as we are and celebrate the love of God and nature that connects us—and all of mankind. People bring flowers, stuffed animals, whatever moves them, throughout the week to decorate the altar to honor God's outdoor sanctuary and our little community who gathers here regularly.

We decided that, as long as Judy's strength held out, we'd also go to brunch at The Lodge after worship to try to create an almost-normal Sunday morning in the Hills. At brunch, Girard, The Lodge's pastry chef, made Judy a raspberry and strawberry pie. So much kindness in this sweet little community of ours. We chose well.

I could see the fatigue behind Judy's eyes and her deliberate movement. She was pushing through, determined to enjoy both worship and brunch. I watched her closely, ready to intervene if it became too much, but I knew better than to interfere. So I stood by, thankful, helpless, hopeful—and awed.

Today, *Jesus Calling* invited us to ask God for what we need—and then to anticipate and trust and express our gratitude that it will happen. Reflecting on the wonders of this beautiful day of near normalcy we so desperately needed, all I can say is *"Amen."*

JUDY: FLAME OF LIFE

This morning's devotional readings include Marc Nepo's assertion that God is "the flame of life" living in my body.

Eternal abundant life is a promise, not just a means of survival. What would my life look like if I took Christ at his word and asked to be filled with his "flame of life"—his Holy Spirit? Would my experience of this journey I'm on right now be more about freedom, openness, and joy rather than anxiety, confinement, and frustration?

Blessings lived into during this time include:

~ Roy's love, support, and tender care

~ My support teams of dear friends

~ Two successful brain surgeries

~ Referral to the Cleveland Clinic

~ I am alive

~ Art as an expression of my life

~ Beautiful home in God's woods

~ Outstanding medical care

In *Jesus Calling*, Sarah Young promises that peace from Jesus transcends intellect. When I put too much mental energy into trying to figure things out—thoughts spinning wildly, without direction or destination—I am blocking this gift to my soul. All the while, she asserts, Jesus's peace hovers over me, "looking for a place to land."

God, please help me be still in your presence. Help me remember to invite you to still my anxious thoughts so your light can infiltrate my mind and heart until I glow with your peace.

Reader's Notes

Summer 2016

Stained Glass

JUDY: STAINED GLASS

Elizabeth Kubler Ross says people are like stained glass windows—their true beauty is revealed by light from within them, once darkness sets in. I'm thinking about this today—the darkness that has set in around us and wondering whether the light within me is enough to shine my true colors.

My reading this morning from *Jesus Calling* picks up on this thread, promising that my journey through this darkness has been mapped for me, step by step. Perfect even in its imperfections.

God, please help me keep my focus on your presence shining within me—and the peace and joy no circumstances can touch.

HOLY GROUND

So grateful for platelet increase.

Also happy to be on the Jin Shin Jyutsu healing quest. Calling upon this ancient Japanese healing art to focus on harmonizing my life energy offers an exciting primary goal to discover my healing capacity. It feels like forward movement rather than staggering in circles in darkness.

I wonder also what God is up to and pray to stay the course with all its twists and turns.

In Exodus 3:2–15, Moses goes to the burning bush and sees that fire has not consumed it. Then God tells him to remove his sandals because he is standing on holy ground.

This famous biblical scene resonates with me particularly today because it is good for me to realize this fire has not consumed me. I believe I, too, am on holy ground, and I trust God's provision in my own exodus.

What of my old self needs to be removed so I can fully take in the energy, power, and wisdom of this holy ground? Doubt? Negativity? Pessimism about an abundant future? Negativity overshadowing blessings?

VICTORY IN THE DAY

Met later in the day with our Cleveland Clinic physician's assistant for my clinical study. We reviewed my medication list and adjusted my dosage and use of the steroid to 3 mg once a day at breakfast. Supposed to take Temador and TRC102 at bedtime, Zofran and other evening meds one hour before I take chemo and trial meds.

We'll do bloodwork each Monday or Tuesday in this treatment cycle. My symptoms are "steady but not declining."

Apparently, some of my parts are healing well, some more slowly. Surgically, she says I'm healing well; the cancer healing is slower due to chemo. Takes a while for my brain to heal from effects of chemo and radiation. Still experiencing significant vision issues—says it might still be due to the swelling in my brain. Or not.

Also concerned about a bit of loss of touch sensation in my left arm. Ordered physical therapy to address this left-side deficit. Parietal brain (right-side) swelling is probably causing this issue. Will likely need progressive therapies to see progress.

PA says that because ENERGY produces ENERGY, she agrees with Tai Chi for exercise in addition to recumbent bike. Also told me to watch my sugar; apparently, cancer likes it, too.

She seems pleased with the alternative therapies and self-care regimen I'm following. She says my attitude is critical, so whatever I can do to stay positive and active will be helpful and good. Art, nature, friends, family, and self-care are also good medicine. Physical therapy and movement of any sort will be good for me physically and mentally. Told us that while focusing on questions, future, and wonderings are natural, it is really important to seize every moment.

Can't help but wonder what that means. Does she not think I will survive this cancer?

ROY: A DEEPER DARKNESS

When Judy woke up this morning, she was full of plans for the day, and dear friends had come to visit us and keep her company while I ran some errands. We were all eating breakfast together, Judy propped up in bed, "a lady of leisure" as she liked to say, when she suddenly began listing toward the left.

"Judy?" I said, jumping to my feet and hurrying toward her from my chair across the room.

"My left arm," she said, rubbing at it, "it just keeps tingling." She continued to lean, slipping from her sitting position all the way down on her side.

"Call 911!" I said to no one in particular.

"No, Roy, just call hospice," Judy said. "They told us to call them first, and they'll decide whether I need to go anywhere or just stay put."

I got Judy propped up with pillows stuffed around her to keep her stable. I kept talking to her, watching her face closely for any signs of the classic stroke symptoms they tell you to watch for—all the while thinking, *This can't be happening.*

The hospice people arrived after what seemed like hours but was, in reality, about 15 minutes. By the time they got there, Judy seemed better, speaking very clearly with no facial drooping.

"Probably a stroke," the young man said, matter-of-factly, as he took Judy's blood pressure and began his assessment.

When he asked her to stand, her left leg buckled beneath her, and in a terrible flash we both realized that she *couldn't* stand—there was no strength in her left leg.

They called an ambulance to take Judy to Fairfield Medical Center, where the telestroke medicine unit at Ohio State University could help evaluate her long distance and tell them what to do.

It was all a blur, people shuffling in and out, checking this, checking that, asking the same inane questions over and over, clicking on their damned computer. Every few minutes it seemed like someone new would come in and we'd start another round. Finally, a doctor beckoned me into the waiting area to tell me that because Judy has brain cancer and has had chemo, she needed to be transported immediately to the Wexner Medical Center at Ohio State.

He went on to say that because of her brain cancer, the medicine they now need to give her to minimize risk of another stroke carries a 20 percent mortality risk.

I stood there, numb and speechless.

"Would you like to talk with her about it?" the doctor inquired.

"Yes," I managed to say. I returned to Judy's side, and everyone scurried from the curtained area.

I looked at Judy. "Do you know what they want to do?" I asked, uncertain of how anyone ever talks about such a thing.

She nodded. "There really isn't much of a choice, Roy," she said, reaching for my hand.

I nodded, fighting back tears. Just when I was starting to have a small amount of hope, this nightmare was taking a hairpin turn into deeper darkness.

"They have to give me this medicine so they can Life Flight me to the Wexner Medical Center," she said as if she were explaining to a small child why we needed to wash the car even if it might rain.

We both recognized that this could be our last moment together. While this drug they were about to administer could well kill her, without the drug another stroke could do the same.

I held her hand tightly as the Life Flight crew arrived—a captain and two other guys.

I listened to the sound of the waiting chopper and watched them transfer her to a different kind of gurney. Because I was not allowed to make this journey with her, I would have to follow by car.

As we said goodbye, I willed myself not to consider that it really might be . . . goodbye.

JUDY: HELD BY PRAYER

So appreciative of everyone's prayers and compassionate hearts over the past few days. These have held us when it has been hard.

My stroke, they tell me, was a "very small one," with little or no permanent damage. The MRI showed that the tumor has changed very little, if at all. This should be confirmed by further testing over the next few days.

I will be transferring to Dodd Hall for intensive rehab for the next 7–14 days. My MRI yesterday and our meetings with my doctors were made easier to bear with all the love and prayers that surrounded us during that meeting. I ask again for prayers for strength, endurance, patience, and progress, as the rehab will be hard work and will take time.

THE HARD ROAD

Dodd Hall acute rehab facility has great, professional, caring people. They are also unrelenting taskmasters to help me progress as much as possible in my occupational therapy, physical therapy, speech, and recreational and psychological therapy/evaluations.

Hard PT session today. Speech sessions were also hard, focused on memory and process thinking. I was very, very tired due to two interrupted nights of sleep.

My "team" met today, and I was told that my projected discharge date is July 8, three weeks from now. More details on Monday. They also said the vast bulk of progress happens in the first 3–6 months of therapy. It's a long, hard journey, but I'm so glad to be able to do something tangible about this other than taking meds.

I will also be bringing home a wheelchair, which will require a ramp to be built at our home. I don't know how much I will ultimately use the wheelchair.

Dear friends are already coordinating our "ramp project" and recruiting volunteers to assist with this construction so it is completed before we get back to our beloved ravine.

I'm also doing other nontraditional care for my cancer; will work and look forward to progress with this difficult therapy and restorative journey. They say by next week I'll be doing things I can't do now—kicking a ball, gripping a glass (for wine, of course!), improved right leg walking, right leg and right arm wheelchair use, sitting centered and steady, shrugs and shoulder blade exercises, and more.

So grateful for all who are keeping us in prayer and delivering all kinds of support. God bless them all, many times over. They are holding us up more than they will ever know.

ROY: GIRL TIME

When one of Judy's closest friends gifted her with a hairstyling session in her rehab room, I wasn't sure how she would feel about that.

In a word, she was *delighted*.

So happy to see how she lit up at the prospect. Thinking about it later, it was more of that dip back into normal that we crave in our world of doctors and treatments and regimens and, now, therapies to try to hold onto and restore what Judy and I now understand that we took so much for granted.

We didn't mean to, of course. It's really an important part of our spiritual practices to remain grateful in small things. However, within that "small things" realm, there's a lot we never think about—automatic things we forget to express specific gratitude for yet now understand as pure miracle. It's a miracle, really, that anything in our body works at all. What an intricate maze of miracles we live in, every single day of our lives, and don't even realize it!

When her hairdresser arrived along with our friends, I was excused. (This was, after all, "girl time"), and I took advantage of the opportunity to run some errands and check in with work. They had been so kind about giving me all the time I need to help and care for Judy.

I realized that as we move forward on this particular stretch of our uncertain path, I'm going to want and need to spend even more time with Judy. Every possible moment, in fact. I can't even imagine, at this point, trying to summon the focus and interest in my job or the demands of it that now seem so completely trivial. Funny how life can shift perspective, sometimes over time, such as with a serious diagnosis like cancer, sometimes in a heartbeat, as with a stroke. Still can't believe Judy is having to deal with both of these things at once. Just not fair.

You hear me, God?

Made a mental note to get paperwork going for a leave of absence. Regardless of how all this goes and on what time frame, I know I want to be by Judy's side every single moment.

Returned to her room to check on the results of the salon session, and I heard giggles as I approached the door. Clearly, this was just what the doctor ordered—haven't heard Judy giggle like that in a long, long time. I waited a bit longer before entering the room, not wanting to disrupt the process that was so clearly lifting Judy's flagging spirits.

When I heard one of them ask when I'd be back, I knew it was my cue. Entering the room, I couldn't help but smile myself when I saw the short, sassy haircut Judy now sported, with its array of pink, purple, and red extensions.

"Gorgeous!" I exclaimed. I meant it. The hair, yes, but the glow on Judy's face even more.

"You really like it?" Judy asked, beaming. "It hasn't been this short in a long, long time."

"I love it!" I said. I smiled at her dear friends, who were looking on with pride. "Thank you, girls, so, so much. This is just what Judy needed today!"

"It is!" Judy agreed, looking at the handheld mirror and turning her head side to side to check it out at all angles.

It was cute. And it lifted my spirits as well just seeing how happy she was. Who knew a hairdo could be such a game-changer?

"What made you think of the colorful extensions?" I asked, not knowing exactly whom to ask about this . . . a little out of character, for sure, but in this case, just perfect.

Judy laughed out loud at my awkwardness. "I did it because . . . I can!" she said, repeating one of her favorite—and most endearing—expressions with a broad smile I haven't seen for quite a while.

JUDY: OFF THE TRIAL

My anticipated discharge date is still July 8, and that dear team of people from Hide-A-Way Hills is making good progress on installing the wheelchair ramp at our house. We're also having other safety items placed in our home with my rehab team's direction.

My rehab team will also offer the training here at Dodd Hall for anyone who wants to and is able to be on my Home Care Team. They'll learn about transfer assistance, specific types of care, and other actions to help increase their awareness and confidence while they're with me. (I'll also continue to receive in-home OT and PT.)

My most recent MRI, when read by our Cleveland Clinic trial doctor, showed a small progression/ growth in my tumor. He also told us he has seen other tumors double and triple in size, so even though it is a progression, it's small. Nevertheless, it did grow in excess of 25 percent, which stops my clinical trial.

It's very discouraging to know it has grown. He already talked with my oncologist at The James about next-step options. We have an appointment Tuesday morning at The James to hear from him and make decisions.

HARDER AND STEEPER

Hard appointment today with our oncologist and his team—and just generally a hard day.

He was encouraged, as are we, that my left side feelings and movement are returning due to work my therapists and I are doing.

However, because of the tumor growth, my options now are to choose one of two treatments, one of which is a longtime FDA-approved chemo treatment and the other of which is an immunotherapy that has been used with some positive results on melanoma, lung cancer, and a few other cancers. This one is not FDA approved for my cancer type. The other option, of course, is to just stop treatment.

The chemo option is a pill taken once every six weeks, with nausea and blood count declines due to the chemo affecting my bone marrow.

The immunotherapy option is a drip infusion every two weeks with little side effects—and would need to get insurance approval for its use for my type of cancer.

My doctors are also applying to have the genetic makeup of my cancer cells examined, which would possibly identify other treatment options.

The goal now, he says, is to stabilize the tumor for a "period of time." They say that they will make efforts to keep to this goal for as long as we want.

GREAT CLOUD OF WITNESSES

Our Hide-A-Way Hills Woodland Fairies, many of whom have moustaches and hammers, have graced our home with a perfect wheelchair ramp. Having it in place before we get home takes a great concern off our plate.

"Thank you" seems so inadequate, but the message it holds is profound and no doubt felt by each of them. Their love, support, gifts, and prayers feed us—and hold us when we are not sure about our next step.
We have now decided for sure to not pursue any chemo treatments from this point forward. Three chemo and clinical trial treatments have done nothing positive, and our oncology doctor said that trying a different chemo would likely not affect my cancer any differently.

We are also considering holistic treatment options, which could be used alongside the immunotherapy—or alone. Soul-searching questions are guiding us as we move toward our choice.

I know the Hills and our little ravine are calling me home, and we're anxious to return to our healing space. So grateful for all the prayers for clarity, peace, and discernment that surround and bless us.

TRIAL RUN

The original plan was to be discharged on Friday, but it has been delayed until Tuesday. This will give us a chance to spend a night in their independent living apartment here and attend Lilyfest on Saturday.

Both will be good trial runs of being at our house and being in public at a busy event, navigating my wheelchair, the drive, the crowds, etc. We will then meet with my rehab team at Dodd on Monday for pointers, "atta-boys," and improvements still needed.

Gathering more info about the immunotherapy medicine and asking more questions of God. Trusting God without answers and clarity.

No chemo, no way!!

Hope to decide between our options this week. I do feel a bit of freedom knowing that we eliminated a major option and are now focused on two options:

1. Clinical trial non-chemo meds
2. Take nothing and focus on living each moment

ROY: EXQUISITE MOMENTS

Lilyfest, which has long been one of our favorite events and beloved traditions, was looking extremely doubtful this year—in fact, I wasn't even going to bring it up. After Judy's stroke and being so unsure of what lies ahead, missing Lilyfest seemed the least of our problems.

Then along came a couple of angels, the "City Chicks," two of Judy's dear friends who encouraged—no, insisted—that we go. They also offered to provide extra help—eyes, hands, hearts, and companionship to help make this possible for Judy.

The deep gratitude in Judy's eyes when they made this sincere offer told me all I needed to know. We were going to make this happen for her—and we were going to have fun doing it!

It was so wonderful to share this special day and event with them. They helped me immeasurably—from avoiding spilling Judy onto grass as I made rookie attempts to push her wheelchair on somewhat rough terrain, to fetching and thoroughly enjoying chocolate truffles with Judy.

We all love Mark Camden's new CD, *Yesterday, Today, Tomorrow,* and being able to hear some of these tracks played live—with these dear friends—made for a day packed with exquisite moments and precious memories to sustain us on the road ahead.

"That's my favorite," Judy murmured as Mark played "The Hidden Place," a song from his new CD. She looked up at me and said, "It's also where I go each morning to find the courage to begin again."

JUDY: GIFTS FROM ABOVE

We came home Tuesday afternoon to the healing woods of Hocking Hills.

The progress I've made has been hard and will continue to be hard. It comes down to perseverance and our belief that it's all worth it. Some days, that belief is difficult to find, to rest in.

However, I am blessed by so many people. It was emotional leaving the 25–30 nurses, PCAs, and therapists of Dodd Hall who cared for me and pushed me during the past four weeks, but they prepared me to come home. Now, a team of in-home therapists will pick up where they left off. I'll also be supported by my dear City Chicks, my Hide-A-Way Hills Woodland Fairies, and "Team Judy," as Roy calls them, as my recovery continues.

We also received good news today that Bristol Squibb Myers will pay for my immunotherapy treatments. It is about $12,000 per treatment, which is already FDA approved to treat melanoma, lung cancer, and kidney cancer. By helping patients such as me, they are building data that could win FDA approval for their drug Opdivo to be used for brain cancers such as mine; that approval will lead to insurance companies paying for its use in the future.

Opdivo has shown strong promise to lengthen lives and improve the quality of lives with few side effects. My oncologist said my cancer has been more aggressive than he anticipated, and he admitted that he is grasping at straws, but at least he's thinking of things to do outside the box for me. He really cares about me, and I can't ask for more.

GOD HAS MY BACK

It's been a while since my last entry, and I've missed the contemplation and reflection in my daily practice.

Last week included several hard days during which I didn't feel as though God had my back, due to everything that has happened. We had to go to The James for an MRI and an appointment with my oncologist about the upcoming immunotherapy treatments, which pushed me back into a heightened awareness of everything and then God showed up.

We received a call late Friday that the MRI showed virtually no increase in my brain cancer when comparing the scans of June 14 versus July 19. It has been stable!!! What a wonderful word. God has my back. I also realized that God has my back via all of my family and friends.

Immunotherapy treatment starts this coming Friday with an IV infusion every two weeks at The James, about 2 and a half hours each time. I hope this makes a difference in my cancer. PT and OT sessions at our home five times a week, while also living with fatigue due to cancer, stroke, and medicines. Hard to push through sometimes.

My prayer for Friday is that God's healing light and energy will be pouring into my body via the medicine.

NOT ALONE

My first immunotherapy session last week was uneventful in and of itself, with my next ones set for August 12 and 26.

However, one of the side effects is potential joint and muscle pain. We found ourselves blindsided by this with my severe right knee pain that took us to Fairfield Med Center at 5:00 a.m. Saturday morning. Good people and a morphine treatment took away the pain. This whole thing can become quite discouraging, which is where I find myself this evening. Helpful to remember that I'm not doing this on my own, even though I feel like it sometimes.

PRIVATE COCKTAIL

The idea of having a "private cocktail" immunotherapy prepared for me every two weeks is kind of funny to me.

This is the strangest bar I've ever been in.

They call it a "private cocktail" because the pharmacist does not mix it for me until the lab evaluates my blood tests, which are done when I arrive each time. Once the results are provided to him, he then mixes my hopefully magic potion, which is given to me via an IV right away.

Also kinda odd to see my name on the IV bag versus a bag that gives only product information.

My next session is this coming Friday at 12:30, followed by an MRI and an appointment with my oncologist on Tuesday, August 16, at which time he'll give us the MRI results. A lot of activity focused on my cancer that reminds me of it being within me.

I pray that it is at least stable again and that my "cocktail" does its job.

TRULY LIVE EACH MOMENT

Yes, I'm still here.

Lots of prayers are holding us tenderly, and they sometimes are the only thing holding us up.

I did not have any ER-type pain with the second immunotherapy treatment received on Friday. I did experience increased fatigue and some aching joints, but better than an ER trip. No doubt many prayers surrounding us helped also.

I have an MRI tomorrow at The James, followed by an appointment with my oncologist to review MRI results, discuss next steps, stay the current treatment course, options, etc., all depending on scan results.

I want to live my life, no matter what the future holds. Truly live each moment.

DRAINED, NUMB, HAPPY

Feeling surrounded by prayers and joined in person today by five dear friends.

Roy and I were told by my oncologist that he believes my cancer/tumor has had no significant change since the last MRI a month ago.

Thank you, God!

There seems to be a slight white spot—white spots aren't good—but he doesn't think it's anything serious. We need to wait for the official word (within 24–48 hours) from the radiologist for his report of what he sees. My doctor said that the white spot may actually be the immunotherapy beginning to go after the cancer. No way to tell this early.

He is keeping me on the treatment, which is good news. He also listened to my need to address my extreme fatigue and constant pain and prescribed a different medicine that may help my mood and periods of depression. He also changed my anti-clotting med from a daily shot to a pill. Wonderful!

These two meds may help improve my life quality and energy, which will also help me more actively participate in my stroke therapy and "live" more fully.

We were prepared to hear hard news but also hoped the stable report we heard last month would be repeated, which it was. Our emotions leading up to today drained us, such that while we were more than happy to hear this news, we were also numb from fatigue.

This journey has been long and will continue.

AROMA TO GOD

This cooler weather has been great. I've been able to get out on our screened porch several times the past few days after several days of extreme fatigue. Gazing at the pasture, wildflowers, and hummingbirds helps restore me.

My third immunotherapy session is this coming Friday at The James. Hopefully, it will be progressively better, without the extreme fatigue. We know how to avoid joint pain via Tylenol and Motrin, which worked last time.

My quality of life is being impacted by continual pain in my left shoulder, foot, arm, and hand, which has been joined by right hip and lower back pain when I move certain ways, which is hard to avoid due to transfers from my bed. I have requested an X-ray of my hip, pelvis, and SI joint, which my doctor's nurse seemed to agree with having done.

My oncologist's impression of the MRI last week showing substantially no tumor change was confirmed by the official report. However, there were new "enhancement" areas that may suggest some spreading. This can only be addressed via repeated MRIs—next one scheduled for September 13—and my symptoms. These suspicious areas could also be caused by radiation that was stopped in January.

Only time will tell.

Today, a dear friend is going to help me start a stained glass project that will reflect my previous "Hidden Places" mandala. It may be something Roy can do with me.

These are the days when it is hard to make the choice to begin again each morning.

Very nauseous for the past 24 hours. Praying it settles down so we can get some much-needed sleep tonight.

TIME, PRESENCE, AND LOVE

Slept well both Friday and Saturday, proving that my prayer warriors and God were working overtime to help me to not get sick during the night.

Because of my getting sick and other things, we met with my oncology team Friday afternoon (accompanied by four dear friends) to discuss the experimental cancer medicine I'm taking. Based on that discussion with them, we have hard decisions to make in the near future.

Reader's Notes

Fall 2016

JUDY: COURAGE TO CONTINUE

Via the crazy plan of Roy and his two accomplices, 86 birthday cards from family and friends, including people I don't even know from Bremen United Methodist Church, graced my home and heart. There were also countless text messages, phone calls, desserts, flowers, and food from our Hide-A-Way Hills Woodland Fairies and pizzas from Utopia in Logan.

I've been tempted to exit this battle a few times, but all of these kind people, including friends and family and people who have begun to follow my story, remind me of why I'm choosing to stay in it. I'm so richly blessed.

We've decided to go ahead with another infusion session this coming Friday, September 9. Last week we were seriously considering not pursuing treatments any further and letting nature take its course.

What a difference a few days can make. I've had additional bouts of nausea, which are rough and exacerbate my depression, and my fatigue is still very present.

Prayers for relief from the medicine side effects and my illness symptoms—and courage to continue on if that is God's desire.

RESERVES LOW

Rough night last night. Got sick three times between 3:30 a.m. and 8:30 a.m., which drains me and causes me to wonder about next steps and this process. This ongoing nausea is also affecting my appetite and lowering my energy.

Thankful to all who are holding me up; my reserves are low.

ROY: OUR TICKING-DOWN CLOCK

Today we went to The James for additional testing and evaluation of our options. The doctors agreed that Judy's cancer was getting more aggressive.

"Well, let's get on with it, then," Judy said, matter-of-fact, green eyes radiating the certainty of her words.

This moment also launched a series of deep conversations, in which we planned her funeral, wrote her obituary, and tended to legal matters. Daily we received visitors from all across the country who had heard the news.

I requested a hospital bed large enough for both of us for our cottage. Our bed would become our new world, where I can hold her, stroke her hair, and talk with her about things that are so foreign and unreal—yet imminent and desperate and urgent. It is a surreal time, compelling us to laser focus on each and every moment we have left in our ticking-down clock.

Judy wants and receives massages and reflexology one or two times every week—and now, every night at the onset of her "anxiety symptoms," as they call it, I put my basic learning of these skills to good use, massaging her feet with essential oils as we talk or just sit together in silence.

This is a time when time is standing still for us. And we are so grateful.

Sometimes she sleeps, and sometimes she doesn't. Likewise for me. We listen to our bodies' rhythms and find ourselves most often in sync, like mothers with newborn babies. There is no morning, evening, night, or day. There is only us and our deepening sense of the preciousness of our remaining time together on this earth.

Home care nurses come regularly, and a case manager comes by a couple times a week to check on us. Physical therapy has stopped, so Judy's energy is completely devoted to living every moment she has left.

On the night when Judy's severe nausea lasted from about 8:00 p.m. to 1:00 a.m., accompanied by intense pain in her head, we both knew this was much, much more than a headache. I called 911 at about 2:00 a.m. We went to Fairfield Memorial, where they checked her in, began IV fluids, and did a CT scan.

Her symptoms continued, so she was transported to Ohio State University's ER at about 5:30 a.m., where they did more tests, including another MRI. They softened her pain with morphine, treated her nausea with IV drugs, and then admitted her to The James Cancer Hospital. At last, she slept, with no pain or nausea at all. I, however, did not.

We met with her oncologist this morning to hear the results of her MRI and other tests. They explained to us that Judy's more intense and frequent symptoms are caused by her cancer now pressing against her brain fluid area, leaking into the brain fluid, and being carried to the top of her brain where the cells block fluid flow. This building pressure is causing her intense nausea and pain, as well as her increased fatigue and confusion. After this interminable barrage of information about this cancer that has become significantly more aggressive, the doctors explained there is nothing to be done short of extremely aggressive, and likely ineffective, chemo treatments that would just beat her up even further.

Judy and I didn't even need to discuss this; we decided weeks ago to stop all chemo-related treatments. They recommended we engage hospice care to manage her symptoms and strive for the best possible quality of life in the time she has left. As a 15-year hospice volunteer, Judy is well aware of the many compassionate services hospice provides and wants to take advantage of them as much as she can. What was unthinkable a short time ago had just become our godsend, our reality.

After her discharge from The James on Sunday morning, we'll return home before going to Pickering House hospice in Lancaster for one to three days to get used to their facility. Then we'll return home with in-home hospice care for as long as we can before returning to Pickering House when she needs their 24/7 care to control her pain and nausea.

While we're both sad that this phase of Judy's journey has begun, we're also comfortable with its wisdom and rightness.

Today, Judy was transferred to the Pickering House for at least a few days to try to get her symptoms under control.

She rested comfortably all afternoon, and so did I, getting some long overdue rest and relief from watching her struggle with the pain and nausea.

Such a helpless, hopeless feeling.

I will stay here with her. God willing, we will get to go back home for at least a little while once these symptoms get under control. Just a few more weeks in our cottage, God. A few more days together before what I know is inevitable will certainly come.

Today, the Pickering House case manager, Tara, and hospice nurse, Becky, are joining Team Judy. This morning Tara was able to help us identify and eliminate several medications that aren't very necessary at this point.

She told me I need to let those who are visiting know that they may notice some confusion. Judy and I agree that our goal now is symptom control, understanding that increasing these medications will likely result in longer periods of resting during coming days.

We also learned that Tara is very familiar with the essential oils Judy has come to love and rely on, so as Judy experienced head pain this morning, Tara reached for peppermint oil and massaged Judy's temples. It was special to see her dive in so personally.

Even amid the rough waters Judy is facing, her goofy/fun side still shows up regularly. That is a huge blessing to us both and to everyone who visits or encounters her sweet spirit in these dark days.

Our dear friend and her young daughter visited Judy Sunday afternoon and evening. Her daughter was playing with her mother's hair, making an array of ponytails at the sides of her head as she visited with Judy.

Judy then surprised us all by asking the little girl for the same hairstyle. The crazy results made us all laugh—and we took a picture to post to Judy's Facebook page to show Judy's sense of humor, still alive and well. Once again, I am amazed at how hair changes everything!

Feeling so blessed and grateful for this respite thanks to these three wild and crazy gals!

JUDY: A MIGHTY FORTRESS

I know my days are getting longer and more difficult. I am so grateful for and gain energy from the outpouring of love, support, and caring. I know God hears our prayers. Together we ARE a mighty fortress.

Roy and I met with our priest today to start funeral plans. Hard work, but I'm grateful I have the opportunity to plan this. The people here are wonderful and caring and mix in humor in gentle doses.

Our tentative plans are to come home Friday as long as my symptoms stay under control, which they have since Monday afternoon due to medication changes.

PRECIOUS LIFE

As we hoped, we're back home from the Pickering Hospice house. At Roy's insistence, they were able to dismantle the wider hospital bed that allowed us to sleep together comfortably and reassemble it here.

The caring staff there is amazing, but there is nothing compared to being home in our woods, alongside our ravine, among friends, cuddling together.

Roy and I will celebrate 39 years of true wedded bliss tomorrow by savoring a heart-shaped deep-dish cheese pizza being shipped to us from Giordano's in Chicago. We'll have a pepperoni pizza also to enjoy at another time soon. There is nothing like their pizza anywhere. Of course a glass of vino will help wash it down as we raise our glasses in a toast to our blessed marriage.

We don't know how long we'll be home by our ravine, but we will do our best to relish and soak in every moment. I haven't been sick or had painful headaches since Monday. Hopefully, my new meds and other changes are working and will do so for a good while. If they return, our hospice nurse will be here quickly to assist us, with the goal of remaining here as long as possible. God's time and God's way.

Reminding everyone I speak with to hug those you love and be thankful for what you have. Life is precious.

READY TO FLY

The outpouring of love and wishes for me and our anniversary last weekend was overwhelming. I often comment that I don't deserve this abundance of love and kindness. Roy reminds me that we all deserve kindness, as that is what God planned.

No severe nausea or head pain issues since we returned home last Friday. However, over the past three or four days it has become clear to me that I'm ready to move on, to join my father, my grandparents, and my aunt, to meet Roy's father and brother and Jesus in heaven.

Being in two places, here and there, is increasingly exhausting. I'm ready and at peace with moving on.

I'm ready to fly.

THE IN-BETWEEN

I have a confession.

This waiting is so difficult, so hard. I've always been more of a destination person. That is true of this journey also. Being in-between is taxing; the waiting is frustrating.

However, events of the past few days are showing why my journey is still in process. So many friends and loved ones have journeyed to pray with us, be with us, and treasure this holy time together.

At one point, I told Roy I feel very cared for. It is for these people and such moments that I'm still here.

Depression sets in at times, which hurts and renders me motionless, emotionally exhausted. I know that love, beauty, light, and joy await me, and they are also here, but they are hard to see right now.

ROY: "IT'S TIME"

Over the past few weeks Judy has had increasing trouble keeping any food down, but mentally and emotionally she is still incredibly sharp. We were able to get out a few times for dinner dates, time with nature in our beautiful woods, whatever she could manage.

On Wednesday, October 5, however, Judy began to weaken dramatically. She just couldn't stop throwing up—it was all reflex, bile—she hadn't really had anything to eat for a couple of days, yet the reflex to throw up was strong and not diminishing with all the medications we could throw at it.

I called Tara, our case manager, who was at our house within 20 minutes. After a quick examination, she turned to me, folded her stethoscope and put it in the pocket of her jacket and said, "It's time."

I nodded, unable to speak. I knew this day was coming. I probably knew it was here. But something inside me wanted to scream, No! Not yet! Just a few more days!

Then, looking at Judy, remembering sights and sounds of her suffering over the past 48 hours, the increase of her symptoms and discomfort that we both hoped against hope we could get under control, just one more time, I knew.

She knew.

It was time.

Tara called an ambulance that arrived way too fast. I thought I might throw up at the sight of it pulling into our driveway. Except I was too numb to do anything but stand silently and watch as they came in with their gurney.

There were two of them, EMTs. They rolled into our bedroom without fuss or conversation. They clearly knew why they were there; Tara must have told them.

As they transferred Judy from our bed to the gurney, our eyes connected.

"Please be careful with her," I said quietly. "She's very precious."

"I will," one replied softly, earnestly, with a tenderness in his voice that was no match for his burly outward appearance.

He helped carry Judy out of our bedroom, out of our home, out of our life together, like she was his mother. Incredible strength but so tender. Never got his name.

Following slowly as they rolled her out of our house, I wondered whether Judy realized she was seeing it all for the last time. Her eyes were closed due to the nausea, but once in a while she would open them. What was she thinking? Was she realizing the enormity of this moment? Or was she so engulfed in pain and nausea and medication that she was simply rolling, quite literally, with the moment? Only she knew the answer.

I realize this was the first of many questions I would be unable to ask her. Or that I could ask and hope the answer somehow floated to me on a breeze, through a thought, a lyric, a picture, an advertisement.

I knew even then that our channels of communication were about to broaden to a place I could not yet imagine. But it wasn't going to be the same. Our years of meaningful, silly, deep, and shallow conversation were coming to their end. The grief of just that was unspeakable in and of itself.

So I followed, numbly picking up my suitcase, already packed and by the door, for the last leg of Judy's journey Home.

As they were putting her into the ambulance, and I had just opened the door to our car to follow him, I stopped.

"Wait a minute," I said. I walked to Judy's side, and she opened her eyes. "I love you," I said. "I'll see you there in a few minutes."

She nodded, smiled, and then closed her eyes.

During this exchange, our burly EMT turned his back, giving us privacy and clearly feeling the intense emotion of this moment. It was a moment that I knew I would always remember, one of those markers that stand out over time.

I arrived at Pickering House first, waiting by their front door as the ambulance pulled into the driveway. Instead of stopping there as I had anticipated, they pulled around to a side door, then stopped, backed up a bit, and cut the engine.

After conferring with the nurse who met them, they walked toward me. "Her room isn't quite ready yet," the smaller guy explained. "So we're going to wait here until she can get right into her room."

I nodded.

They disappeared into the ambulance, and after what was probably 15 minutes but felt like 15 hours, they emerged. They opened its rear doors, lifted Judy's gurney out, engaged its wheels, and rolled her in my direction. As she came closer, I noticed her eyes were open; we looked at each other with a tenderness that has no words.

The EMTs stopped the gurney and waited. Their silent understanding and reverence for this moment required no words to pass between them as they stood, looking down, waiting. I reached for her hand, and she clasped mine in response, our fingers settling naturally into their familiar entwinement.

I held her hand as they rolled her to a place just outside her room. After conferring with the nurse standing there to greet us, they rolled Judy into her room.

"Give us just a moment to get her settled," the nurse said, but with a tenderness in her voice and tone that conveyed far more than routine instruction.

As they started to leave, the EMTs rolled by me with the now-empty gurney. I made eye contact again with the tender, tattooed linebacker.

"Thank you," I whispered.

He nodded. I couldn't help but notice the tears in his eyes.

ANOINTED TO FLY

We had been at Pickering House for the better part of five days. In addition to peaceful management of Judy's symptoms, long periods of rest with intermittent moments of quiet conversation, there has been an endless parade of dear friends and family.

Judy welcomed them all as she could, visited as she was able, and wanted me to be sure, if she couldn't, to tell each of them how very much it meant to her that they were there—and how much their love mattered to her and brought joy to her life.

On Sunday evening, Ellen, our caseworker, who was filling the role for us that Judy had filled for so many—and we both knew and appreciated her immense talent for knowing when to lighten things up and when to just be quietly present—turned to me and said, "Roy, have you been for a run lately? Have you gotten out of here *at all* in the last few days?"

Ellen knew that I ran and exercised for stress relief. "Put on your running shoes and shorts and get out of here," she said. "You need a break!"

So, of course, I did as I was told.

Just before I left for my run, a hospice nurse named Patsy had come into the room and had asked Judy, "May I give you an essential oil bath?" Judy, somehow in her deeply medicated state, acknowledged the question and said yes.

When I got back from my run, Patsy was still preparing and getting things ready for this "essential oils bath." The bath, she said, would begin as a regular bath but would end with a special blend of essential oils.

As Patsy began Judy's essential oil bath, I realized this wasn't just a bath—Patsy was anointing Judy for her death. Everyone in the hushed room realized we were sharing one of the most holy moments any of us had ever witnessed. That room had become holy ground, right before our eyes.

Patsy was whispering and humming to Judy as she massaged, caressed, and treasured her. Everyone in the room was in tears—so deeply touched and overwhelmed with the beauty and sanctity of what we were witnessing and therefore part of. Not a word was said as Patsy prepared Judy's body for death—and her soul to fly.

That evening, I laid beside Judy in her bed, holding her anointed, tired, precious body in my arms, listening to her shallow breathing, stroking her hair with my fingers. "I love you, Princess," I whispered repeatedly. "Fly home. Be free."

At 8:46 p.m., her last breath left her lips, and we kissed for the last time as she flew home.

Reader's Notes

PART III

How to Survive

2016: An Unwanted Journey

The first three months after Judy died were a complete blur of quiet sobs, outright knee-buckling breakdowns, and trudging through the tasks of daily living. I got up. Got dressed. Exercised. Ran errands. Tried to get out among people.

Memories of Judy and of our lives together were everywhere. Being in her studio, reading her writings, looking at her art with new eyes, seeing photos of our life together—all both comforting and pouring salt in my gaping wound.

I dreaded going to bed alone, dining alone, and being "odd man out" at parties and gatherings. I especially abhorred going home to that empty cottage on Friday nights. I soon made a habit on Friday nights of going to a movie, then to a restaurant or bar. I also picked up Judy's habit of journaling.

How do I do this? How do I go on? What am I to do now?

What I did find, more surely as time went on, was the immense help it was to journal, to pour my heart out onto the page each day. I also found help in the wisdom of spiritual directors and others trained and experienced in the grief process. I sought out opportunities for reflection and contemplation.

To live. Whatever that means. These next chapters of our story will tell you how I learned some answers to these questions—and so much more—in my journey through grief.

Fall 2016

I've decided to follow Judy's lead of starting my day with a devotional, followed by my own reflections in journals. "My time with God," as she called it. I know keeping this practice will help me remember that starting every day with God is the only way I'm going to get through the coming days—and sometimes hours—at all.

I know Judy would agree.

The second reason for starting my days in this way makes me feel closer to Judy and helps me believe I am somehow carrying on *for* her—even in this strange, new, uncharted journey *without* her.

Today, I started with Psalm 23. "Lie down in green pastures" seems to point to God's desire for me to rest, to be at peace.

I'm trying. I ask for peace; it is elusive, fleeting at best.

Judy's presence here, in our home, is palpable. It is terribly painful here without her, reminders everywhere. Tears, smiles, gentle feelings, memories. Having real trouble sensing God's presence, even though I know God is beside me, as is Judy. My heart is so full, waves of intense emotions.

Had several crying jags as I began the torturous process of canceling appointments, closing Judy's accounts, and stopping subscriptions—it hurts so terribly much to say it out loud to strangers.

Went for a walk. I felt Judy urging me to go, get out in sunshine, and spend some time under her blue "Judy sky." She was right.

As I walked, I took a few calls, people saying how much they miss, or are going to miss, Judy. One expressed her gratitude for being there with us when Judy passed on. It was a holy time and event for her, yet she didn't know why God had placed her with us.

"To pray," I told her. "To be with us."

Talked to Judy's dear friend who misses Judy terribly. She told me she spent yesterday afternoon in her own "studio" Judy encouraged her to create, reading letters from Judy over the past 20 years. She is growing into the listener, spiritual director, woman Judy saw within her. She talked about what a lesson it was to see how Judy lived every moment—for herself and for others. Judy taught and is still teaching.

Went to the monument company in Abbottsville today. Couldn't stop my chin from quivering as I said aloud the date when Judy passed on, relaying her instructions and the decisions we had made together a few short weeks ago. Butterflies, cross, "MTY (Me Too You) Beyond Forever," interlocking wedding bands, "Life is too short not to eat pie." Coral blue, which in a certain light takes on a purple hue.

Afterward, I visited Judy's gravesite. It hit me hard to enter the cemetery, knowing that she is now there. I know she is *not* there, of course, but as I stood/kneeled over where her urn was buried, I sobbed and placed my hand on her ground. I miss her beyond words.

Joined some friends at The Lodge for dinner at their invitation. Ordered an extra wine glass, a new tradition I started last week in Bar Harbor. I let them lead our conversation. Eventually, the conversation turned to Judy, and they told me how reading her obituary made them feel as though they knew her better. She wrote it with her life.

Began to set up our trip to Sarasota and Gasparilla to spread some of Judy's ashes on the beach with her dear friends, fellow students, and instructors from Expressive Arts Florida Institute. She will be there, I know, to help us honor her and her work there.

Stayed up until about 1:30 a.m., then fell into something fitful that bore little resemblance to sleep. The pillows I cling to are a terrible substitute for holding onto Judy.

Cleaned and straightened up Judy's studio. Felt right to be in her "sanctuary" . . . tearful and right. I sense I'll be there—that I'm *supposed* to be there—often.

Found a few of Judy's art journals, including one from Gasparilla in 2012. Her art and words there were beyond incredible. In one entry she described a busy day, but then said that all she really wanted to do was "walk under the blue canopy of trees and sky with my beloved." That's when I lost it, crumpled to my knees.

Writings and words of others say to turn it all over to God. How do I do that?

Where am I to go, God? Where are you leading me? What am I to do? I don't sense or feel your presence. Too deeply hurting, grieving. Where are you?

Today, I read another of Judy's art journals. Her courage and passion to give more to others, to do more, to do it longer, for God, is incredible.

"All will be well!" . . . "Trust you, God, Jesus, as you are ahead of me." . . . "Please give me more time to do more, to serve, to love." . . . "I believe in this being cured." . . . "I claim healing."

Did she mean only the cancer in this earthly life, or did she know deep within herself that her words and prayers also contained an eternal meaning?

As I read her words, her prayers, I broke down again and again. She did not receive on earth the time we pleaded for. We knew the likely end, but we pleaded anyway.

Why were we not allowed to grow old together? To brush and play with each other's white hair, go for walks under our "blue canopy" of Hide-A-Way Hills, and spend our golden years holding hands, cuddling, talking, laughing, sitting on our porch . . . . *Why?*

Did some yard work this afternoon and pictured Judy sitting on our front porch as she often did. I remembered how I'd look up at her as she sat there while I worked. She'd smile and sometimes wave.

Repotted our wedding fern a few days ago into a larger pot. Room for it to grow, to continue on, as will our love.

After finishing the yardwork and house chores, I settled onto our porch, across from Judy's empty chair, to write in my journal, sip Maine blueberry wine, and listen to our Nora Jones CD, remembering how we danced to these songs on Judy's sixtieth birthday. If only I could dance with her again.

Devotional speaks today of being grateful, expressing thanks repeatedly to God, and how we will then be better able to sense the Spirit's presence. I believe this is true.

There aren't enough or proper words to fully express my gratitude to God for the gift of Judy in my life. I am thankful she said yes to my first date request, to my marriage proposal, to me at the altar, and so many more times over 41 years. Judy made me a rich, blessed man.

This is the first Thanksgiving without my princess, and it is excruciating.

On the way home from dinner, I pulled off the road to watch a beautiful, full "Judy moon" rise through the trees. We watched many moonrises together, holding hands. My deep pain is from our deep love. An eternal blessing and gift.

"Thank you, God, for this deep pain."

I never thought that sentence, those words, would come from my heart and mouth.

"Where do your words come from?" Sister Noreen asked. We were sitting in her favorite meeting room. She had been reading some of my journal entries from the days and weeks following Judy's death. She is one of the special women from the Sisters of the Dominican Order of Peace who loved and cherished Judy for many years—and by extension loves and has graced me today.

"It is painfully honest, real," she said. "You don't hold back. You show your pain and your love, your loneliness for Judy. You also show your hope and belief that you and Judy will be together again." She also noted that the setting of me dining alone in a restaurant is real, a picture of life for so many, a picture of our life together.

"The words come from deep within me," I said. "From a place where I don't plan the words or sense them when I write. They just come."

I felt I was on holy ground in Sister Noreen's presence. She shocked me toward the end of our time together when she said, "You give me hope. Your relationship with Judy and your willingness to be so vulnerable give me hope."

Her words humbled me in a way I cannot describe. *What does God have planned for me? Are these writings somehow to be a tool, a resource for others?*

Had breakfast with a dear friend from church today at his invitation. I told him about our Bar Harbor and Sarasota trips and Judy's presence in both. I showed him the picture of the naked, broken tree at Jordan Pond House, telling him I felt like that tree—bare, broken, and missing a huge piece of myself.

He heard me and then told me what he *also* sees in that imagery: a strong foundation in the silhouette of that single, leafless tree. And that when I see that tree as a reflection of me—bare and broken—I need to remember that it is winter. The tree will be lush and colorful again with time and the seasons' changes, as will my life with time and the seasons' changes.

We talked about God's presence with me in all of these times—and my painful, angry, and relentless WHY questions:

Why so young?

Why would God let this happen to such an incredible and faithful woman who gave so much, who would have done so much more?

Why did God allow a stroke on top of her cancer?

"No answers to your questions this side of heaven," he said.

Reader's Notes

Winter 2016-2017

Judy always put our ornaments on the tree. I sherpa'd boxes upstairs, and she decorated. It's what we did for 42 Christmases. Beautiful, treasured. Not nearly enough.

I put luminary bags on our driveway and the lane last night for Judy, remembering how much she loved them. I'll do this every year for her. Our neighbor across the lane texted me saying they were awesome.

One of Judy's spiritual direction classmates sent me a text saying that she prayed for me last night in church on Christmas Eve and continued to hold me in prayer during my first Christmas without Judy. She also said she was celebrating Judy's first Christmas celebrating Christ's birthday with him. What an amazing, holy image that brought to my mind and heart.

I'm really struggling to live in God's peace—and not to let discouragement settle in. This still seems so unreal. Judy's presence permeates our cottage and my heart, both comforting and wounding me. Relentless.

God, you are seen and known in your son, Jesus, in friends and family, in nature, in random acts of kindness, in the sunrise and sunsets, in the stars and moon, in kind emails, texts, and cards I've received, in colors, in art, and in Judy. She lived for you by living for and caring for others, even as she was transitioning to join you and your saints. You gifted me and so many others with her life, her love, and her compassion.

Went to The Lodge for its annual Colonial Dinner. Mark Camden, who played at Judy's celebration of life service, playing background music. I sat at a two-top table, two glasses of wine, and Judy's picture leaning against her wine glass. We danced in my heart and mind as Mark played.

Some friends invited me to join them at their long table. I declined, telling them, "Judy and I are dining together tonight." I think they understood.

I saw a couple about our age from across the room. At one point she leaned over and put her head on his right shoulder. It made me smile even as it cut into my heart.

I overheard a conversation in a nearby booth between two men, one saying how frustrated he was with his girlfriend. I wanted to turn around and say, "Just be glad she's still here to frustrate you."

Also saw a friend whose wife also passed away recently. Only the other widowers "get it"; they understand this kind of loneliness—and the deep *aloneness* this journey brings. He brought up how "couple friends" look at him with those sad puppy dog eyes. We are their nightmare—the vision of what they will likely experience one day. And just as we are not comfortable around them, they are not comfortable around us. Nobody knows what to say and what not to say.

Attended a candle-lighting memorial service this evening. All the candles were in glass vases with pictures of everyone being remembered, about 40 people, including Judy. A reader read short paragraphs people had submitted about their loved ones. We were then supposed to go up and light the candle for the one loved and lost.

Almost couldn't get up and walk to the altar to light Judy's candle. Perhaps I still don't want to admit that this is real. The candlelight within the vase behind her picture cast a beautiful glow on her face. An abyss has been opened in me that will never be filled.

So grateful for all of my memories of Judy. They're both-and, now-always: grief and joy, smiles and hurt, joys and tears. *It all belongs.*

"Thanks for meeting me, Roy."

June is our friend and fellow Maine-iac who has had some rough turns in her life. At her request I had arrived at the coffee shop near St. Albans just after church.

"My pleasure," I replied.

"I just need to talk to you," she began. "I just . . . well, I still miss Judy so deeply. I just don't know quite what to do with all these emotions I'm having. I can't even fathom what you must be going through."

"One day at a time," I replied, trying to appear stoic. "In fact, some days it's one hour—or even one minute—at a time." I shrugged. "I know I'll get through this; I just don't know how." I decided to stop talking because I could feel the tears starting to rise up within me.

She nodded. "Judy did so much for so many people in so many ways," June observed. "For me, she unlocked an art-related creative spot within me I didn't even know was there." She paused. "I also really miss Judy's contemplative prayer and art sessions—and the wonderful conversations we had before and after." She looked across the table at me, a deep compassion and concern in her eyes. "I always admired the relationship you two had. It was really something special."

"It was," I agreed. "It *is*."

"I can't begin to imagine how much you must miss her."

"No words for it," I managed, the lump in my throat growing. Nothing like sympathy to set things off again. Just when I think I've got the crying jags under control, another test of my will comes along.

I tried to channel Judy's listening skills to deeply listen to June. I also really wanted to take the focus off me. She was clearly hurting—and for whatever reason needed to get these things off her chest.

"I'm still just so angry at God," June said. "And that is not a feeling I want to have." She looked down at her folded hands. "I'm not proud of myself at all for feeling this way," she continued. "But I also can't help but think that God made a HUGE mistake here. Why would God destroy something so perfect as your marriage, your amazing relationship with Judy? Why Judy? Why not someone who did nothing for others? There are still a lot of bad people walking around in the world—people who don't care about anything or anyone but themselves. Why would God allow this to happen when the two of you were doing so much good together?"

"I don't have any answers," I began, "and I have some of those same questions." I looked up at her as she struggled with this pain I am too familiar with. "As I said, one day, one moment, one question at a time. A lot of time outdoors, a lot of time with God, and a lot of time just trying to figure out what in the world I'm going to do . . . now."

June went on to add she was also mad at *herself* for not being able to see Judy in her last months. With such a deep connection to Judy via her art, her encouragement of her creativity, and her love of Maine, she felt like there was so much more to talk about, so much left to say, and she would now never be able to have those conversations—and this grieves her deeply.

I listened, nodded, just let her get it all out. When the conversation rolled around to Maine, I felt on more solid emotional ground. I told her about releasing some of Judy's ashes in Bar Harbor—and also in Sarasota. She understood the magic of all that without my having to explain it. By the time we parted ways for the day, I sensed that our conversation helped us both.

We agreed to meet again in a few weeks to talk about resuming contemplative prayer at church. I told her I'd pick out some pieces of Judy's art that could work in sessions designed for people to engage God via art.

She seemed excited about this and said she would appreciate getting to see whatever pieces I choose as well as the opportunity to offer her opinion.

"I really am starting to understand the importance of seeing our world's beauty through grief-stricken eyes and missing a loved one," I offered. "So maybe this would be of help to someone else going through a loss." I didn't say "a loss like this," because there *is* no loss like this. But perhaps it would be relatable to any feelings of loss or grief in some way.

"I hear something within me whispering that I should use Judy's art to help others," I added. "To flesh out and develop practices and disciplines that will help people reclaim 'eyes of wonder' after a devastating loss."

I held it together fairly well throughout my conversation with June. Then I cried all the way home. It was raining when I got home, and I sat in Judy's car for a while as tears streamed down my face, leaning my head against the door window and watching the water gently roll down outside the window, illuminated by light from inside our cottage. A reflection of the tears rolling gently down my cheeks. Tears of pain, sadness, loneliness, and beyond forever love.

An exchange today felt especially harsh. Two men and I were talking about a business item, and one asked me how I was doing. When I answered that I'm all right, still hurting, and my grief is still strong, the other man offered his "wisdom."

"It'll stay like that until you make the decision," he said.

He delivered this matter-of-fact advice with no compassion whatsoever. I knew even before I asked the "decision" he was referring to.

"The decision to move on," he said.

"I make that decision *every* day," I declared, emphatic yet polite. "*Every day* when I get up and move into my day."

The flash of anger within me was quite intense, but I managed to contain it. Later that evening—much later—I prayed that he:

~   somehow realizes what he said and how wrong it was;

~   never utters those words and tone to anyone ever again;

~   never *experiences* those thoughtless words and tone in this circumstance;

~   if his wife dies before he does, his own deep, holy, adoring love explains this level of grief to him.

If only people would pause for a moment in these conversations *before* they speak and remember that if you're not sure what to say, just say "I'm sorry."

Judy used to say when I got this upset, "What can you learn from that person?" From this person today I learned to be careful what I say in such circumstances, to listen more carefully, to consider his question, even if the delivery is beyond rude. It was a question worth answering.

And, yes, I believe I have made "the decision" to move on, confident in the passion and purpose God and Judy have planted within me to serve others. However, the incredible pain and grief are still overwhelming me most of the time. How can I move on from that?

Judy would say to me right now, "Both-and, Roy—it all belongs."

Took a walk to visit with the horses today, as Judy and I often did. I missed holding her hand, walking on the traffic side of the road to shield her, talking with her, hearing her voice, helping her up small inclines in the roads.

As I walked, Judy's presence with me was unmistakable. Several horses stood at their fences and gazed at me. Did they see Judy's spirit walking beside me? Do they sense my grief and loneliness?

I stopped to listen to the wind singing through leaves of the tree across the field, near the chapel. I responded by saying, "I love you, Judy," right out loud.

I pictured her holding onto me as I went down the final incline toward our cottage, remembering how we held onto each other so we would not slip on the loose gravel.

We'll go for more walks. I pray Judy will keep whispering to me.

I met with Kermit, the grief counselor at the Pickering House, again today. He asked about our last five months at home together. I told him there were some good memories—and some hard memories. How I loved caring for Judy, even when we sometimes snapped at each other. We never stayed mad for very long, and we always said "I'm sorry."

He told me he believes Judy and I have a special love he rarely sees. That she and God will guide me in this different life, this unwanted new normal. He reiterated that my sadness and pain will come and go.

Just as Judy loved bathing people when she was a hospice volunteer, I loved massaging Judy's feet, reading to her, holding her, tending to her personal needs, holding her as she stood between transfers between bed and wheelchair. I also told him that our love deepened because it was a sacred honor and blessing to love and care for Judy. He said that in his view only about 20 percent of Christian couples have what we had. I hurt for the other 80 percent.

He says he sees the same indifference I'm feeling toward work tasks and other "priorities" in people all the time. Priorities change, he explained, especially with caregivers who go through a long period of caregiving with their spouse. He encouraged me to listen to and trust my heart. To move *toward* things versus away from them and not to quit anything without something else planned and new goals.

I met with Katherine, another of Judy's dear friends and spiritual director today. I took her up on her offer to sit down with me due to her love of Judy and to tell me about her first husband, Hugh, who also died of a brain tumor.

She shared stories about her decision to retire, her decision to become a wellness and spiritual life coach and spiritual director. She also told me about the first time she introduced herself as a widow.

We talked about the sacred journey Judy and I walked, not just during her illness but during our marriage—a match created by God for us. How sacred and holy our journey together was, even during her illness.

During our session, Katherine asked me to tell her more about our Bar Harbor trip last October. I did so with details about Judy's presence there and nudges she gave me. She was touched deeply and told me about her experience of the nudges and presence of Hugh, after he died.

Katherine asked whether I was still angry or upset about anything. I told her that while I treasure all of the time we had together, I'm angry and in ocean-deep pain that we did not have more time together.

She told me that my repeated listening to songs and music that hurt me and remind me of Judy is likely a way to hold onto the "sacred container" of my love and adoration of her. Hurt and love. Pain and special memories. It all belongs.

Telling her about our Bar Harbor trip and our Sarasota trip to spread Judy's ashes helped me. She believes I'm journeying as is best for me, with Judy and without her. She believes I should keep being open and vulnerable through my pain so Judy and God can best reveal to me the next steps of my life.

Katherine agreed to meet with me more, and I will take her up on her offer.

In today's spiritual direction session with Katherine, she recommended I have a conversation with God—and to write it down in a back-and-forth exchange as it comes to me, as if God and I were having coffee and talking to each other.

In this four-page conversation I got to write down all the questions that had been rolling around in my head—burning within me in endless loops—since the day Judy died. And after I wrote each question, I waited, then wrote down what came to me.

Words flowed out on the page, sometimes going in directions I hadn't imagined. Were these words coming directly from God? I like to think so—or at least from that God-spark living within me.

By the end of this exercise, I felt a sense of peace that had been elusive. I asked what I needed to ask, railed when I needed to rail, argued, listened, and, in the end, left this conversation with an assurance of God's love, Judy's love, and my own strength and resilience. I felt a deep sense of God's forgiveness, redemption, and compassion—and the certainty that God's spirit was planted deep within me and that Judy's spirit remains with me as well.

In the end, my trust was restored, my anger was tempered, and my "path to walk," as Judy often described finding one's own way, felt just a little more solid beneath my feet.

Katherine noted that a large, tender part of me has been taken away and will never be replaced. She speaks from experience, with gentleness, and I trust her.

I told her a few people have suggested that I find my *own* passions. The trouble is my passion and joy have always been serving with Judy, watching her grow and touch hearts. Katherine wisely replied that continuing Judy's work will fill a passion within me, will honor her, and will continue to serve others. She also shared with me about how she gradually grew into her new existence and that I will do the same in my own time.

I then admitted to my fear of somehow leaving Judy behind.

She replied, "That will never happen. Both of you will continue on, just as you did, together and as individuals, when Judy was here."

I repeated a few questions I asked of God in my written exercise. She understood them yet offered no answer, as spiritual directors do.

Sitting in Starbucks, writing in this journal, I sense Judy is with me. For me, journal writing has become another way to talk to her.

How did one of Judy's long red hairs get intertwined in my sweater? I found it as I started writing this afternoon. I have it in between two pages so I can take it home.

I see two ladies easily over 70 talking. Both with wedding rings. Why weren't we allowed to grow old together? Watch each other's hair turn white, walk hand in hand with hands that had grown knobby and frail? Why weren't we allowed to tell stories of our 50-year anniversary? We had so much more than many couples, I know, but I selfishly want more. What we had was beyond measure. And still not enough.

I felt a nudge to have dinner at The Lodge. Kat, our usual server, was genuinely happy to see me and gave me a big hug. It brought tears to my eyes when she brought out our dessert with two spoons. Judy should be across the table from me. Friday nights were for dining together at The Lodge, looking at each other, talking, treasuring our time together.

I then went out to our Subaru and sobbed like a baby for almost 10 minutes before I could even start the car, praying for help as I sobbed, missing Judy so very deeply.

Visited Judy today at Abbottsville Cemetery. Placed a blanket of evergreen branches adorned by purple ribbons and purple ornaments by her gravestone. It's a chilly, foggy day. Fits my mood, my overcast heart.

I knelt so that I could touch a part of where Judy's ashes lay buried. I know she's with me, but not in a way that I can see or touch or hear. I can't feel her presence, feel God's presence, even though I know both are with me in this pain. As I sat beside her grave, the traffic on Route 49 passed by busily, completely unaware of my presence here, of my grief, of the grief of millions of people around the world.

God, please help me to sense you and Judy always and live as such.

Drove through an intensely thick, sudden fog due to rapidly rising temperatures and wind that moved across snow and ice and farm fields along I-70. Dangerous. As I write this now, I realize the parallel with my life right now. Driving through that fog, I could not see more than 50 yards in front of me; I couldn't focus on what I could not see ahead of me in the fog. I had to slow down and focus on what I *could* see— the road right in front of me—and stop trying to see what I could not see in the future.

People all over the world do this, I reminded myself. It's not bad. It's life. The wonder, beauty, and tragedy of life, all together, all present. It all belongs.

Valentine's Day. Our first one apart since the first one we shared. I drove to Abbottsville cemetery to place flowers on Judy's gravesite. I talk with her often—all the time, in fact—yet there is something different about being *there*, to talk and write to her from my lawn chair.

I recall holding, clutching Judy's urn during the service here on October 15 because I did not want to let go of her. It was so horribly painful. I remember sitting on the grass after the service, touching her urn. Now I visit here monthly, bringing flowers, just to sit with her.

It's a special, sacred place.

This still doesn't seem real at times. I still talk to Judy. I think I need to call her, text her, pick up chocolate or flowers for her, turn over in bed to hold her. But at other times this is all settling in—her absence, her passing on to heaven, our quiet and empty cottage.

I'm so incomplete without her.

My devotional time this morning is focused on "peace." Feeling God's peace is my deepest need right now. It still escapes me how to find and feel that peace.

IT'S SO HARD TO PRAY AS I USED TO. Very difficult to feel God's presence.

I know she needed to leave to be with God. Her body was done. Her leaving broke my heart beyond what I ever considered or imagined possible, inflicting wounds that will never heal. And I don't know that I want them to.

As I try harder to "turn it over to God" and "relinquish control into the hands of Jesus," I realize that I would have to *have* control in order to relinquish it. Right now, I feel like I have no control over my life and circumstances. I also have very little control over my deep, authentic feelings and reactions—and explosions of grief that come out of nowhere.

Feeling this vast emptiness now, I try to imagine what it would be like to be filled with peace.

Turning my attention to gratitude for this day of life, I recognize that somehow, even this horribly lonely life is a precious gift.

When we talked about what Judy thought heaven is, she said, "Love." When I asked her what heaven looks like, because I so wanted her to have an image in her heart and mind during her last few weeks, she said, "Love, beauty, light, and joy."

I remember this precious conversation of about 10 minutes. Judy had her eyes closed, and it seemed as though God was guiding me to allow her to picture heaven. Then I asked her what "love, beauty, light, and joy" look like, and she answered by pointing to me.

This was perhaps the most sacred moment in our life together. In that moment we were both focused on each other and our beyond forever love. We'll be together forever, I know, yet I miss her now.

On a positive note, I will say that it is getting more frequent that I can hold closely and appreciate special moments and special memories of Judy without falling apart.

Sometimes I stare ahead and see nothing, even when I'm surrounded by people or nature. I hear people and catch random words. Life passes by constantly, and I'm alone in a cloud or daze. My eyes and brain see colors, but land and colors God creates for us don't register; sounds, voices, and laughter pass through my ears and keep moving along, not relating.

The past few weeks have brought an elevated loneliness, a sadness that is rooted deeply and firmly. It has taken hold with a vise grip and will not let go. My desire to produce at work is numb. My will to do much of anything is weak. Yes, I exercise, eat right, do what I'm supposed to do at work and more; I write, call, text friends and family; and there are moments of joy and satisfaction. But this constant overcast fog remains.

Had lunch with Sister Carole, another one of Judy's mentors, today. She asked several questions about how I'm getting along, to which I replied, "I'm getting along. The pain is not easier, but it's a bit softer."

I told her about my possible retirement and how lately I don't seem to have the same tolerance for my work, for the reports, paperwork, sales production goals. It's valuable work, honorable work. I've enjoyed it for many years, but not now. I told her how a coworker cautioned me not to make big changes too quickly, as he remembers how he didn't care about work at all for at least six months after his first wife died about eight years ago. I appreciate his concern, but I don't feel right that I can't devote as much work and focused energy to my coworkers. I am distracted by my focus shifting to Judy's nonprofit, her book, and serving people in need.

Please, God, guide me, whisper to me about where I am to be for your plans. Please help me listen.

Spring 2017

The day I first met Judy, when I climbed to the top of those stone steps, up that curling stairway, over 42 years ago, my heart and life changed forever. My heart knew that it had met the heart God created to be my beyond forever love. Everything about her captured me without her even knowing it. Becoming her friend was a lovely piece of our foundation and God's plan. I had no idea how deeply I would or could love her or how deeply she would or could love me. Perhaps neither did she.

In the autumn of '75, after Judy graduated from Massey and came home, we were sitting on her parents' love seat in their family room. Her parents were not in the room. We were talking, kissing. Judy was telling me about a conversation she had with her mom about us.

She told me that during their talk, her mom asked her whether she loved me. As she was telling me this, I held her in my arms, facing me. Her head was leaning against the left side of my head with her arms around my shoulders and neck. As my heart started exploding with anticipating joy, I asked, "What did you tell her?"

She answered tenderly, "I said, 'Yes, Mom, I love him.'"

As I'm writing this, I'm smiling with watery eyes. I remember moving her head away from mine so I could see her face and her eyes, at last saying out loud what I had whispered, undetected, from the moment we met, "And I love you!"

We embraced with joyful electricity that lasted 41 years. That electricity is still alive and increasing in power, even now. We looked deeply into each other's eyes with smiles that would not, could not stop. Then we held each other tightly, as though to never let go.

Our declared love had to make God smile. God was certainly with us in that moment, even if we were not aware of it. God continued to support us throughout our lives together and bless us with each other and so much more than I could have imagined.

We were flying high together at that moment—and from then on. When Judy's body was nearing its end, I prayed over and over again to God to let her fly, be free, go home, even as I knew I could not go with her. God was with us then, too.

Judy's last breath released her, shattered my heart, and answered my prayer for her to fly. I released her into God's arms.

IT ALL BELONGS!

I met with Katherine this evening. "How are you doing?" she asked.

"I don't know," I replied, which was an accurate statement. My mind and heart fluctuate so much and so frequently. "I'm not at peace," I added. "I know I should be more at peace because I know where Judy is and who she's with and that she and God are with me in my heart and soul. But I'm not at peace. At all."

"What do you know about Judy's peace?"

"It was deep and perfect," I said after thinking about it for a moment, looking for words to describe the complete sense of peace Judy felt and emanated and how this peace calmed everyone around her.

For Judy, peace wasn't a feeling. It was how she lived. Her trust in God was complete, even during her darkest days on earth.

"I remember that even when she was ready to go and very, very weary of having, as she said, 'one foot in heaven and one foot here,' she was still giving way more to others than they were to her," I reflected.

Katherine nodded her agreement, adding, "I witnessed and felt this peace whenever I was with Judy, when I was in your home. This always encouraged me to think about it and reflect on Judy's peace."

Katherine also told me a bit more about when she realized she was not only a widow but also a single woman. I had asked her about that because it was something she mentioned when we last met. She said it was a process of some moments for her that included keeping her promise to her husband that she would "be all right."

I told Judy the same thing. Katherine said she had cursed that promise many times. So have I.

It took her a long time, she said, around two years. Her explanation resonated with me and helped calm me because I detest being a widower and a single man.

"I'm glad you're writing to God in that journal," she offered, "and that you're allowing your emotions to come out rather than just keeping them stuffed inside." She paused, looking at me intently. "This is all helping you to journey this path authentically," she said.

"There is no other way," I replied. How I wish I was not on this journey.

God, I know that you love me, all people, all creatures, all existence. You created it all. You came to us, left heaven to be with us in Jesus. You gave up your human life for us. You promised an eternity with and for us.

You ignited Judy's heart for people in crisis. You graced so many people with her heart and soul. You placed her in the lives of people and enabled her to awaken the art and creativity within them.

You allowed her to be stricken with cancer and a stroke, to bless and grace others even through that. You watched her in pain as her body betrayed her, as she got so sick and when food would not stay in her.

You cried with us, just as you cry for all of your children around the world who are dying—and for their caring loved ones. You were with us in our tears as Patsy anointed Judy with that tender essential oil massage and we witnessed that holy moment between them.

Your tears flowed as my grief exploded when Judy passed from us. You felt our pain and then cried tears of joy as you welcomed her home. Holding all that joy and pain at the same time, you're walking with me as I learn to live this new life without her.

It's so hard to feel your presence when I'm so preoccupied with missing Judy. Help me to seek you.

Am sitting at our Hocking Hills winery tonight as I write this. How I wish Judy was here with me. A very good musician is playing, and people are dancing, enjoying music, and being with one another.

Many couples. A few tables of married women, probably out while their husbands are watching tournament basketball. They played "My Girl" and "Ain't Too Proud to Beg" by the Temptations, bringing tears and memories of us, dancing together.

Reminded me of our Ohio State days and a place called Char Bar, where we used to hang out with friends, fraternity brothers, and Little Sisters. I had a sudden memory of kissing Judy across the Char Bar table and her friend Karen throwing her hands up in the air as if to say, "I can't stop them!" Dancing to "The Locomotion," laughing, and hugging—such precious memories.

We shivered in cold winds together, planted flowers, built a family, created legacies, loved each other, loved others, and grew in God. WE LIVED! WE LOVED! Judy was so gracious with her love, her heart, her smiles, so generous with her hugs, her compassion, and her art. We are *all* better because of Judy.

I've asked God many times *not* to remove this grief and pain, but to allow me to be with Judy again in my dreams, to hear from her in a memorable conversation or presence. I want to have a dream of Judy and me together in a tender way, a simple way I could easily understand and cherish.

As I sped along freeways, on my way to visit my brother, David, and his wife, Melinda, in Texas, I rested my hand on Judy's seat cushion. The songs on our CDs spoke deeply to me about us and to me now in my loneliness for Judy.

I pictured us dancing as we did so often in our cottage, close to the fireplace. I'd hold Judy gently and whisper-sing to her as she rested her head on my chest. I wish we had danced like that more often, our bodies moving as one, treasuring this special nearness. And, yet, even as I write this, I realize that we "danced" together in all the aspects of our lives we shared, large and small. That sense of nearness was always present in all we did, and now we continue this dance on and on, even if only in my mind.

Made it to Fort Worth safely. Went out for key lime pie with David after dinner. He wanted to check in with me. Assured him I'm writing and journaling. I ordered Pinot Grigio for Judy and me. The waitress brought the glasses, and I poured the wine into our two glasses.

Went with Melinda and David to be with their three horses today. Melinda said I could choose the one I connected with most and groom him.

I followed Judy's lead and how she interacted with horses. I entered the large pen where they were. Sam, the largest one, came right to me. He looked right at me, and then the other two pushed him away.

We led them to a smaller round pen, and Melinda tied them to the fence with ample space between them. I stayed with Sam. When I asked whether he sensed whether Judy was here with us, he nodded, two or three times. How could I not stay with him?

First, I used a round curry comb to clean the mud from his coat. Then a large brush to brush him, then a mane and tail brush to get the knots out. As I brushed, I talked to him and to Judy, as if she was standing there beside me, offering guidance.

Afterward, I held onto him, wrapping my arms around his strong neck, my head against his. He leaned his head against mine. I felt him sigh, relax his back leg, lick his lips—all signs of relaxation and trust, as Melinda told me later.

It was a truly calming few hours. I felt Judy's presence; I believe that somehow Sam was with Judy—and Judy was with both of us.

David and I took Melinda to lunch. David and Melinda have a deep and adoring respect and love for each other. It's obvious. It's a true pleasure to be around.

I told them about the text God sent to me via Judy's phone back in June; the text said, "Know you are loved. Be at peace."

It came from Judy's phone after her stroke, when she was admitted to the therapy hospital and we were apart for a few hours. I explained that there was no way Judy could have typed that text. She didn't have the physical capability to type it, yet it came from her phone.

Got back home yesterday. Took an hour and a half walk today through our hills to the mailbox and then to the outdoor chapel and back. Stayed in the chapel for about 20 minutes, listening to the breeze in the trees.

My session with Kermit at Pickering House today was helpful. He gets to know Judy more and more each time we meet, even though he never actually met her. After the initial pleasantries, he said, "Update me on your grief."

"It rolls up and down, valleys and hills," I replied. "Sometimes steep and sudden, sometimes rolling and gentle." I paused, looking straight at him. "My grief is still deep," I said. I told him how the familiar sight of Cincinnati's skyline on the way home from Texas had unexpectedly broken my heart open, with deep, gut-wrenching sobs punctuating my rush of memories of our Cincinnati years. "It just sneaks up on me when I least expect it," I added.

I'm sitting here looking at a picture of Judy from 1996 when we were in Bar Harbor. Tan shorts, white turtleneck blouse, looking straight at me through the camera.

She was sitting in the sun and green grass on a double Adirondack chair with a table in between on which she had placed her tray of books. She had been writing in one of her journals after breakfast, cup of coffee beside her. Wish I knew what she was writing, but I guess it doesn't really matter; seeing her smile is more than enough—it always was.

Spent a few hours at the Hocking Hills winery today. Kristin, the waitress who thought so much of Judy, sat with me for a while just to catch up. She told me how she remembered when we came to the winery last April, almost exactly one year ago, just after Judy's two brain surgeries and chemo/radiation treatments.

Kristin said that when she saw us walking toward the door, Judy with her hat on (she had never seen Judy wear a hat before), she suspected something was wrong and went into the back to collect herself before she waited on us and Judy told her about her cancer. She took our picture on their covered patio that day. She later told me she cried when we left and again at home that night.

They've gotten used to me coming here to write, remember, and reflect.

It's a Judy moon evening, and as I sit on our porch, I raise my glass of Pinot Noir to Judy and her moon. No sounds. Just the deep, Sunrise Ridge quiet.

I remembered that same quiet on the night Judy died. As I walked to the car, I stopped to listen to the stillness. Then I heard an owl hoot three times. Some cultures believe the owl escorts the soul of the recently departed, a protective presence to accompany them home. That night, I knew it was true.

Good Friday 2017, our first apart. Service was quiet, as always. A large wooden cross lay on the communion altar area for us to approach, kneel, and pray. Others seemed hesitant, so I went first. I kneeled and placed my left hand just below the cross intersection, uttering silently my prayer of gratitude for his life, his sacrifice, his love, Judy's life, Judy's love, his resurrection, Judy's new life in heaven.

Angels Watching over Me

Live well, die well, love well.
All precious gifts.
Given well, received well.
Holy living, holy dying.

"Judy taught us how to live . . . and she taught us how to die," someone said shortly after her celebration of life service. Judy *did* live well, so well.

Even in her introverted way, Judy cared for and loved so many people with compassion and passion that inspired all who knew her. She expressed this and set an example for the rest of us in how she created art, laughed, was honest, had fun, and was driven to care for others.

Judy also died well. She engaged with her caregivers and invited them to journey with her. She asked and allowed so many people to be with her in this sacred time, welcoming their hearts and souls into her journey. She also allowed me to love her more and more deeply.

Judy spoke often of her path—and others' paths. She held their hands as they cried, created art from her joy and pain and doubt and uncertainty. She pleaded with God, thanked God, and blessed God. And so she blessed us all.

"Do you think that Judy was at peace as she lived into her last days here, as she passed on to heaven?"

When I last met with Katherine, we talked about whether I was at peace or feeling any peace. She continued that thread into our next meeting.

"I don't even know what peace is right now," I replied.

During her last few weeks here when she was tired of "having one foot here and one foot in heaven," I also remembered Judy's sense of peace with it all. Her life was not how she had lived for six-plus decades.

It was time.

Today I know I'm at peace with Judy being in heaven, not hurting any longer, and experiencing things far beyond what we can even imagine there.

Yet my heart is not as fully at peace now as it was when Judy was here with me. That peace went away when she fainted in our shower, when her premonition about "not being long for this world" became reality, when they told us about her large brain tumor.

"I believe in the love and protection of God," I told Katherine, "but my heart is not at peace."

"Belief and trust need to be enough for now," she said.

Met with Kermit, which is always beneficial. At one point I told him, "The grief is deepening. It is sinking deeper. While this grief was at first like a sharp spear thrust into my chest, now it is more like an infection slowly spreading within my heart and soul and every cell to take up permanent residence and become a part of me."

Love, too, is an infection, first surprising us with its energy, depth, power, and excitement—and likewise spreads through every fiber of our being, taking up residence as a permanent part of who we are.

Love is an Infection. It Changes Everything.
Grief is an Infection. It Changes Everything.
It all belongs.

Driving to Abbottsville cemetery tomorrow. The concrete base is in place at Judy's gravesite. Our gravestone will be on it before Memorial Day. I'll be back to see it and sit with Judy then.

A couple about our age was cleaning up around a gravestone close to ours when I got there. They put a small yellow flower and wreath with a helium balloon on the gravestone.

Also saw a man in his 70s preparing fresh flowers to put in gravestone vases. For his mother? For his wife? Other cars were driving around, carrying people doing the same for their loved ones.

Driving away, I heard "Over You" by Miranda Lambert on the radio. Had heard it before but did not listen closely until now. This time I did, and it slammed me in the gut, especially because of how well it described the final reality of our gravestone.

My devotional today emphasized that spending this time with God every day is essential for my well-being. Not a luxury—a necessity. Judy knew this, and now so do I.

I know my time in the past, present, and future is precious. Time and time again, my prayers, walks, and writing have been times when God has spoken to me via images, thoughts, writings, and nudges. Sometimes it happens while I'm running, shaving, showering, porch sitting, resting in bed before sleep, or just after waking up.

I must confess, however, that my time with God lately has mostly been about Judy, my whys and my sadness that she is not here. Sometimes when I'm listening for God, I feel distracted, which sometimes brings up guilt.

God, help me to hear you better when I spend time with you.

In today's devotional I focused on God's unlimited capacity to bless us.

This statement is beyond true. I could fill this entire journal with my blessings, small and large, all the miracles, throughout my life.

God, forgive me for not thanking you more often for your abundant blessings. Time and time again you have and continue to grace me with love and miracles and people who love and care about me—and people for me to love and care about.

And your blessings continue: Smiles, flowers, lightning, sunshine, breezes, snow-covered trees and bushes. Sunrises, sunsets, Maine-blue skies, wine, porches, lobster, kayaks, concerts, dancing, dating in the '70s, Judy walking down the aisle. Hawks, walks, marathon races. Blue Volkswagen beetles, Mustangs, lilac and verbena, cherry vanilla perfume, young love, rolling thunder, baseball, poetry, stories within country music songs, ice cream, pie, friends, rocky beaches, white sand, Hocking Hills, expressive art, maraschino cherries. Rainbows, a comfy chair, giggling and slow dancing, roller coasters, fields of wildflowers, beyond forever love. Dancing at an outdoor concert, hot coffee, mountains, fireflies, a first house, Christmases, Thanksgivings, and family gatherings, grief, prayer, promises, helping and being helped, life.

This list is just getting started and could go on forever. These are my blessed realities.

A phone call today brought a different layer of reality: "This is Missy from Abbottsville Monuments calling to tell you that your wife's monument was placed on its base yesterday."

A week from today my banking career stops and the next phase of my life becomes a special place to honor Judy and God through her nonprofit, publishing her books, and one or two other projects close to my heart. One of my coworkers, Dave, really understands—or at least he's the only one to express it verbally. He told someone else today that I'm not retiring; I'm only retiring from my *banking* career to go on to the next phase of my life. It's true.

When I leave the bank next Friday, my corporate career will be over. That pace is go, go, go—nonstop client and internal meetings, reports, fire drills, computer data entry work to track activities, boom, boom, boom. I've been doing this one way or another for over 40 years. With God's blessings, I have done it well with many wonderful coworkers and supervisors and, most of all, with Judy's support and love.

Praying that God and Judy's spirit will guide me to the right priorities, tasks, quiet times, serving paths, and methods. Also praying that I will learn to listen better, to respond more fully—and that when I don't, they will nudge me to stop and listen.

As I was getting ready to go for a run on Mt. Zwingli Road, I started experiencing heart-related sensations. I went through my normal personal evaluation of whether to go to the ER. When my symptoms began including pain in my left arm and lightheadedness, I went. They triaged me quickly and kindly. Two flare-ups happened shortly after I got there.

Being in the hospital alone is a sample of my new reality. This unwanted journey has many twists and turns, with new circumstances every day to navigate without Judy by my side.

Busy morning here at Fairfield Medical Center with heart tests and waiting. My mind is racing. I imagine Judy in my room, in the hallways as they transport me from place to place, kissing me, being kissed by me, holding hands, putting in my eye drops, talking with her, praying with her, for us. I have never missed Judy's physical presence more than right now.

What am I to learn from this waiting? This experience? The last time I was in this hospital was with Judy as she/we moved closer to her passing from this world to heaven. Our bodies wear out in so many ways, or they are destroyed in accidents or from another person's thoughtless or purposeful actions. We have no idea of how this will happen, when it will happen, when our bodies will breathe our last breaths of this beautiful, awesome, tragic, mysterious life on earth.

Yet we do believe that God, our greater power, receives our soul, our heart, our love. Souls, hearts, and love created by God. What if we devoted our God-created, God-provided abilities, passions, hearts, intelligence, skills, and compassion to preparing for our transition, to preparing others for their transition? To place the needs of others before our own?

What if the filters for our decisions—individual, personal, corporate, societal, community—were simply "What is the best for people everywhere?" We show amazing compassion and capabilities when tragedies happen around the world. We come together, ignore our distances, remove obstacles, remove borders to save and to serve, hold one another, speak with each other via hands, hearts, tears of joy, tears of pain. We give and forgive and act and sacrifice. We help each other grieve, love, and rebuild. We put others' needs and pain before ours, before our own comfort and pleasure.

Aren't we all, every single person, struck at some point with the sacrifices and miracles we thought impossible, miracles we never saw coming? When we experience and witness kindness and compassion that are unexpected? We become moved to join in, contribute, do something beautiful, different, something that adds to the groundswell of joy.

What will it take for this to become the norm for all of us? We see it, we do it, we smile and cry tears of joy when we experience it. We have such an amazing capacity for good, wonder, joy, and sacrifice within us.

It seems that this is an individual decision, moved by our values or interactions, similar to a spark or sparks, small embers that grow into flames, sometimes bonfires, fanned and fueled by hearts ablaze with divine love for others. It starts with a spark—one heart, one soul who sees what needs to be done, what can be done, what should be done. Judy was and is that spark for me and many others. I pray that fires she lit, sparked by God, will blaze again to serve other people. Every bonfire starts with a spark.

Released from Fairfield Medical Center in the early evening. Blessed news is that this episode was not caused by my ticker. Thank you, God.

In my devotional time today, the focus was on approaching each day with a desire to find God—and the path God has set before me for each day, including hidden treasures along the way for me to find.

Today, I saw God:
~ while running on our treadmill with no issues after spending the past few days in the hospital
~ when I saw the first firefly of the season from our porch
~ when I heard the first sounds of night.

As I reflect back, I did see God in my life today.

God, please help me to remember to look for you, find you, and thank you more in my daily words, thoughts, and deeds.

That first firefly was sweet to see, to experience. I asked Judy whether she was here with it on our porch and those in the field, all around us. I believe she is here with me in some way, more than I realize. I believe there is a permanent thin space between loving hearts, similar to God's presence.

This thin space is a holy, divine place in our dimension we are allowed to access once we believe it exists and hone our hearts to be aware of it. We never know when it will open, but when it does, we need to be ready. Ready to be enthralled, to be touched by mystery and love on the other side. Judy is the energy, love, and light on the other side of my thin space.

Thank you, Judy, for sending a firefly into our exercise room in our cottage tonight. I saw it in our room and let it out through your art studio's glass door. I know it was you signaling me that you are near.

Slept in this morning. Feels very different to be able to do this on weekdays. I awoke slowly, to gentle and soothing memories of those days when Judy and I slept in. Coffee and breakfast on our porch or in other settings throughout the years: Bar Harbor, brunch at The Lodge, Mountaintop in Virginia, Sarasota, Orange Mango, on and on. This extra pillow is only something to wrap my arms around without having Judy's warmth, curves, long wavy red hair, soft skin, her head on my chest.

As I sat outside with my coffee, Judy visited me on our front lawn via a magnificent bluebird that landed right in front of me. I haven't seen one in a few years. I had to take a deep breath and just sit there, completely still, watching this beautiful messenger that landed here to let me know Judy is right here with me.

"Thank you, Princess," I whispered.

Reader's Notes

Summer 2017

Had dinner with my cousin Kim today. I arrived early with my journal. She saw me writing when she came to our table.

"What do you write about?" she asked, gesturing toward my open journal.

"Everything," I said. "Thoughts, feelings, reflections, hopes, dreams, where I see God and Judy. How much I miss her."

"I don't know," she said, dubious. "I could never see myself writing because of all the hard things I've been through in my life." She paused. "I want to write, but I'm just very . . . leery of it."

"Why don't you start simple?" I suggested, knowing without a doubt that Judy was guiding me. "Write five good things that happened today. Write five blessings. Write five gratitudes."

I hope it helped her. I also told her how much I need my writing—and how much of it happens *as* I write, not before.

Today was a "Judy activity" day, beginning with my facilitating a contemplative prayer session at St. Alban's; I tried to channel Judy and how she led such sessions so well—and so effortlessly. To prepare for this session, I had spent time in Judy's studio, praying and listening to her about which art items to provide. I wanted to do my best to create an environment that would help release their subdued inner artists.

After the opening portion of the session, when it was time to transition from discussion to "creative play time" using expressive art to listen to, create, and find their own meaning in their chosen words or phrases, I watched as the participants circled the table of Judy's art supplies I had chosen for them.

As they touched the items assembled and searched for just what they wanted, I was reminded of children picking through toys, crayons, or pieces of candy—or the flavors of ice cream at Graeter's—searching for just the right one. And then, for 45 minutes, with the scent of lavender filling the air, each person kept their mind, heart, and hands busy, creating and playing with artistic expression. It was a sacred time and freedom to listen to the words they had chosen.

Now I know what Judy meant when she said watching people, listening to them in retreats and prayer sessions, was a precious gift to and from God. It was beyond delightful and soul warming to watch and listen, each in their individual moment, their own sacred space.

I missed Judy especially deeply in those hours. Such sessions and services at St. Alban's were things we did together. I was her Sherpa, her encourager, her admirer.

And now, with so much to say about my own experience of leading this session, I had no one to tell.

Got up early today to go to St. Alban's for its church service. It's not getting any easier to be there without Judy. Somehow, I trust Judy is with me, sitting beside me, walking in front of me for communion, kneeling beside me, praying with me.

June sat with me again, as she often does. She's heading to Maine for two months. So jealous! June and I enjoy our Maine conversations, even though they are bittersweet, as they bring back exquisite memories of being there with Judy. Smiles, joys, and sadness—it all belongs.

Judy visited me again today as I was sitting in pebble dirt, chopping open plant holes. A small, beautiful, soft lavender butterfly flitted about, to my right and in front of me. It landed two or three times well within my arm's reach. I smiled and said, "Hello, Princess!"

I've never seen a lavender butterfly anywhere, let alone here. A small, soft lavender butterfly, Judy's favorite color. Such a sweet, undeniable reminder that she's still here, somehow.

It's not just the big dates and events; it's a constant parade of living and doing little things without Judy that is excruciating. A steady stream of reminders of her absence.

Even amid good things—beautiful "Maine skies," rain on our roof, time with family and friends, hearing people speak of Judy with tender affection—my sense of her absence is profound. Sometimes it's the good things that actually intensify my loneliness for Judy.

Friends tell me I seem to be better and look better. I'll trust them—and continue to live with this abyss of loneliness inside, hidden from view.

Kind neighbors stopped by to check with me about watering our flowers and ferns while I'm gone on my extended road trip out West next week. Sat on the screened porch with them.

I couldn't help but notice Judy's empty chair while I talked with them on our porch. That chair should not be empty, but I can't bring myself to sit in it. It's HER CHAIR and always will be. When I sit in mine, I reach out and touch the left arm of her chair as if I'm touching Judy. I always envision her sitting there as we enjoy the night sounds, the night music of our Hills.

Travel and road trip day. Made it from Terra Haute, Indiana, to Moriarty, New Mexico, almost 1,200 miles. Beautiful forests, rolling farmland, scrubby landscape that changes continuously as you travel through it. Looking at the mountains and plateaus in the distance, I can envision this land covered by ancient oceans, teeming with sea life. What changes these lands have seen over the millennia, but the land itself never changes. Barren, dry, and yet full of life that strangers and passers-by can't see at first.

> Landscape changes so much as you travel through it
>   Life changes so much as you travel through it
>   The true land doesn't change
>   Mankind adds to and subtracts from it
>   God doesn't change
>   Mankind adds to and subtracts from views of God.
>   True cherished love is beyond forever
>   Grief, deep true grief, lives with love
>   Souls do not change, divine souls
>   Bodies change, strengthen, grow, tire, fade.
>   Land, God, Love, Souls—holy constants.
>   Land, God, Love, Souls—eternal gifts.

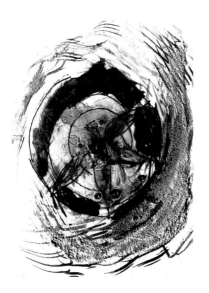

An Enduring Center

A clear night in the desert. Drove under brilliant starlight, the Big Dipper, and Polaris on some desolate stretches of Route 66. Occasional stops for truckers and souvenir stands for tourists, all-but-deserted towns of broken-down homes, shutters hanging loosely, with gas stations, cafés, bars, dusty roads, pickup trucks, and untold stories. Stark beauty.

As I dined alone in Sedona tonight, I observed several couples, young and mature. As the piano player softly entertained us with ballads and love songs, thoughts about marriage began to flood my heart and mind. Did we have a perfect marriage, "everything and then some," as the phrase goes?

It starts with that first look; we never know when it will happen. And when it does, we know it. Confusion, joy, giddiness, conversations that never end, walks in the rain, tingling kisses, a breathless gasp when she answers her door in "that" dress . . . and on and on.

Then comes the question and answer that everyone knows are coming: he's nervous, and she's waiting; he's sure and unsure. Both belong. Then he asks, and she whispers (or shouts) "Yes!" with tears of joy. He grabs her, picks her up, twirls her around . . . neither wants to let go of that moment or each other.

Then there's the wedding. Plans and details somehow magically fall into place. A short walk that takes eons and they are now one. One divine love, shared by two. Families smile through tears of joy, God smiles, and heaven celebrates.

Everything and then some. A "perfect marriage" experiences everything: giddy love . . . a first home . . . new jobs . . . a baby's cries . . . vacations to discover "favorite places" . . . disagreements, hurt feelings, saying "I'm sorry" more often than they thought possible . . . tears of joy, cries of excitement, shared grief when loved ones die, always too soon.

Fear-filled eyes and hearts when a suspected diagnosis is confirmed by medical tests. Plans and lives changed in the blink of an eye. Caring for, being with, holding closely, feeling helpless, seeing overwhelming weariness in those same eyes that gave him "that first look" so many years ago.

One leaves this earth; both knew it would happen. Now this perfect marriage continues on two planes, until they are rejoined for eternity. *Everything and then some.* Love and joy. Pain and grief. It all belongs.

As I was writing this, a busboy stopped at my table and asked what I was writing about.

"I'm writing to God and my wife. She passed on a little over eight months ago. I've been writing/journaling since then, just about every day." I paused. "It helps me a lot."

"I'm so, so sorry," he said as he touched his heart.

When he brought my crème brûlée dessert, he said, "It's on the house, for you and your wife."

Stooping beside me, he showed me a picture of his 15-day-old baby girl. "Her mother just decided she no longer wants to be with me," he said. His eyes revealed his deep hurt.

"Do whatever you can to be her daddy," I said gently. "She'll need you."

He nodded. "I'm fighting every day to get to do that," he said.

Pain and joy, love, grief, and confusion. It all belongs.

Talked to the front desk manager about hiking the Sedona vortexes.

"What are you hoping for?" he asked.

"Rest, contemplation, listening," I said. "I'm on a road trip to listen to God and my wife, who passed on recently."

"I lost my wife in 2000 and miss her every day," he said.

"It sucks, doesn't it?" I commiserated.

"Yes, it does."

"You will realize that the sensation or feeling you're hoping to find in a vortex is actually already within you, ready to guide you," he advised. "If you feel a leading to turn down a road or stop at a certain spot on your hike or climb, trust it, follow it."

He understands.

When I got to Bell Rock, a vortex site, the "dry heat" was in the high 90s, heading to triple digits. Noting that the heat didn't feel as stifling as the same temperature would have back home, I made sure to follow the desk manager's advice to stay hydrated.

My ascent began, and I climbed about three-fourths of the way up the rock mountain. While I didn't find the route to a high spot the front desk manager suggested, I did find a wonderful shady spot under a small outcropping, near a small, scraggly tree. As I sat on the red gravel, reading Judy's journal entry about "Centering Prayer with a Pilgrim's Soul," I pondered its advice to "breathe in new life."

How do I do that?

Quietly sitting on Bell Rock in the 100-degree shade was strangely calming. Before I left, I stacked five or six rocks near that scraggly tree, a small red rock altar on the north face of Bell Rock. I hope it will be there for a long time.

Woke up at 2:30 a.m. to be at the Grand Canyon by 4:00 a.m. so I could hike into it at sunrise. Stopping on Route 66, I got out of my car to see the Milky Way in all its glory, billions of other stars, and distant galaxies. Life, mysteries, answers, beauty, darkness, light, divinity. Do we slow down enough to see, hear, feel, sense this totality of ours?

The hikers' shuttle dropped about 20 of us at the south trailhead at 4:15 a.m., and I headed into the canyon by 4:30. Ooh Ahh Point is well named—an amazing, incredible, indescribable view!

With sunrise still about 50 minutes away, there was just enough "dawn light" to see our trail. As two horses carrying riders and five fully packed mules passed us on the trail, I wondered how they could manage this steep and narrow trail with four legs; I was having trouble on two.

Sand and loose rocks made the footing slippery; in some places the trail was so narrow and close to the edge I wanted to turn around. After about 2.25 miles I could feel my anxiety building as our trail became narrower and even closer to the edge.

As a novice hiker, I was very satisfied that I managed this terrain as well as I did, but I recognized I had reached my limit and headed back up, stopping at Cedar Ridge to watch the sunrise and take pictures.

Sitting in palpable quiet, I took in the stark beauty of the canyon's muted colors laced into its twists and turns. As the sun rose higher, varied strata of canyon walls became increasingly visible, along with its valleys and floor thousands of feet below. At once calmed and inspired, I realized how this place challenges body and soul, even as it offers natural limits and checkpoints along the way. Pretty much like life.

My climb back up was steep and hard. Leaning over my feet and stooping slightly forward for balance, I realized this was much like leaning into life to find balance and gain traction over pain.

Taking this parallel even further, I considered the hard and steep climb out of the abyss of grief. It can take much longer than you expect, and because of how a journey changes you, the trip back up will bring you to a new normal. Even as landscapes around *you* remain the same, you will never, ever be the same.

After lunch at the circa 1902 El Tovar hotel, the first hotel in the park, I traveled Route 66, stopping for the night in Williams, Arizona. Traveling without Judy is harder than I thought it would be. More than once I thought of something to tell her or point out to her before bitter reality rushed back into my heart.

Today was a travel day from Williams, Arizona, to Grand Lake, Colorado—about 10 hours. As I continued through Arizona and into Utah, I encountered red rock mountains, high cliffs, and short, horizontal mountains that looked like they had been dug out with an ice cream scoop. The landscape in that part of Utah was a mixture of beautiful and odd.

Nearing Blanding, Utah, I felt myself smile and take a deep breath when at last I saw some green grass and crops. The Southwest landscape is magnificent with its mountains, mesas, and stark beauty, but grass and green breathe life into me.

WOW!!

That word is inadequate to express my gut reaction, my soul-deep amazement as I took in the Colorado Rockies for the first time. These mountains feel so life giving and inspiring to me.

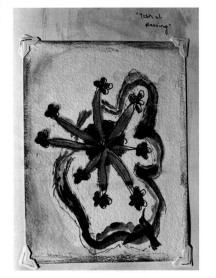

Path of Blessing

Pine greens and earth greys.
>Red dirt and cerulean sky
>Wide valleys of rolling fields
>Streams, creeks, rivers flowing
>Log cabins at the river's edge
>Snow Capped peaks, pillars above it all.
>Presiding over their shorter cousins,
>Mountains rivers cliffs fields
>Suddenly, I can breathe . . .

Dinner at the Grand Lake Lodge. I imagined Judy sitting across from me, our excited conversation about the incredible views of mountains, pine trees, lake, our duplex cabin, and this small, quiet mountain lake community.

In my devotional time today, surrounded by this spectacular beauty, I reflected on the assurance that as long as I am conscious of God's continued presence, all will be well.

I know Judy visited me this morning when a hummingbird came to hover within three feet of me. I was startled to the point of shooing it away because it was so close. It came back, hovered close to me again, and stared right at me.

Hello, Judy.

Yes, I know all WILL be well. This I trust. Yet right now, all is most definitely NOT WELL with my heart and soul.

How long does it take? I feel my grief softening, but I can't help but wonder when and how I will ever be fully *well*. There is and will be joy and laughter, thrills and contentment—but will my grief, longing, questions, and confusion also remain? Will a part of me always feel lost and lonely for Judy?

Birth, life, death—it all belongs. If only it could be just the first two, only those two.

Attended a "Chapel in the Rockies" worship service this morning, high up on the mountain overlooking Grand Lake. The service was led by four college-age employees of The Lodge who also volunteer for the Christian ministry in the National Parks Program. One young man named Seth spoke about being bold for Christ. A young woman spoke about St. Stephen, who was martyred for his faith. I was immediately reminded of how Judy glorified God throughout her illness and death. I also remember how together we loved and glorified God on that journey. Not perfectly but faithfully, tenderly, and with devotion. Their closing song was Judy's favorite hymn, "Amazing Grace."

I felt Judy with me today—in this place, in the service, in her favorite song, in her hummingbird. I will live with these thin-space nudges and touches from Judy and God. I will honor our love and Judy by living, loving, serving, praying, and being present.

I will live—with a piece gone.

Woke up listening to birds singing in the pine trees behind my cabin. Lay in bed for about an hour, hugging an extra pillow and just listening.

After breakfast, I walked down the "billy goat trail" from The Lodge to Grand Lake. One section was not very identifiable at all. I veered off the path, which almost caused me to go back up the hill. I kept searching for and eventually reconnected with the path.

Certainly another metaphor for finding our way on the path of grief. Stay on the path chosen by people you trust who've gone before us. When you get lost, keep searching and moving forward, trusting that you will reconnect with the path when you move in the right direction.

Walking back to my cabin, I mused aloud, "I can see why people drink to numb the pain. How else do we live alone after decades of having our divinely created love by our side?"

I felt Judy's presence three times when I hiked the Adams Falls trail. Once when I was sitting beside a hanging swing for two, once when wind brought the fragrance of a spiced verbena bush to me, and a third time as another hummingbird visited me. As it fluttered in front of me, I stood, motionless, delighting in how she can reach through the thin veil that separates us. Judy reveled in nature, and she is still sharing that with me today. It hurts and soothes. It all belongs.

Tried and completed something I wasn't sure I could do—a 10.4-mile hike in the Rocky Mountain National Park. Started at about 9,200 feet above sea level and ascended to over 11,000 feet one way on the hike.

It was a wonderful thrill. Pristine quiet, whispers and wafting scent of Rocky Mountain pines, a mother moose and her baby, a lone moose grazing as I stepped into its meadow. Horseshoe prints on the trail. Broken-down shepherd cabins. Charred and barren pines from a long-ago fire. Brilliant blue skies with cotton ball clouds, the deep green forest floor, beautiful wildflowers of yellow, violet, white, and orange. Tall meadow grasses dancing in the breeze, creeks babbling downhill, fed by inlet springs. At the top, a cascading waterfall roared over fallen rocks and trees.

Sat near the fall to read Judy's journal from January 2014 through September 2015. Paralleling her art journals, she recorded her responses to various devotional writings and then often also commented on her life's happenings. Those were special and crazy times—our cottage was being finished, we were moving into it, and we were handing over the keys to our previous home. Reading this now, I could see that she seemed to sense the illness within her not yet identified and how few her remaining years.

Her words and heart were wise, vulnerable, honest, prayerful, compassionate. It was soothing, painful, and special to read this. She knew it was all from God and for us and those we loved and served. It allowed me to reminisce about the unexpected gift of our cottage in the Hills. Why did God allow us to see the slower, peace-filled dream of our cottage come true—and then have her leave it so soon? Perhaps God brought Sunrise Ridge to reality to grace us with a glimpse of the heaven she now enjoys. Many times she said of our place in the Hills, "My soul was born here, many years ago."

Last afternoon in Grand Lake. I read some more and took a nap as suggested by a more experienced hiker when he heard what I had done over the past few days. I knew this was solid advice when I woke up several hours later.

Went to the Sagebrush BBQ Grill to hear the Peggy Mann Band, a local group that played rock 'n' roll, folk, and ballads. It was clear they truly enjoyed performing together and cared for one another deeply.

A lot of life and energy were in the crowd, too. Six young men for a bachelor party; a family from Australia with two little girls who could not stop dancing; couples of all ages relaxing and enjoying each other, their food, and Peggy's band.

No doubt others in the room are dealing with a problem no one else knew about. Yet they are here, living, laughing, listening, hugging, eating, cracking open peanuts and throwing shells on the floor. We're all just taking one step at a time. What a perfect place and way to end my stay at Grand Lake.

Back home, I've rested for a couple of days and attended to chores in our too-quiet cottage. I decided to go to yoga for the first time since Judy and I went in April of last year, while she was still receiving treatments for her cancer. I have been feeling a need to reenter this group. I saw only two people from that class we went to last April. I greeted them and purposely did not engage in conversation. I did not want to talk about why I was there alone. In a few sitting and meditation poses, I could easily picture Judy there on her mat beside me, red wavy hair, eyes locked forward as she breathed smoothly and slowly.

It's taken me nine months to get to this point, but today I decided to take Judy's hanging clothes to Goodwill so other women could wear them. I knew she'd want me to share her clothes with other women. I kept several blouses and shirts that were my favorites or that she wore in some of my favorite pictures of her. When I gave the bags to a Goodwill employee, I felt as though I was saying goodbye to yet another part of her.

After dinner I waited for Judy's full moon to rise. When I saw it peeking through our trees, I went outside to see it better. Looking to my left, I noticed a neighbor's bush across the lane, bathed in moonlight. I walked over to stand in front of the bush to see her moon in all its splendor.

After an unexpected torrent of tears and pain that followed and needed to be released, I went back inside. Knowing that Judy's full moon would move through the night, I rearranged the pillows on our chair-and-a-half so I was facing the trees and waited patiently for her "Judy moon" to emerge from the leaves.

I knew she was there with me. After talking with her until I was too sleepy to continue, I left our chair and went to bed, hugging pillows as I still do each night. As I slept, Judy's moonlight flooded the wall of our room and our chair, just as she flooded my heart with love, so many years ago.

Your Full Moon . . . You

Your full moon captivated all eyes,
     Gently, peacefully, humbly
     Lights up the dark sky
     Hiding stars and planets

Your full moon rises through the trees,
     Peeking in and out of leaves and branches
     Announcing your presence quietly
     Climbing peacefully higher and higher

Your full moon does not intend or plan
     To light up the night landscape
     It just . . . does, with its shy smile
     Everything, everyone, smiles back

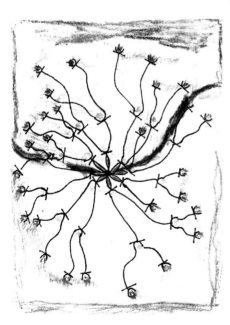

Life Energy

Your Full Moon . . . You *(continued)*

Your full moon reflects the sun's light
      Illuminating the earth below
      Your light reflects off the ocean waves
      And lake ripples. Hearts are stilled.

You are your full moon in our lives
      Captivating people and hearts, humbly
      Unintentionally, peacefully
      Moving in and out of our lives, our souls

You are your full moon, shyly smiling
      Giving hope and dreams
      Creativity and compassion,
      illuminating possibilities.

You are your full moon, announcing your presence
      quietly, gently.
      You do not reflect the sun's light.
      The Son's Light shines through you!

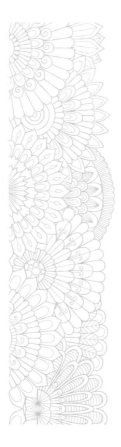

I had my last session with Kermit at the Pickering House today; he's moving into their chaplain position. I'll start to meet with another grief support person soon. We talked about my long road trip out West. About how Judy showed up in the Rockies and nudged me.

Kermit said that he senses an increased, deeper peace within me, even after I told him about sobbing on our lane last night as I breathed in Judy's full moon. He said my grief is still evident *and* a new peace has settled within me. "The road trip, Judy's nudges, your writing, and God's grace all have contributed to this peace," he said.

I'll let his observation rest within me.

On the way back home, I saw an almost black sky over toward Hide-A-Way Hills. After driving through a hard storm to reach our back gate, I learned that it didn't work because the power was out. I drove around to the front gate.

From there I could tell that our cottage, our sanctuary, the sanctuary for so many, had likely been hammered. The whole area had no power, trees were blown over, uprooted, some of them splintered, and many roads were blocked.

A neighbor called to see whether I was all right, but I couldn't return her call due to "no service." I was then stuck on one particular hairpin turn in our Hills for 15 minutes while trees were being removed.

I was so afraid that our cottage had been severely damaged, maybe even destroyed, because of all the fallen trees.

Once that blockage was cleared, I made my way to Papago Lane, only to find it blocked, too. I left my car and climbed over trees to get to our haven.

It was all right.

"Thank you, God," I sobbed in relief, realizing I had been holding my breath. Branches and leaves peppered the front of our cottage like measles; our neighbors lost two trees, and two other trees had their tops ripped off. One of our trees had its top ripped off, too.

It looked worse than the hurricane winds that came through there two years ago. Our neighbors who had weathered the storm huddled in their bathtub described how it got really quiet, then very noisy for 10–15 minutes, followed by hard rain. I have no doubt that a funnel cloud came up from the golf course and right through our lane.

Thank you, God, for sparing our houses and people's lives.

I spent about half of today cleaning and clearing the storm litter and, while I was at it, clearing the overgrown weeds, brush, and sapling trees from our porch-view gully today. It had grown much more than in years past; I realized I had not cleared it since Judy was ill.

As I worked, I remembered watching Judy sitting on our porch in her wheelchair the last time I cleared this gully. I remembered wondering what she was thinking about. Gazing out at the pasture, she was obviously in prayer, in deep thought, maybe crying because of what the stroke had taken from her, maybe expressing gratitude for all of God's blessings in our lives. Perhaps she was asking God what heaven would be like—how it would be to see her loved ones already there. Maybe all of this and much, much more.

Tonight, I'm going to turn out the porch light, place my right hand on Judy's chair, watch the fireflies, breathe in the scent of trees, grass, and shrubs—and picture Judy there beside me.

I spent some time today on my regular tracking of expenses, which Judy always said she was glad I did but wanted nothing to do with; numbers weren't her thing. I noticed that this memory made me smile today, rather than reducing me to a convulsion of heaving sobs. That's progress, I suppose.

Had a realization about my writing in restaurants, bars, parks, and coffee shops, and even on our porch. Writing *about* Judy in these places is my version of talking *with* her on our dates. With my journal and pen I can connect with my memory of our talks, observations, memories shared.

Now when I leave our cottage and I don't take my journal and pen, it feels a bit incomplete, just as it did when I had to leave our cottage without Judy. A different way of dating, I suppose, given that we're now in two different worlds. Also a different way of keeping her with me. Suddenly, this behavior makes more sense.

Amanda said today that she sees healing within me, within my words and descriptions of the western road trip, while also seeing continued grief. Both are true. She noted that Judy and I tasted the divine experience of heavenly love, that we believed it was real, and that too many people don't believe that heavenly love is real because they haven't tasted it in this life. I'm sad for these people.

Over lunch, Deb offered that I am honoring Judy and how she lived from her passions and how she would want me to now live from my passions, as well. She also said that doing things I've never done, such as the road trip and hiking in the Rocky Mountains, also honors Judy.

She added that in getting Judy's writing and art published, I am being her loving Sherpa again, carrying her materials for her as she continues to serve people in need from her words and her art.

Mowed grass and avoided the ground hornet nest. They've stung me twice. Not again.

A couple drove by and slowed to a stop in front of the cottage. He rolled down the window, and I walked nearer to see what he needed.

"You did a wonderful job redoing your cottage," he said. "We knew the previous owners and remember how it used to look."

"It was my wife," I said. "She dreamed it up perfectly."

"She obviously had a great vision for it," she ventured.

"Yes, she did," I said.

I clipped some daisies and black-eyed Susans and coneflowers from our garden to put in a vase at our gravestone. Judy's flowers for Judy. I'll never get used to seeing that stone with Judy's name and life dates on it.

I invited Jim, my friend from Pickering House whose wife, Pat, just died, to dinner tonight so he could talk. I sensed from our previous conversations that he needs to talk with someone living a similar grief journey. I asked him how he and Pat met, and he shared a lot of stories about their family, camping, cruises, and, finally, her death.

At one point, he said he couldn't remember the last time he talked like this to anyone. He also said he thought his "heart's ears" were growing since Pat died—he heard and sensed people's words and emotions much more. He asked me whether this was the case with me.

Told him that I, too, was learning to listen with my "heart's ears." And, yes, a different and deeper level of sensitivity has developed in me since Judy became ill and passed on.

In the evening, after dark, I opened a small bottle from June that I thought was white wine; it turned out to be a *sparkling* white wine. As I tasted it, my heart and mind raced back to our wedding reception, where Judy and I entwined our arms and champagne glasses as a symbol of our entwined hearts.

Images of that moment, our wedding reception, flooded my heart and mind. Dancing and the Sigma Nu sweetheart song. Our families, the silliness of removing the garter belt from Judy's leg, Judy tossing her bridal bouquet. The gorgeous woman who had just become my wife. How deeply in love we were, only to grow deeper over the next four decades. The clarity of those images made me believe Judy was sitting right there beside me on our porch, sharing those memories with me.

Entwined

Joy

Traded glances and subtle winks.
Entwined arms with champagne glasses.
Wedding cake held and offered to teach other.
Much more, so much more than seen.

Treasures hidden in cherished traditions

Entwined hearts and souls never to be separated
Entwined futures beyond forever
Treasured dreams known and unknown, together
Linked arms, hands, and bodies — perfection.
Wine glasses full and tender toasts.
Long kisses.
Manhattan-soaked maraschino cherries, shared.

Beaches strolled, mountain peak seats
Dinners for two, then dinners for three, four, five
Waves, sea glass, full moons, new moons.
Fireflies, visiting cows, adventures.
Holding hands under trees, under stars, in the snow

Discovering God's heart within us and others
Uncovering your God-created heart for others
Watching you blossom again and again and again
Journeying together, with others, on your last path.
Till death do us part.
Till our next wedding in heaven..

"You've got this!"

Out of nowhere those three words recalled a memory and wracked my heart with pain.

Those three words had been written many times by medical professionals, caregivers, and visitors who wrote on the notepad Judy offered. It was her request of all who cared for her in some way to share their thoughts and notes of encouragement. These words were written to Judy to imply that she would survive the horrible, life-draining cancer.

The bitter truth was that Judy's body did not "got this." Despite her strong spirit, her body wore out. Bitter, angry, sarcastic tears erupted and overwhelmed me.

Then I realized that maybe those words, "You've got this," did apply, after all. Cancer took her body—but that tender, gracious, beautiful, loved, and loving eternal spirit—the essence of Judy—prevailed and *did* "got this"! Just not in the way that I wanted.

God's "got this"—all of it—as well. *Thank you, God, for this insight.*

Woke up remembering how an owl called out three times the night Judy moved from this world to the next as I left Pickering House with her belongings. A special call to Judy and to me as her spirit, her soul, flew to be free, to join God in heaven.

Sometimes we differentiate between God and nature as though they are separate. I'm more and more convinced that nature is an incredible expression of God, a facet of God's spirit on earth. The owl's call is a perfect example of this truth to me. As are beautiful butterflies, hawks, and the abundant variety of life coexisting with us here on earth.

I'm also convinced Judy often nudges and says hi to me via nature, just as other loved ones have done for all time to those of us who are still here, temporarily separated, with eyes and ears and souls awake and aware of this "thin space," nature in all its glory.

My devotional reading today described the desire of grieving people to go back, to return to the past, to turn back the clock when their loved one was alive, healthy, and beside them.

Do I want to return to the past when Judy was here? A big part of me says yes, of course. I want Judy bedside me, with me. Yes, I want OUR life back. I passionately want her here, now, in this time and place, in our cottage with me, on this earth.

However, it cannot be. I know this. My mind and soul and heart and body know this. Even as I know this, I still want her beside me. This life is full, abundant, AND incomplete.

I went to see the movie *Wind River*. Edgy, deep story with a social message about missing girls in our Native American population. Many well-presented scenes. Two were very personal for me. Both involved two grown men who had lost their teenage daughters.

As a Native American father opens his door, he sees a dear friend who had lost his daughter long ago. Acknowledging the Native American's life-altering pain that will never go away, he encouraged him to allow the suffering to happen in order to live through it.

Toward the movie's end, the grieving father has been contemplating killing himself; his pain was just too great. Again, his friend arrives and goes to where the desperate man is sitting and sits down beside him.

No words followed. None were needed. Simply his presence, being there. Sitting with his friend was all he needed to do.

This scene struck me because even though I've been blessed with incredibly supportive friends since Judy died, I don't recall anyone appearing and just sitting beside me, being with me. Nor have I asked anyone to "just sit with me." There is such healing, comforting power in just sitting with someone who is in deep grief.

God, open my eyes to ask. Open my heart to sit with others who can't ask that question.

Fall 2017

I decided a while back that we would celebrate our 40th wedding anniversary with a trip to the ancient "thin space" of Iona, Scotland. Packing for one, not two, tonight felt so wrong. Finished my final packing for my Iona trip last night. Packing for one, not two, felt so wrong. We always traveled/flew together; the idea of going to Scotland without Judy feels like some kind of betrayal. She should be going with me.

Walking down a concourse toward the gate at Columbus International, I was suddenly and unexpectedly gripped by Judy's absence; yet another new layer of loss hit me so hard I had to stop for a few minutes and lean against a wall. Already this trip is sending my heart even deeper into darkness than it has been so far. I didn't think that was possible.

Long travel day to Oban, Scotland. Jets to Chicago, Dublin, and then Glasgow. Then a bus ride to catch the train at Glasgow's Queen Street Station, then a four-hour train to Oban.

The countryside of Scotland's Highlands is breathtaking. Some mountains are steep with rocky crags, but most are gently rolling inclines rising up from wide, verdant valleys that twist and turn in all directions.

After dinner in a local Oban restaurant, I went back to the hotel and ordered a pint of Belhaven, a beer from Scotland's oldest brewery, and a shot of Bruitschladdich single-malt Scotch. Sitting in the bar and writing, I noticed a delightful mix of people around me—from Scotland, Ireland, Italy, Belgium, Great Britain, France, Switzerland, Canada, and this one American. As a small band with a bagpipe began playing Scottish and Irish music, everyone was tapping their feet, clapping, and singing along.

I've heard that we are all born with a desire to play, to love, to be loved, and to play with others. This gathering of people, including the musicians, was a perfect example. Play happens spontaneously if we let it, billions of times every day, throughout our world. God's world.

Today would have been our fortieth anniversary. We talked and dreamed many times about celebrating 50, 60, 75 years together. Instead of celebration, terrible pain marks this day.

Got up, dressed, and went to get on the ferry to the Isle of Mull. Settled on a seat in the rear of the ferry, I watched Oban getting smaller as we moved through a small channel and then toward Mull.

Leaving Oban behind is a visual reminder of not only leaving my life behind up to this point but also moving toward a new land, a new unknown, and a changed life. As I move toward places I've never seen or experienced, I trust God and Judy to be with me. My heart is still broken, yet it also feels pregnant with a new life of some type; a new life that includes our separated life and love.

The bus ride across Mull wound through majestic green mountain slopes and wide, lush valleys. I looked out in wonder as we passed sheep grazing in the fields, Scottish cattle with curved horns and long hair that covered their eyes, calm lochs, and small villages of only a few homes.

I took in the sloped terrain that was dotted with sheep and cattle, some of which meandered onto our single-lane road. Then I saw a dark-feathered hawk perched on a black stone outcropping as we passed.

"Hi, Judy," I whispered to myself.

Low stone walls and aged stone cottages were from a less hectic time, not without its own stresses and harried moments. It seemed as though I was in another time, but for vehicles, utility poles, and some more recently built houses.

Gentleness

The Creator's Waves

As the Creator's waves have massaged beaches and rocks
Since water and rock existed, and will repeat
Their dance until both are no more,
Our life has and will continue in the calm
Under the sun and moon, in the storms.
Yet, one day the waves and shores will exist no longer.
Our love will grow and continue past that moment,
Our love will go beyond the waves,
Beyond the shores and rocks,
Beyond forever.

Our short ferry ride to Iona was a whispered entry, a gentle call to this adventure. As our ferry approached, I saw the Argyll Hotel, a stone abbey, and, facing the road, 15 or 20 two-story stone and plaster homes lined up in a single row. Peaceful solitude enfolded me, as it did countless times on retreats with Judy. A few small boats, row boats, and a single sailboat in the small bay.

Judy.

Dinner on the Argyll's enclosed porch, beside the one-lane road coming in from the hotel. Afterward, I walked along the dark road to take in the starlit sky above and drink in the rhythmic sound of the waves caressing the rocks. I prayed for peace and presence these next days and nights, to receive what God and Judy have for me, my heart, and my soul.

On my first full Iona day, I woke to music from waves. After breakfast I walked along Iona's northern half. I wanted, needed, to ease into Iona, its land, its ancient body. I trusted Judy was with me each step, even those that took me into hidden, small bogs that soaked my shoes and socks. For over seven hours we explored heights, views, shorelines, and aromas of Iona.

Our day included gazing at Highland Mountains across the Sound on the Isle of Mull. Judy would love the beaches, ocean, water, and surf with mountain views on grand display on this small, prehistoric isle.

I walked on white sand, watched waves splash on black rocks and crags, talked to Scottish cattle and grazing sheep as they wandered wherever they chose, climbed higher to see the island's four views from Dun I, the island's highest point; I let my hair blow in the wind.

For centuries and centuries, Iona has been purported to be a "thin space," a place with a thin veil between earth and heaven, between us and God. We must be willing to receive, be open to reaching through the veil, be open to being touched by God.

I don't know exactly what that means, how it works, or how it feels. What I do know is this is completely a matter of trust as I enter this foreign land. The mystery is in God's hands. As Abram said, "Here I am, Lord."

God and Judy, lead and guide me as I'm able. Here I am.

I believe God has plans for me, that something is growing within me, something of God and guided by Judy. Only God and Judy know what it is, what it is to become, and how it will take hold and give life on earth to God's plans.

"Your movement is free-form and always shifting,
which can make you feel like a foreigner.
Remember this is your pilgrim soul spreading its wings
to explore edges where new life and possibilities reside.
Know that you are held. You may not see the safety of the container.
But I am there, I am strong, I am solid.
You will not fly off edges where there is no one to catch you.
Breathe. Slow down. Reside in the present. All will be well."

~JUDY'S JOURNAL, 7.5.15

*"I feel very much a foreigner on this pilgrimage
that I don't recall embarking on with intention.
I have to trust there is a container holding this seeming chaos
to know that I am 100 percent held
in some manner as I spread to unknown edges."*

~JUDY'S RESPONSE TO HER OWN WRITING, 7.5.15

These words were not only a call from Judy to herself with her amazing courage and honesty. They are also a precise and prophetic message to me.

There's a community no one acknowledges until they're in it. It's populated by billions of loved ones since the first wife or husband lost their spouse. We both knew one of us would embark on this journey alone. Yet neither of us anticipated it happening so soon.

It's a new season of life for both of us; me still here without Judy, Judy in heaven without me. It seems that Judy's is a return home to God, a home of joy, of celebration. This new season for me is joy and grief, pain and smiles, tears and sweet memories, unanswered whys and why-nots, loss and longing, gratitude and confusion, shattered hearts and broken dreams.

Went on a guided pilgrimage tour of sacred sights of Iona today, led by a charming young lady from Uganda. She started our tour by the Iona Abbey at St. Martin's cross, which has been here for 1,100 years. This three-and-a-half-hour excursion also took us to Martyr's Bay, St. Columba Chapel, the Pink Rock, the Crossroads, the Hill of Angels, the Nunnery, and Machair Beach on the west side of Iona.

Having read *The Rebirthing of God* by J. Phillip Newell while here, I have a much better appreciation of Iona, its sacred places, and the Celtic crosses. Because the Celtic cross is a combination of the Christian cross, representing Christ and our loss of his life, with the Celtic circle, representing how everything is connected and interrelated, it is powerful. The cross and the circle also share the same center point, the One Source of all people and all things.

A rainy, gray yesterday in Iona, with a gentle and peaceful rain that increased off and on in intensity all day, gave me the opportunity to relax, visit three or four shops here on the island, and climb a hill west of the Nunnery after lunch.

I'm reminded of a quote by Vicki Harrison about learning to swim when you're in the ebbing, flowing ocean of grief. However, as I think about it, there *is* another option: choosing *not* to learn to swim.

Vicki doesn't mention it, but some people choose to let grief overwhelm them permanently, choosing instead to drown in their turbulent sea. Some just tread water. I can completely understand and empathize with everyone, the swimmers, the treaders, and those who choose to be overwhelmed. My heart has done all three.

After the stormy, cloudy, rainy day of yesterday, Iona's skies are crystal blue today, populated with white sheep wool clouds. An Atlantic breeze is playing with the bright sunlight, bouncing the temperature up and down.

To take advantage of this bright, clear day, I hiked for about six hours to the Hermit's Cell, the western beach, Machair, by the open range community golf course, St. Columba Bay, the Marble Quarry, and back to the village.

I hiked to the Cell and sat in it. It's a 20-foot-wide circle of large stones piled two to three feet high. It sits in a low-lying area between two rocky green hills crisscrossed by sheep trails. Looking west, I see the Atlantic Ocean spread across the horizon before me.

There is a small entrance and exit space in the wall, leading into and out of its grass floor. Reminds me of a labyrinth entrance and exit, which reminded me how Judy guided so many labyrinth journeys for people. What thoughts and prayers and conversations have been held here in this labyrinth over the centuries? A place to listen in solitude and/or with another. A place to listen to God, to the person with you, to your own heart.

I'm sitting in the Iona Abbey tonight for their communion service. A picture of Judy and me from 2002, standing in Mom and Dad's dining room at their lake house, is on the hymnal counter in front of me. I fervently wish she could be sitting beside me in this holy Medieval church. The service was crowded with Iona people, people on retreat at the Abbey, tourists, and retreatants like me, here on their own.

The service was informal, joyful, and special in this holy cathedral. Even though the Abbey Church and its other buildings are reconstructions, people have been worshipping on these grounds for over 1,800 years. Receiving communion with other Christians from around God's world touched me deeply.

Going back to today's hiking pilgrimage, which ended up being almost eight miles, I walked a very short distance to a walled well that had served people for hundreds of years, or maybe more than a thousand. Then I hiked up and down hills and pastures, mostly on narrow sheep trails. Through murky bogs and clumps of heather, I headed south to St. Columba Bay.

As I came down a hill into a clearing, I asked Judy, as I often do, "Where are you? Are you here with me right now?" I had seen a few small violet-colored flowers here and there, and as I bent over to pick one of them, I suddenly sensed Judy to the extent that I had to bend over to place my hands on my knees and catch my breath between loud sobs.

After about a minute I stood up, stretched out my arms to receive her, and then wrapped my arms around my shoulders, pretending that I was holding her and she was holding me. During all of this, I kept my eyes closed. When I opened them and looked around, I was standing in the middle of a solid field of those small violet flowers. In all of my hikes over the past four days, probably over 32 miles, this was the only patch of these flowers I saw. She was surrounding me.

From there I walked due south over more up-and-down terrain on Iona's west side, including a community golf course at Machair Bay where sheep and cows are given free range; they also help keep the grass trimmed with their grazing—an Iona landscaping team.

The views of the land, hills, and bay are spectacular. I snapped a few pictures of the course, its tees and greens, and its four-legged groundskeepers.

As I climbed up a hill on the course's south edge, my path was very rocky, muddy, and wet—and continued for quite a while until I began a downhill descent toward a green flat pasture. Seeing this pasture framed by rocky hills on each side was magnificent.

Just beyond the pasture was St. Columba Bay, where Columba set foot on Iona in 563 AD to bring himself and a few followers here with his intent to introduce Christianity to Iona's people.

The beach was completely covered in stones washed up by ocean waves, varying in size from very small to about 10–12 inches in diameter. Pure white stones, green stones, red-orange and white ones, dark gray and black ones, some that sparkled in the sunlight, and many others.

I also noticed four or five mounds of stones that had been built by people. A larger one reminded me of the stone mound at the foot of a cross on the Compostela de Santiago.

At first I thought about building a small mound for Judy. She whispered to me the memory of her love of the scripture about a cloud of witnesses—and how she always preferred to be behind the scenes helping others grow and develop their gifts, not out in front.

A three-inch or so dark, flat rock caught my attention as I approached the mound. It sparkled on both sides and glistened in the sunlight. It reminded me of how Judy sparkled—and brought peace, joy, love, faith, and passion to her own life and to everyone she touched. I climbed the five-foot-high mound, kissed her sparkling stone, and placed it about a foot below the peak.

Just as Judy chose to do in her life here, her sparkling stone was placed among many other stones, adding its beauty and place to the collective of colors, shapes, and sizes.

As I started to leave the beach, I chose a most attractive green stone and walked to the waves. Not to throw it in to represent something I needed to leave behind a practice, done by thousands of people over the years. I threw it in, returning Judy's green eyes and pure heart to the ocean she loved so dearly.

Once I moved past the stone beach, I saw names that had been laid out in stones in the green field. "Judy" is now one of those names.

Looking at the map, I located a grass labyrinth outlined by sizable stones from the beach. Judy no doubt has walked a labyrinth such as this in the past 11 months with God and others. Retreating to the rocky beach for a moment, I chose two stones to carry with me on my own labyrinth walk.

As I walked the labyrinth's narrow paths, a few small piles of sheep dung seemed perfectly placed in the middle of the path at various points. Walking toward the center, sojourners have to watch for them to avoid fouling their shoes or boots.

I smiled, thinking how this parallels with the messes and crap that happen in our lives at different times as we move forward. We cannot always easily step around them, even though sometimes we can and do.

Most of the time we have to walk through, straight ahead, directly into the crap in our lives. Crap happens, and we live in it, sometimes alone. Most often with the comfort and love of others. We then come through it to see once again the light and lush green fields that await our next step, our presence.

As I reached the center, remembering what Judy taught each time she guided our labyrinth walks, I reached for my two stones; one had hues of red orange and white, which reminded me of her hair, and a smaller one had shades of green and hazel, which reminded me of her eyes. I kissed the stones and placed them beside each other in the labyrinth's center. They represent Judy, there among many other stones, many other people no doubt remembered as their loved ones placed their stones in this labyrinth.

Instead of offering a prayer to leave something from me in the center, I offered a prayer of gratitude to God for the holy divine gift of Judy and a prayer that God will continue to journey with me, shape me into who I'm to become, what I'm to do while I'm still here without Judy beside me. I also prayed to be able to hear God's whispers, feel Judy's nudges, hear her voice with each step that takes me through the crap of life *and* its lush green grass.

My return hike to the village included an eastward jaunt through more hills and pastures of sheep trails, rocks, bogs, and thick heather bushes. I could have started my return by retracing my steps, but I chose to go through new areas traveled by people and animals for thousands of years.

As if in return for this extra effort, Iona graced me with wonderful views of small valleys that led to ocean waters and trails less traveled for about an hour. It was not lost on me that in the past almost year, I could have started my return to life by retracing my steps, but instead I have chosen to go through new areas, traveled by people for thousands of years as they journey through grief and transformation.

Breakfast on the Argyll's porch was special, sitting next to Jan and Roz, two women I have enjoyed talking to each time our paths have crossed. They're leaving this afternoon, and after two days in Mull, Jan will return to Sidney, Australia, and Roz to northeast England.

Jan gave me a small card of geese flying against an orange dawn sky. "If I rise on the wings of the dawn and settle on the far side of the sea, even here Your hand will guide me, Your right hand will hold me fast" (Psalms 139:9–19).

On it she had written, "My prayer for your journey, Roy."
        — Jan, 2017 on Iona.

She had placed this card on my table as she left to go to her room. When she returned, I asked whether I could give her a hug to thank her for her card and words. We embraced tightly as our eyes moistened, hers 75 years old, mine 62.

Today is a blustery day of writing, stillness, reading, and listening. For more than three-and-a-half hours this pen has recorded images, thoughts, experiences of people, places, feelings, wanderings, and more on these pages, into this leather journal, while sitting in this charming Scottish small hotel's north lounge.

This quaint lounge holds two couches, a chess board, four padded chairs, a stone fireplace with a blazing wood and coal fire, and two windows offering views of thrashing wind, white-capped waves, and nearly horizontal rain. A perfectly offered and received day of stillness. I pray my heart and soul receive and hear God's whispers.

I went to the St. Columba Hotel to register for the April 2019 John Philip Newell Pilgrimage on Iona. All of the pilgrimages prior to then were sold out. As I left, I looked up to the left and saw a copy of *Celtic Treasures* by Newell on a ledge. I had forgotten he wrote that exquisite biblical journey that I read to Judy so many nights in her last two years.

The last stop before returning to the Argyll was the Iona Community Book and Gift Shop to find and buy the Iona Abbey worship service book that we read from in last night's communion service. I'm planning to use it in our closing reading at Judy's ashes ceremony at our cottage.

As I was waiting in line, surrounded by their books about Celtic spirituality, pottery, and jewelry, I was listening to a deeply peaceful, holy piano music CD they were playing. I had to catch my breath. I *felt* Judy and her presence come over me, from somewhere deep within me. I turned away from the line of people for this private moment with Judy. That CD is now purchased and tucked into my suitcase.

Strong southern winds are dancing today with the ocean water at the Sound of Iona, creating surging and pulsating waves, whitecaps, and white sprays. Peaks and troughs rise and fall in their eternal rhythm. Small boats and hand-crafted wooden row boats anchored in the sound rise and fall, rise and fall like the heartbeat of ever-moving waves. Gray, ocean green, and white water everywhere.

Seagulls offer wisdom to willing observers. Do they hide from the storm and pounding waves? Not at all. Do they hide from these 40–50-mph winds? Not at all. Facing the powerful winds directly, they spread their white and gray wings without any need to move them up and down. They ride the wind and storm, hovering above ground and water, their eyes scanning waves below in search of nourishment, in search of provision. Held by an unseen wind, they hover and remain in place, expecting, waiting, trusting an unseen provider's hand and promise in this storm. Suddenly, their trusting, waiting, and expecting are fulfilled. They dive headfirst into crashing white-capped waves, and gray-green seawater welcomes them without hesitation.

Together, gulls and ocean water applaud, creating splashes of seafoam rising in the wind, celebrating their union, thanking their unseen provider for nourishment received. The seawater thanks the provider for being asked to care for needy gulls. Countless times, again and again, their unseen provider smiles, nourishes, and comforts.

It seems as though the storm actually *stirs up* more provision, more fish for the hungry gulls than normally present. The gulls move headfirst into the storm, and their eons-old friend, the sea, offers its presence silently: "I'm here for you. Come and be with me. Let me care for you."

Seagulls leaning into this violent storm, strong winds, white-capped waves, churning seawater. They lean in. Do we see it? Are we listening to their silent wisdom?

I've never seen gulls do that before. Today, I was meant to watch and learn from it, to make this connection. When we lean into *our* storms and trust, ample, extravagant provision arrives, along with a deep, caring presence.

The gulls didn't run from the storm because they knew there would be extra provision there.

As the day moves along, strong winds are increasing, as are choppy waters and waves. The rough water of the Sound has greatly decreased the ferry trips, which has reduced the number of visitors from the morning to the midafternoon. "Our Iona" is even more so today, thanks to Mother Nature and Father Neptune limiting trips to the island.

After walking through the small village and visiting the Iona Abbey, I learned that while the museum was closed, church cloisters and several other buildings were still open. The small and modest St. Columba memorial stone chapel, with room for only four chairs, was also open. There I prayed for peace, comfort, and healing for people who are ill and grieving. I thanked God for Judy and for all of our family and friends who have loved me and invested in my life.

This place, this island, this church, this open reverence and joy for God remind me of Judy's joy and reverence—how her eyes would water at times as she sensed God, as God responded to her in her heart.

I braved the winds to walk to dinner at Martyr's Bay, where I enjoyed a front-row seat watching waves splash above the 15-foot stone wall and spray the windows at least 30 feet away. Gale-force winds, much stronger than before, combined with high tide to create an exquisite show for us, with powerful white-capped waves, seawater washing our windows, and the sound of the wind against the walls. I noticed a black seal bobbing in and out of waves just beyond the stone wall. Just like the gulls, it was playing in and being nourished by the storm.

While I was eating my sticky toffee pudding with vanilla ice cream for dessert—and struggling to place both ice cream and muffin on my spoon, a memory arose of Judy trying to learn to eat with her right hand after her stroke. Her frustration hurt me then and still haunts me. I remember wondering whether Judy was asking God the same question as I was: *Why a stroke, too, God? Wasn't brain cancer enough?*

Without warning, my grief wound reopened, along with my anger and tear ducts. My memory of all of it—of bearing such grief and pain for and with her, praying so earnestly for her earthly healing, learning it would not come, realizing that Judy was soon to leave me, that our time together here was almost over—raced through my mind and heart.

Suddenly, the joy and laughter all around me became just too much; it hurt and angered me. I had to go outside, where I could only hear the wind and the waves, where darkness offered cover for my tear-streaked face.

Back in my hotel room, storms raged as I clutched my extra pillow, the storm of Iona meeting the storm of my heart. At last, peace from sleep guided me to rest, and my storm also passed sometime during the night.

It's a gray day over the Sound and Iona, as well as over my scarred heart. The explosion of grief last evening taxed both my body and my emotions. It purged grief that had been simmering below the surface of memories, activity, and prayers. An exhausted calm now occupies this space within me.

"Be at rest," I commanded it. And myself.

Last day on Iona started with breakfast on the Argyll's conservatory porch. Will soon walk up the lane to the Iona Abbey's Sunday service.

The sermon was "Departure, Initiation, Return; Manna from Heaven" (the Exodus story), delivered by Fr. Alistair MacIntosh. Subtitle: "God does not always answer our prayer for manna." This intimate communion service in the Iona Abby was holy, meaningful, hard, and touched by Judy's presence, the presence of God, Jesus, and their Holy Spirit.

Alastair's message framed the manna provision story from Exodus, tender and powerful as it rose from his Scottish lilt. He spoke of pilgrims and this journey many are embarking on this week in Iona as well as the pilgrimage we all move through each day in terms of DEPARTURE, INITIATION, and RETURN.

DEPARTURE: No matter the pilgrimage, our departure, or better said, our decision to depart, is usually the easiest part. Whatever our reason or impetus, we decide, we prepare, and then we begin.

INITIATION: We're tested when a fierce obstacle is planted in our pilgrimage path, and we may long for what we left behind, even though we know we left it for good reasons. When the Israelites appealed to Moses for food and comfort, God responded by providing quail and manna for nourishment.

RETURN is being guided to God's promised land and to God's comfort and safety.

Alastair was also wise and honest enough to remind us that God's response is not always what we request on our pilgrimage. Throughout his message, the question plagued me:

"What about the pilgrimage forced on us, that we don't want or choose, that we never intentionally decided to begin?"

The communion was joyful and reverent, led by a Scottish Presbyterian minister from the United States. As instructed in that beautiful lilting voice, we passed bread and wine to one another, a Canadian on my right, an Australian on my left.

Music in the ancient chapel included hundreds of voices and a piano, flute, trumpet, and violin. As these sounds blended and echoed from stone walls and high, carved ceilings, Judy's presence touched me several times with the image of her smiling with closed eyes and silent tears as this music was offered to us. It came to me, deep in my soul, that my requests of Judy and God have blessed me here in the Abbey.

Our closing hymn was a Gaelic hymn in English of St. Patrick's Breastplate, one of Judy's favorite tunes and poems. My heart ached for her deeply; I had trouble singing all of it.

This beautiful service, with the presence of Judy and God extremely apparent, was hard, tender, and vulnerable. That question within me about forced pilgrimages would not leave me, my heart, or my soul.

I had to speak with Alastair about it. I asked one of the women who helped guide the service whether I could speak with him privately. As if sensing my desperation, she agreed to seek him out, and after a few minutes she returned to escort me to him.

We stood together near a cloister wall, a bit away from most of those lingering in fellowship and conversation over tea and oat cakes. Alastair explained that he has difficulty hearing and asked me to allow him to clip a device on my shirt that would allow him to hear me more clearly.

This afforded me a brief pause before speaking to him. I could feel the difficulty of expressing myself rising with the lump in my throat. As my fingers fumbled with the device, words began to escape from my bruised heart:

"I arrived on Iona last Sunday and celebrated what would have been our fortieth anniversary," I said. "She passed on last October, thrusting me on a pilgrimage I never wanted or requested. We journeyed together through her illness and treatment for almost a year before she passed into Jesus's arms."

These words were delivered haltingly, not nearly as easily or smoothly as written. My voice quivered as I fought back tears and took deep breaths. Not once did Alastair interrupt me. He tenderly listened and waited.

"In your message you did not address a pilgrimage thrust upon us, that shatters us, one never wanted, a forced departure from the life we were living. How do I live in and walk through this pain-filled pilgrimage I never wanted?" I asked.

Alastair looked directly into my eyes as he placed one hand on my left arm and held my right hand with his other.

"I have no answer for you on how to do this," he offered softly. Then, while squeezing my hand he told me of a personal tragedy he and his wife suffered 30 years ago.

"I'm so sorry that happened," I whispered to him. That was all I could muster.

Tapping my chest, he offered, "'God, come into my heart' is what I learned to say and pray and plead, over and over." He paused, then said. "May I suggest that you offer that prayer when your sorrow overwhelms you?"

He said that he learned that prayer when he was in India about 20 years ago from a holy man who uttered a phrase in his native language, which Alastair happened to understand: "God, come into my heart."

Alastair then cited a passage from Kahlil Gibran's *The Prophet*, where Gibran described each level and recurrence of grief as scraping a piece of wood until it forms a beautiful bowl that ultimately yields music for others.

After a soul-deep hug and "God bless you" for each other, I walked for about an hour under Iona's clouds to reflect on this tender exchange. I realized my grief eruption had calmed, my pain subsided, and I knew that Judy is still deep within me and my thoughts—and always will be.

There was something about Alastair's presence, his listening ears, his eyes, his touch, his compassion, his stories, his offered prayer, his patience by not rushing me, even though we were surrounded by people who wanted to speak with him. Alastair journeyed with me for a tender moment and didn't try to fix me. He led and listened to my heart and my story and my pain. He was Christ to me, to us. Judy was certainly beside me the entire time.

This was holy ground—Judy, Jesus, Alastair, and me. A gift I will never forget. A gift I will forever treasure.

Thank you, God. Thank you, Judy. Thank you, Alastair.

That evening at the Argyll Hotel, my last on Iona, I spent some time on the hotel lawn, facing the Sound and its waves. Gulls flew overhead and then grouped on a black rocky crag in the Sound. People around me rested at round picnic tables and benches, soaking up the peace.

A young couple sat close to me, likely from France. As she read a book, he painted on a small artist's pad with a 4 × 6-inch paint tray of about 12 colors and fine brushes. It's easy to see that they're deeply in love. I pray they have the treasured love that we did and still do.

During most of my dinner of Mull scallops and cod coquettes, followed by a glass of 10-year-old port (some of it drizzled over Mull ice cream), I wrote about this day. A younger lady I had seen in the village the past few days came into the conservatory porch to look through their small bookcase, and then she left with a book. A short time later, she returned to replace her book. As she turned to leave, our eyes met.

"Are you journaling?" she asked. "I noticed you writing on the island these past few days."

"Yes, about my time here and experiences," I replied.

"Is it a diary, or are you writing to someone?"

"Actually, both," I said. "I'm talking to my wife and God, writing poems and essays as they arise, asking questions, praying, trying to listen."

I learned her name, Shuna, also a local island's name. She said she wants to journal but has trouble starting because she keeps hearing voices from her school years telling her she's not a good writer.

This admission reminded me so much of what Judy told people—*everyone* is an artist—so I shared Judy's wisdom about that. Shuna smiled and connected with it. I felt Judy's nudge to encourage Shuna to start writing from her heart; her writings are for her, no one else. Shuna noted that she gets up early already and will try to clear those critical voices from her mind.

Shuna's husband, Cammy, soon joined us, probably wondering what was keeping her. We three then had a special and vulnerable conversation about Judy, and then I learned about Shuna's recent cancer diagnosis and her decision to not use traditional medical treatments for now.

We also talked about their 17-, 14-, and 8-year-old sons, her uncle, who lives on Iona, and her father, who lives on a nearby island. Shuna shared that she had suspected that my wife had passed on recently. "There was something about you and your wife that I sensed," she added.

Shuna admitted that her diagnosis scares her, even though she's confident in her treatment decisions. As she told me this, her blue eyes teared up, and in that moment with our eyes and hearts connected, I felt her fear.

"Hold each other and never let go," I said, turning my attention to Cammy. "Be sure to take care of her, and also yourself, Cammy. Do you mind if I hold you both in my prayers?"

I knew that God had brought us together for this moment.

"I would cherish that," Shuna replied.

"Bless you, Shuna," I whispered to her as we hugged tightly, exchanging much more than a hug. God brought us together for this moment.

Predawn clouds blocked most of the stars as I walked through this quiet, dark Scottish village to its pier. Soon, a few others joined me, including school children saying good morning to one another.

As our ferry pulled away from Iona, I smiled for all gifts received here from God, from Judy, from strangers, and from this Thin Place. I will return, and Iona will always be with us!

Ferries, trains, and busses today, propeller planes and jets tomorrow, then back home to our cottage. Rolling through Scottish highlands from Oban to Glasgow, I drank in the countryside—charming views of foggy, lush mountains, mirror-smooth lakes, and quaint villages.

God, please help me move into disciplined meditation and prayer as Judy did so faithfully. Help me not to let this time in Iona slip away. Guide and nudge me. Sit with me; hold me in your mysterious holy way through the Veil.

After 20+ hours, including layovers, from Glasgow to home, I went straight to bed and slept until I woke up. Spent the rest of the day and evening on laundry, grocery, and other errands, sorting through bills and mail, unpacking and settling back into my solitary life at our cottage.

Thinking about and reflecting on my journey through this past year, with a growing awareness of the upcoming anniversary of Judy's death, I wondered whether my Iona trip and spiritual activities there would soften everything a bit. We'll see.

People have told me the second year is harder than the first for most spouses. In addition to the difficulty of the dates themselves is a new layer of memories of not only two years ago but also last year. I know without a doubt that my next few months will be yet another intense roller coaster of emotions.

The Other Side of Why

Why so soon, only 62 years?
Why not more years together? Only 41+
Why not more time in your hills and forests?

Why silence her voice, her retreats?
Her passion for shepherding people
Why silence her creativity?
Her art, her laughter?
Why take away our walks together?
Under your cerulean sky and whispering trees.
Why allow cancer to silence her?
To shatter our hearts?

Why 62 amazing years gracing us?
Why 41 years of love, passion, and bliss,

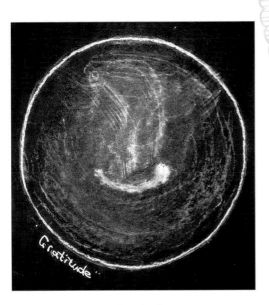

Gratitude

The Other Side of Why *(continued)*

Tenderness, laughter, heaven on earth?
Why the gift of her to so many?
Hearts, people, sunrises, sunsets?
Why create her voice and passion and compassion,
Her gifts for so many people?
Why bless so many, including herself with
Her art and creativity, her wit and wisdom?
Why gift us with her "because I can" hugs
Why gift me with countless walks in the hills,
Among loving homes and white beaches, holding her hand?
Why smile at us as we cuddle, spooned,
Loved, slept in each other's arms?
Why gift us with such a deep love,
That spawned such deep grief
Why receive her into Jesus arms
To cure her cancer eternally?

Why? Your Love Runneth Over . . .

Last day before October. Dreading October. At least this year.

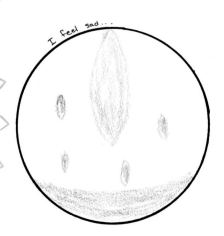

I Feel Sad

October, Not Your Fault

October, you came along innocently, gently.
Cooling days, sweaters, changing leaves.
Breathtaking colors. Jack-o-lanterns
Homecoming, corsages, parades.

Falling acorns, walnuts, dry leaf mounds.
Harvest dust, silos and bins filled.
Ghosts, goblins, princesses, superheroes.
Witches' brew, warm cider, s'mores.

October, Not Your Fault *(continued)*

Ambulance carries a precious princess.
Hospice angels surround you, anoint
And bless you, us. You bless them, caress
Them with love, compassion for their tears.

You and our son sleep, hands linked forever.
Heaven's arms open. Tears of joy flow, welcoming you.
Jesus' arms clasp you. "Fly, go home!" whispered.
Last kiss. Tears of pain erupt. Hearts shattered.

October, it's not your fault.

I took a big step today by attending a small group Bible study. Ten couples . . . and me. Everyone I spoke with was warm and welcoming. Two people asked me whether my wife would be coming with me. I told them about Judy's passing last October, which made them very uncomfortable and prompted their condolences. I hate these sorts of questions and having to answer them by speaking about Judy's death—and how uncomfortable they feel when I tell them.

Afterward, a question came to me:

~ Will my presence and story make other couples so uncomfortable that it be best I not attend?

And that question led to two more:

~ Is this a self-protective question masked in concern for them?
    Or
~ Is this a genuine question that I need to be aware of and act upon?

God, please help me with this one!

Lately, the BIG steps seem to be coming in bunches:

~ Flying overseas and vacationing alone

~ Judy's birthday, alone

~ Our anniversary, alone

~ Anniversary of Judy being taken to Pickering House, October 5

~ Anniversary of Patsy anointing Judy with essential oil, October 8

~ Anniversary of Judy leaving my arms and flying to heaven, October 10

~ Anniversary of Judy's celebration of life services

~ Small group gathering with 10 couples, with me as the only single person there

Lunch with June (the MAINE-IAC!) today. Answered a lot of questions about Iona—why go there, was it worthwhile, what did I do, what did I receive/hear, and more. Told her about my conversation with Alastair, and she listened intently. She said if I wanted to read any of my writings to her, I was welcome to do so. Responded by letting her read several poems and writings, which helped her receive what God and Judy were revealing and bubbling up within me, within my heart.

Then we talked about her family, and as June told me stories about the three most influential people in her life, a "Story Listening" session from a few days ago came to mind.

"Who are the most influential people in your life now?" I asked.

"That's a good question," she replied, pausing to consider the answer. "I don't know. Have to think about that."

I just let this question lay in the air, in her mind, and on her heart with a prayer for it to prompt some discernment that feeds her.

Looking out at the outdoor plaza, fountains embedded in the pavement shoot water into the air in irregular intervals. It's an unusually warm day, and small children are laughing and getting wet and loving the bursts of the refreshing water that shoots up unexpectedly, then disappear. Their parents, looking on, are smiling and laughing, too.

A young mother and her daughter are enjoying a chocolate birthday cupcake with a candle in the shape of a number 4 a few tables from me. With her ballerina skirt, long blonde hair, and fair skin, chocolate icing on her lips offers the image of pure joy.

This is what life is all about. How do we eat more chocolate cupcakes and heal our hurting hearts?

Woke up this morning to my friend's email about his wife passing away overnight. Tears for him and his family flowed freely as I surrounded them in my prayers.

God, thank you for placing my friend and his wife in each other's hearts and lives, for creating them for each other. For blessing so many people through them, their love, and marriage. Thank you for comforting him, their children and grandchildren, siblings, and dear friends. Please guide me how to walk with him to the extent he wants/needs and to learn from me. You gave him a tender heart, a wise heart. Thank you for helping him as it breaks into pieces and he, like me, has to learn to live without his bride by his side.

As I hiked our hills today, thoughts of Judy ran constantly through my mind and heart, as they almost always do. Although we did not know it at the time, and even though we knew very well what was happening, we did not know that this day last year was going to be our last day together in our cottage, our last full night together in our special bedroom with its wall of windows. I recall holding her as we slept as I always did, my left arm across her with pillows arranged to support her in her special bed.

We say to Love, "Bring it on. Bring it all. Everything. No matter what comes, I want to be with her/him, *no matter what*. I want *everything*. Leave nothing out. Do you hear me, Love?" And, yet, we don't have the ability to know what "everything" entails. When we fall in love, we invite everything, sight unseen, to take up residence within us. Somewhere we understand that this is an eternal journey, one that Love, Beauty, Light, and Joy win every time.

"Yes, Love, we want it all. Grace us with special moments that are holy, life-giving in every circumstance. Surround us even with grief, when its time arrives. After all, Love, you were birthed within us, and you, Love, will be with us beyond forever. Grief will not."

One year ago today we decided it was time to move Judy to Pickering House for her final days on earth. We knew this day and decision were coming, but that didn't make it any easier.

Picturing these moments as though it's happening now; I know I need to replay and release this sweet and terrible scene from my mind. It still all seems so unreal, like a nightmare from which I will never awaken.

Waking up, holding Judy. Gazing through our bedroom wall of windows, looking out at our trees and the increasingly colorful leaves. Saying, "Good morning," "I love you," and kissing. Bringing Judy breakfast, half of one of her favorite scones. She was tired. So tired.

Calling Judy's hospice nurse, answering her questions. Her tender exam, how she looked at Judy compassionately, directly into her eyes. Judy turning her head to look at me with a slight, sweet smile, then back to her nurse, saying, "If you think it's time, then yes, let's go."

Judy's acceptance, love, tenderness, and courage as I called the Pickering House, then Hide-A-Way Hills security about the coming ambulance. Holding Judy as we waited, I sat with her up against her bed's raised top half.

The tender-hearted EMT, fully realizing the "holiness" of his work. The compassion in his eyes, posture, and reverent demeanor. Saying to him, "Please be careful; she's precious."

His reply, "I will," with a full understanding of what was happening. Lifting Judy onto his gurney as if he was lifting and holding his mother, his sister, someone he loved and adored.

Following the ambulance to Pickering House, sobbing and numb, praying for peace and comfort for both of us. Arriving, getting Judy settled into Room 9. Her hospice nurse's holy hug goodbye as Pickering's onsite team assumed Judy's care.

Our last five nights and days there together, Judy's soul transitioning as her body was preparing to die. Praying over and over and over for God to take her home, to release her from this physical struggle while also dreading the moment when it would happen.

As I finished writing all of this, I looked out to see Judy's beautiful full harvest moon gently blazing above the field. I ended this difficult night under her moon, falling asleep on our deck.

This morning, a pain-filled year later, dear friends came together at our cottage to remember Judy with songs, scripture, flowers, prayer, and presence. People from Columbus and Hide-A-Way Hills gathered with me to remember and honor Judy as I placed some of her ashes in her "Grandma's Garden" along with flowers from each of us.

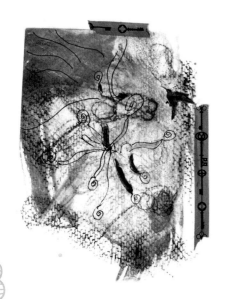

Carried Toward the Light

One year ago

One year ago, you flew.
One year ago, you left us.
One year ago, you breathed your last,
In my arms.
One year ago, we cried and wailed,
Loudly and in silence, as you passed.
One year ago, God cried for us, with us.
One year ago , God smiled and hugged you
"Welcome home."
One year ago, you cried with your daddy,
Tears of joy, as you embraced each other.
One year ago, my world, my heart, my soul
Shattered.
One year ago, I whispered, "Fly."
You flew.

Numb is my dominant feeling today. Most "firsts" have come and gone, and now, all the "date" or "anniversary" firsts have happened.

This first year was filled with shock, raw grief, and adjustment. My second year, I'm told, will be harder somehow, as long-term reality starts to settle in and the false hope of waking up from the nightmare vanishes for good.

After walking to our community's Lake of Four Seasons, I sat with a glass of wine on a boat pier in the evening mist. I toasted Judy, remembering our last night together on this earth, remembering the moment her body entered eternal sleep and her soul flew into God's arms. I remembered the owl's call to Judy's soul to help guide her home.

One year ago today was the first night of my life without my princess, my wife, my best friend, and my lover in my arms. A single autumn leaf floated by me, illuminated by my flashlight.

"We don't learn how to live until we learn how to die." I heard that over and over from all who visited Judy, especially our dearest friends and her hospice team.

For the past 40+ years, 17 has been our special number because we first declared our love on September 17 in Judy's parents' living room.

A year ago today, on October 17, I picked up Judy's ashes from the funeral home in their lovingly created urn and then went home to organize pictures and pieces of her art I sensed would best tell her stories—Judy's loves, passions, and creativity. Never did I think I'd be doing those things so young in her life and our marriage—not for at least another 10–15 years.

When I was entering college with my future looming before me, I was not planning on falling in love in college and getting married shortly after. I remember telling Judy that I was not going to get married until at least age 25 and did not plan on getting serious with a woman while in college. Grad or law school would follow graduation, I thought, with a year or two working overseas. All those plans changed when I met and fell in love with Judy.

Then on November 21, 2015, my plans were again changed forever, and the finality of that change happened less than a year later. Two times in my life Judy and God changed my life plans. Once, beautiful beyond words. Once, painful beyond words.

On this day a year ago, many, many loving people gathered at St. Alban's to hug one another, cry, and celebrate Judy's life and love. It was surreal, a nightmare from which we all wanted to wake up. It was also an outpouring of love and compassion and stories and laughter and deep support and tears.

Dinner afterward at Shaw's; I recall my brother, David, saying that we were there to tell good stories, share our precious memories of Judy. I remember telling them, between gasping tears, how deeply I needed their stories and memories. My mind and heart were so filled with pain and images of Judy's last few weeks. I had nothing to give; I could only receive.

One year ago today, we gathered at the Abbottsville Cemetery for Judy's graveside service with close friends and family. I remember carrying Judy's urn and ashes across the drive and standing under a large tree, tightly holding onto her urn as though I was holding onto Judy, talking to her through my tears.

I remember how Judy's mom came up behind me and put one hand on my left shoulder and the other on my right arm wrapped tightly around Judy's urn, saying, "It's time, Roy," and then how, together, we walked slowly, haltingly, across the lane.

After a few words, a special blessing, and prayers, we lowered Judy's urn into that small square hole; we each tossed in a handful of earth. Then I sat on the ground beside the hole, holding onto her urn until our priest, too, whispered, "Roy, it's time. You have to let her go."

On this day, this year, I still feel incredibly isolated, whether I'm alone or with people. This feeling is stronger at some times than others, not always dominant, but still with me in some form most of the time.

I, along with billions of other people who've been left behind, live in a cycle of falling down, getting up, falling down, getting up. From time to time, an extended hand of family or a friend helps pull us up when we can't do it on our own—until one day, hopefully, we're able to get up and stay up. There is no specific time frame for "getting up" and back to living; sometimes we never fully "get up." Tragically, some never get back up at all.

How can we intentionally support and love and hold one another through these times? How can we learn and remember to reach out when we see someone struggling to get back up?

Every time I sit with Sister Noreen, I see why Judy and so many are moved by her strength and compassion. She truly lives from the God-center within her. Today, she caught me off guard when she showed me a picture of a multicolored leaf. Its colors were graphically arranged from red to orange to yellow to deep blue and then green at the bottom. It was not a naturally colored leaf, yet it was beautiful all the same. Below the bottom's green section was a long stem.

"Which color are you right now?" Sister Noreen asked.

I stared at it for several moments and still nothing came to me. "I don't know," I replied. "My favorite color is red, but that was not your question." I paused, thoughtful. "I don't know what color I am."

As I continued to reflect on her question about the leaf, still no color came to me. As I handed it back to her, I pointed to the bottom of the stem and said, "I feel like that stem, disconnected." I let this idea settle for a moment, then continued, "Disconnected from my energy, my life source, my strength."

Sister Noreen listened without offering any platitudes or fixes. "That is an honest answer, a deep truth," she replied. She then read me a poem about the leaf, a meaningful reminder that even though colors fade, the leaf will return, full of life. "This is the cycle we know and believe in," she added quietly, "a source of hope."

She then told me she senses that God is taking me on a higher, deeper, longer journey that will benefit others as well as me. "We don't know our part in the whole," she said, "but we need to play our part. God's dream and plan for us, for all people, is yet to be realized."

"What does that mean?" I asked, puzzled.

"We were all created in God's image, male and female, equal in God's image," she replied. "We need to live from our Inner Authority, go in our direction, even when everyone else is going another way. We each must believe in our consciousness and inner authority," she added. "It is of God, planted and developed by God."

Amazing wisdom, such a gift to receive it. These points are critical aspects of peace in our families, communities, churches or places of worship, workplaces, nations, and world.

God, come into my heart. Heal me as I walk this path you've prepared for me. Help me to bring your Love, Beauty, Light, and Joy to others, to help them see Love, Beauty, Light, and Joy within themselves, within everyone.

I talked with Amanda today about my Iona trip and shared my experiences from being there. I also let her read several of my writings from my time there.

Her gentle smile grew as she read. "For the first time, I'm hearing and reading a balance of love, pain, and hope in your writing," she observed. "Whereas your previous writings were heavily weighted with grief and pain, those feelings are not as dominant here." She looked at me as she emphasized, "Your pain and grief are still obvious, but now there's so much more."

Her comment rings true. Grief's fog is slowly, ever so slowly lifting and letting the light of our love, of our life before her diagnosis, return to my mind, my memories, and my heart. Sometimes I sit and replay images, pictures of Judy, of us. God blessed us with innumerable glimpses of heaven throughout our life together, both in good, loving times and in hard, painful times. I believe Judy and God are opening up wells within me to soften my grief and possibly serve others who are walking, or will walk, this unwanted, uninvited journey.

Had lunch with Jim from Pickering House. We both talked more easily about Judy and about his late wife, Pat. Similar journeys and similar pain.

Jim, however has a lady friend, and they are seeing each other quite frequently. They're developing a sincere affection for each other. I am immensely happy for them, two special people who have been widowed.

Then came the question I had been told would come at some point.

"Would you like to meet some women, widows, she knows?" he asked. "She can help with that."

"Tell her, 'Thank you, but no'!" I replied immediately. "Not now and probably not ever. I can't imagine myself with anyone else."

Woke up at about 5:30 this morning, deeply shaken by a dream about a painful conversation with Judy in which she used a word she NEVER used: "*hate*."

And she directed it at *me*.

"A part of me *hates* you for what you did," Judy said to me in the dream.

It was so real—I even recall the softness in her voice and disappointment in her eyes as she said it that made it infinitely more painful than if she had screamed those words at me while throwing something my direction.

I woke up, stunned, rattled, and scared. "How could Judy tell me that she hates any part of me, even in a dream?" was the question that burned within me all morning. That dream of such a horrible verbal exchange stuck with me all day.

Judy told me many times that people and words in our dreams are reflections of something within us we need to address. So what was that statement in *my* dream saying to me, about me, from me?

Of course, I know there is no way any part of Judy hates or hated me. After all, she's the same woman who pointed at *me* to describe Love, Beauty, Light, and Joy.

Then somehow Judy and God shook loose what this was likely about. There was someone at the workshop I attended yesterday who once hurt Judy very deeply. Although they eventually reconciled, I was never able to completely let go of the many times he hurt her, betrayed her, and walked away from their friendship and all she did for him. My deep anger at him was not a good thing, not pretty, and to this day is still well entrenched within me.

As I thought about and reflected on this uncomfortable memory in light of my terrible dream, I began to understand what I was saying to myself *about* myself in that dream.

Judy said she had let go of all expectations of this person; I have not been able to do that. I now believe *I* hate that part of me that won't let go of my anger. That person's presence at the workshop was likely a nudge to address this unhealthy anger once and for all.

As I continue my way on this unwanted path, I realize this deep anger must be jettisoned somehow in a faithful, honoring manner. It is an old, monumental weight on my soul and heart. Even though it is far from conscious thought, it remains a seeping wound I must lance, remove its disease, and heal. It is an obstacle to my moving forward along the path God knows and desires for me.

Attended the Dominican Associates of Sisters Annual memorial mass to celebrate friends and family who have passed into eternity the past year or so. It is terribly hard to see Judy's name in a memorial program and especially to hear her name read aloud. I felt a physical reaction within me as I heard it, an all-too-familiar stab to the center of my chest. I don't think that reaction will ever go away; at least I hope not. This pain is a reminder of our divine love.

During the mass I sat between Sister Noreen and Sister Joan, two incredibly special souls to both of us. I felt enveloped in love and protection with them on each side of me. Family members were invited to stand as one person went forward to light a floating tea candle. When Judy's name was called, I stood to go to the altar. Sister Joan stood up with me, and Sister Noreen would have if she had been able. My legs weakened with this realization as I walked to the altar.

Joined some Hide-A-Way Hills neighbors at a local church to help serve soup meals to clients of Good Works, an organization devoted to helping people who struggle with homelessness and poverty.

Met Jeanne, a Good Works client, a 75–85-year-old lady with full makeup and a lovely purple and black sweater. All of five feet tall and about 100 pounds soaking wet. Her husband died about five years ago.

The gleam in her eyes told me this weekly meal is a special social event for her. I saw so much love and affection among people who come regularly, clients and volunteers. Genuine, divine love everywhere I looked.

In our contemplative prayer session this morning we explored more history of Zen Buddhism and parallels between scripture and Zen Buddhism writings. Further demonstration of the Holy Mystery, God revealed to all people in different ways and different times.

Our discussion leader also talked about writing haiku, a traditional Japanese three-line poem of 17 syllables, written in a 5-7-5 syllable count. Judy wrote these many times, including in her *Praying the Hours* booklet I still use sometimes.

The haikus below flowed out of me quickly as I became "The First Reader" of these words from God and my heart.

> Scottish sheep trails call
> footsteps to follow; peace and calm
> wild heather blesses

> longing for you . . . us
> memory palm against palm
> never again touch

> hazel green eyes—yours
> captured my heart . . . soul . . . forever
> together we will be

Painting Beauty in the Ashes

After I read them out loud, Robert said they painted vivid images for him.

"I write what I see and feel," I said. "My words are spurred, mused by Judy, by life."

Church service at St. Alban's with June sitting beside me. Amma Nicolette gave a sermon with a well-reasoned and very different explanation of the parable about the master who gave his servants five, two, and one talents, respectively.

She said the servant who buried his one talent was the hero who decided not to pursue ill-gotten gain. The master was a greedy man who wanted unreasonable gain, no matter who may suffer for it. A powerful paradigm shift from other explanations of this passage I've heard before. A mystery to consider.

Two years ago on this date, our GBM (glioblastoma multiforme) cancer journey and horribly difficult path opened and called us forward.

Two years ago, Judy fainted in our shower. We heard those words that changed everything: "You have a large mass in your right temporal lobe."

Two years ago today, Judy looked at me from her ER bed, and our eyes and hearts connected as never before. She knew. We knew, yet we still hoped.

Two years ago, I prayed for a miracle.

Two years ago, Dr. Elder and his team removed the large mass from Judy's brain one day before Thanksgiving and confirmed it was indeed a GBM tumor; they referred us to oncology doctors for treatment options.

Two years ago, we began our final year together on earth. Two years ago.

Two years ago, on Thanksgiving night, Judy rested and recovered in her ICU bed amid tubes, wires, and beeps, wearing an eye mask and a surgical turban.

Two years ago, I slept fitfully in a chair by her bed when I wasn't awake, staring at her, talking to her, praying for her.

Two years ago, we were so grateful she survived her first brain surgery.

Two years ago, we were so deeply terrified. We prayed. We hoped. We were thankful.

Sitting with me in her favorite meeting room, Sister Noreen handed me back my writings, telling me that she read them at least three times. She then asked me to read aloud my poem "Are You Dining Alone?" I did and then asked, "Why that one?"

"It is painfully honest, real," she said. "You show your pain and your love, your loneliness for Judy. You also show your hope and belief that you and Judy will be together again. Roy, you hold nothing back from within you."

She also noted that the setting, dining alone in a restaurant, is a picture of painful reality for so many.

"Where do your words come from?" Sister Noreen asked.

I paused, then replied, "From a place deep within me. I don't plan words or even think when I write. They just come."

"Where do you see this going?" she asked. "Your writings."

"They will go where God wants them to go," I said. "I'll trust my responses to prayer, nudges, and the observations of trusted loved ones."

"Your raw vulnerability will touch people," she said. "Your relationship with Judy and your willingness to be so vulnerable in your grief gives me hope."

Being in Sister Noreen's presence always feels like holy ground. Her words surprised and humbled me.

What does God have planned for me?

Are You Dining Alone?

"Will someone be joining you?
Are you dining alone?"

"Yes, I'm alone."

I said it out loud, my aloneness,
Even as others, couples, surround me, hear me.
We are not "us" any longer.

You're Here,
You're not.
Our hands touch in memories.
Our souls and hearts touch always.
We dine together no longer.
We will drink nectar together forever.
One slice of pie with two forks, without you.
One slice of Heaven, together, Beyond Forever.

Winter 2017-2018

This holiday season feels harder than last year, as I was told it would. Last year I was numb and in shock. This year's reality of Judy's absence is palpable.

A woman sitting across the room from me at a meeting here in the Hills was peacefully knitting while also participating. It caught me off guard, a sentimental reminder of watching Judy knit through conversations, in meetings, in our home, on our couches.

My continuous prayers have been for strength on this journey. This second holiday season, it's the little things—scenes, words, overheard phrases, smells, music, pictures, and on and on that cut even deeper than before.

Even through outward smiles and inward thoughts of gratitude, a continuous lump in my throat remains. Unexpected tears, soft sobs, loud, deep, anguished crying, all still with me this Christmas. Swimming in a sea of happy memories while submerged in a well of grief—it all belongs.

My sensitivity to pain within others seems to be increasing. Conversations have become more meaningful and vulnerable.

Had lunch with a longtime business friend who is going through the same spiritual direction program Judy did many years ago.

"Are you good?" he asked, referring to how I'm doing this holiday season without Judy.

"Right now? Not really," was my direct and honest reply.

He listened and truly heard my description of this holiday season versus last. "I'm so sorry for your pain," he said. Then he told me how a painful death in his family almost 30 years ago still hurts.

"As it turns out, time does *not* heal wounds," I said. "It actually makes them more painful."

"Whoever said that does not know true loss," he agreed. "That's a bunch of shit!"

He's right.

I read in the past year that it helps a grieving person to talk about their loved one with people who care. That is so true. Talking about Judy openly and honestly with someone who really listens and cares is such a gift. So many people, out of fear they won't know how to react if I get upset, avoid talking about Judy with me at all. That just makes matters worse.

Katherine noticed my increasing sensitivity to hurts and joys, pain and treasured moments, expressed and denied love. Images and holy interactions. Messages and nudges from God.

"But it hurts, so much of the time!" I responded. "Even delightful moments contain sadness and grief."

"Compassion is a danger to anyone open to its journey," she offered. "You choose, as did Judy, to live out of your compassion for others. You're continuing to do that, even without her here.

"Your heart is not shrinking," she continued. "It's expanding. And Judy's heart was, is, and always will be with yours. Her heart and compassion are living on within you." She paused, musing. "Perhaps your sensitivity is increasing because now it also includes hers."

Judy and I did believe God joined us in a mysterious, divine way that included our love and passion for each other, our individual and mutual dreams, and our desire to love, serve, and guide others.

While I've always been sensitive, Judy was always much more so. She saw things in people and in nature more deeply than I did. She developed a habit of saying "Thank you, God," for big and little things. And she meant it. She modeled that for me and others.

Katherine's right. Now when I see, observe, or feel something more deeply than I did as a younger man, memories of Judy's words, actions, writings, art, and dive-in approach return to me.

"Has your writing always been so vulnerable?" she asked.

"I have been sensitive all my life," I replied, "but not to this depth."

"After all the years of living and loving *with* Judy," she observed, "I believe her heart is guiding yours."

Makes sense. With Judy no longer here to act on her heart's messages and desires, it's up to me now to carry her words, her passion, her sensitivity, her compassion. My heart is expanding because it is *our* heart now, living and loving only within me. What a humbling treasure.

My conversation with Katherine then explored how compassion, once felt and acted upon, almost always beckons memories of painful and similar experiences, regrets, and tragedies. She said that when we welcome our vulnerability, the deeper the grief or pain or regret, the greater or more intense our compassion. She adds that the decision to welcome vulnerability, once acted upon, also yields irreplaceable beauty.

Now I understand. When we make the decision to walk with compassion, it becomes a living, growing passion within. Beware of compassion's invitation. Danger, pain, beauty, love. It all belongs.

Lunch with "June Bug," our fellow "Maine-iac," who shared pictures of her recent trip to Switzerland. I felt I was serving her by listening to her, asking questions, truly being engaged in her joy. Her year there as a young woman was full of amazing memories and relationships that have spanned the past 46 years. I could sense her excitement to share all of this with me.

She had listened to me in our previous conversations, offering her support. This was me, returning her kindness. I examined the picture of her standing between her "Swiss brother" and her "Swiss best friend's" husband. "You look so happy in this picture," I said.

This caught her off guard. She blushed.

On my hike through Hide-A-Way Hills today, the loudest cacophony of wild geese I've ever heard rose from the Lake of Four Seasons. This enormous group of geese had at least seven or eight V-shaped gaggles with 10–25 geese in each one.

They took off from the lake, heading south, and then turned east, flying directly over me before turning northward. I stopped and drank in this experience, trying to decipher this message from nature.

A short while later, a red-tailed hawk also flew right over me, gliding low. The hawk looked directly at me.

I descended the hill toward another small lake on my right, and a smaller group of geese lifted off, headed north, and then turned west, also flying straight toward me.

These three visitations by nature overwhelmed my heart, soul, and mind. Realizing there must be significance in of all this, I spoke aloud the questions rising from somewhere within me:

"Are you talking to me?

Are you singing to me?

Are you anointing me?"

I shared the geese and hawk visitations with Amanda today. "Amanda, I don't know who I am," I said. "I don't know where I fit, what my purpose is. I'm lost without Judy, without *us*, but I also have a sense that I have much to do to carry on our work. These questions have arisen intensely in the last few days, then this morning these geese, this hawk, this awareness of a message. But what is it?"

Amanda listened. When I raised my head to look at her, her eyes were misty, her right hand was on her heart, and a slight smile penetrated her sadness. She got up and went to her bookshelves and retrieved a book. Opening it, she turned to a particular page and then asked, "Did you know that geese are the Celtic symbol for the Holy Spirit?"

"Is that why that word came to me me this morning?" I asked, incredulous. "Were they *anointing* me? And for what?"

She closed the book. "Are you able to stay in this place of not knowing who you are, your purpose, your place?" she asked. "Do you know that God and Judy have something special planned for you?"

"I believe I can wait—and that they are both walking with me and have a plan for me," I said, then frowned. "This fallow time is so hard, though. I know it needs to happen, will happen, but I don't want to become 'me' without Judy. A huge part of me died when she died. How can I be fully 'me' without her here?"

"As Judy went deeper with God," Amanda said, referring to earlier conversations with Judy while she was progressing through Wellstreams, "she, too, was unsure about who she was becoming, blossoming to be."

Amanda said it was Judy's courage and deep desire to grow and serve God, to become who God planned for her to be, that kept her moving through that uncertainty. "Judy told me that at times she wanted to return to 'her box' of who she was before Wellstreams," Amanda added, "but she knew she wouldn't fit back into that old box."

Like Judy, I want to return to *our* "box," our life together, before death separated us, before cancer changed everything. I never imagined how hard this could possibly be, even with the brief glimpse of this ocean of grief—and my heart's immediate, visceral reaction—when Judy said, almost casually, "Roy, I don't believe I'm long for this world."

Now, more than a year after Judy's strange prophecy came true, I still feel ripped apart—and now I'm being put back together. I feel like a heap of complex, jagged pieces, an emotional puzzle God is slowly putting together to make a new picture of my life. I know this has to happen in order to somehow live the rest of my life without Judy here beside me.

We promised each other that we would "truly live" after one of us passed on to heaven first. This unwanted, painful journey I am on will end only one way—when I leave this earth.

Meanwhile, I will "truly live" as best I can: absorbing joys and praying continuously for wisdom, receptive ears, eyes, and hands to serve. I will pray for my soul to be aware of God's leadings and Judy's nudges. I will pray my vulnerability and sensitivity manifest themselves into words and deeds. I will pray my life honors our promise. I will pray I will find a new way to live and to love.

Long Walks in the Hills . . . Alone

Long hikes/walks up and down hills, around bends
Passing naked, leafless trees, white-tailed deer
They watch and listen to me, my footsteps, my breath.
Crystal blue skies, puffy clouds, or grey,
All are above me. Do you watch from them, watch me?

Quiet shallow breezes, wind gusts, chilly air.
Quiet, hawks screech, woodpecker tapping,
Cardinals calling to each other. Quiet. No
Electronic distractions. No "to-dos" interrupting.
Pine needles whistle as their wind partner
blows through them.

Quiet. My breath is rhythmic, shoe soles rhythmic
Arms rhythmic, gravel scrapes the road.
Loud thoughts race around mind's oval track.
No thoughts sometimes. Try to . . . listen to
God, you, nature . . . my heart . . . my soul.

Questions, statements, wonderings, pleadings, prayers.
"I love you. I miss you. I need you. Where are you?
Do you see me? Are you watching? Are you beside me?
Do you hear me? Do you miss me? Please . . . visit me"
"Why, God? Please God! I trust you, God. Help me, God!"

Hands swing freely in time with rapid steps
In time with paced breathing
Hands swing freely, holding no . . . other hands, your hands
No stopping to steal a kiss, to gaze into your thrilling
Seas of hazel-green eyes, to see your smile.

10,000, 12,000 steps, up and down, around bends
10,000, 12,000 steps; two feet, not four.
Horses watch one walker, not two. Two eyes, not four.
Survey your beautiful forest wild geese, swans.
Two hands, two feet, two eyes walk . . . alone.

fire walker

Firewalker

Drove into Grandview for my monthly gathering with "the Guys." I prayed to listen with God's ears as we updated one another about our lives, families, seeing God in our lives, and more.

One spoke about his difficulties with his sons. He shared a dream about telling them he needed to "take his life back." He also said he was having trouble praying.

"Two things come to me as I listen to you," I told him. "One, your dream *was* a prayer. Two, don't answer the following; just listen: What does 'your life' look like, the one you want back? Maybe write down what it includes, what it doesn't include, what you want to do. Try not to have an agenda; just write. Over a period of days and weeks, scribble down what your heart and soul tell you."

He responded with three things he believed would interfere with doing that.

"Each of those things you just mentioned could be added to your list," I said, praying that God's words, coming through me, were connecting with him.

Another of "the Guys" is hurting deeply; his wife of over 50 years died very recently. "I feel like I'm not being productive," he said, looking right at me as he spoke.

"Don't worry about being productive or efficient," I said slowly, answering his silent plea. "I still don't feel as efficient as I was before Judy died." I paused, looking straight back at him. "You've been deeply wounded. Try your best to just 'be,' not 'do.' This is your time to 'be' in your new and different life."

I pray that my words soothed him in some way.

Meeting with Katherine today was special and helpful. What a blessing she is with her heart, her tender listening, and her compassionate willingness to walk with me. I told her about reading *Kayak Morning*, a journal of sorts about the author taking up kayaking in early mornings after his adult daughter dies of cancer. Poignant. Scattered. Honest. Raw. Angry. Lovely. She had not read it but said she would like to.

"What did you receive from this book?" she asked.

"Well, it took him two and a half years to engage in something, his kayaking, that started to revive him and his heart," I said. "His writings and thoughts are very scattered at first. Memories, anger, literary recollections, counselor sessions, grief, degrees of depression, bitterness, love, and more."

It comforts me somewhat that even though I'm still very lost, it has not been anywhere close to two and a half years. His scattered writings are a perfect picture of my mind and heart most of the time.

"I STILL don't know who I am, what my purpose is, or where I fit in," I said.

"You know who you are *not*?" she asked me, gently and matter-of-factly. "You are *not* a couple. You are *not* married any longer in this life. You are *not* with Judy in this life."

"I know who I am *not*," I replied, echoing her tone and emphasis. "Who I *was* is no longer."

I realized I don't want to think about or say out loud who I am *not*, or even who I *am*, in this life.

Who I'm Not

Not married, not a husband, not hers
Not a couple, not her walking partner
Not with my princess, not held, not kissed
Not her holder, not a dinner partner
Not her hand holder, not her porch partner
Not her travel partner, not her listener.

A widower, a single person, someone who
Now eats alone, walks alone, travels alone
Grocery shops alone, talks aloud very little
Thinks alone, drinks wine alone
Goes to movies and pubs and restaurants alone
Goes to church alone, prays alone
Receives communion alone . . .

Cleans our cottage and cooks alone.
Does not buy flowers or cards or presents or sparkles
Clothes, knick-knacks, art, dark chocolate . . .for her
Talks to her with no audible replies
Writes to her, emails her—no replies
Reaches out to her—touches nothing
Not sure who I am. Part of me has died.

A gigantic tender part has died.
Not sure what my purpose is
Not sure where I fit, what my place is
The completed puzzle of my life has been ripped apart
A father, yes. Father-in-law, grandpa, and son.
Brother and friend
All treasured and cherished
Still, I'm not the me I was. But who am I?

Calm My Storm

Heard about it. Read about it. Hoped it wouldn't happen. Was told by several people they would not let it happen.

They said they would stay in touch. And then they didn't.

I know everyone is living their own lives and has their own responsibilities, just as I am living, or trying to live, my life and have my responsibilities.

They may not be sure what to say, or what to talk about. They don't want to infringe on my life and my time. Most were much more connected to Judy than they were to me. Even "the Guys" don't touch base with me outside our monthly meetings.

I feel abandoned. Friendship is a two-way street, and it feels like I'm doing all the driving.

Where are they? Why do *I* always have to make the call or initiate *every* get-together?

Where are their calls, their messages, such as:

"Let me know when you'll be in Columbus next so we can get together."

  Or

"We'd like to see you. Can we get together soon?"

  Or

"Want to have lunch or dinner one day next week?"

I'm almost interested to see how long it would take for them to contact me if I didn't reach out to them. That would not be right, but it *would* be interesting.

Katherine related how she had experienced the same circumstances with her own family and friends. She said that she then started getting involved in new "people circles"—events, classes, etc., to build friendships that were *hers*, not theirs.

I realize I need to do the same. I don't want these relationships to decline, dissipate, or end, but this new life of mine will likely involve new "people circles," and the energy I'm expending on relationships would likely be better directed in that direction, rather than continuing to pursue those that seem to be slipping away.

Sister Noreen started today's conversation by asking, "How are you?"

She had read some of my recent writings and was referring to my many comments about "she's not here."

To which I replied, "Numb. Not sure who I am, what my place is in all of this." I also told her about my recent off-the-chart sensitivity and that I'm not at all OK with this transition time between two lives.

She smiled, then said, "God will reveal in God's time what God is working on within you." She paused, then asked, "Can you write Judy's responses to what you write? Listen and write *her* words, in response to yours?"

"I've never considered that," I replied. "I do very often imagine her words in my thoughts."

"Oh, Roy, she is *so* present to you. She's working hard to tell you that in so many ways," Sister Noreen said. "If you want to hear from her, in her voice, start by writing her words—but only when you're ready."

Following up on Sister Noreen's recommendation, I decided to launch my "listening" conversation with Judy.

Judy: Roy, I'm here with you, always will be. I know you want to see me, hear me, touch me. I know you at least want to see and hear me in your dreams. For reasons I'm not able to tell you because it's beyond me, that can't happen right now.

Me: But do you miss me? Still love me? I know you love me, as I do you, yet it hurts to not hear you say those precious words to me. We said those words so much; we *lived* those three words beyond anything I thought possible. I miss saying those words into your ear, over the phone, as we drift off to sleep.

Judy: Roy, I will never leave you. You used to say, "Our souls and our love live on after we die." I used to say, "Our bodies don't have souls; our souls have bodies." If only I could show you where I am, where my soul is. And my love for you, my love for us, this dimension called heaven. Your soul and heart are still connected to me, to my soul and heart, separated by a thin veil.

I know you're in deep pain, which I wish I could remove and cast into the far reaches of space. I know this is so hard for you, as I predicted when we talked. I know how deeply and passionately you "treasure, adore, love, cherish, and are utterly mesmerized" by me (my code word for this sentiment was TALCUM, and I said it to her often). You've shown me. You were and are my Love, Beauty, Light, and Joy. Please trust me. Trust God. I do love you and will always be with you, and I'll be with God to welcome you home. We'll hug and laugh and walk and hold hands, beyond forever.

Me: God, I trust you. Judy, I trust you. I don't understand how our hearts can hold such love and pain together. We had and have so much, and we have no more together here. We didn't deserve or earn the life and love that God graced us with, which is why it is so exquisitely precious, why I miss it and you so much. Our love and this grief are eternally linked. I will never fully recover from your death. You still envelop my heart and soul.

I don't feel like being with people. I need, and that is the accurate word, to be alone, trusting that God and Judy are with me.

Not sure why being around people is at the bottom of my desire list right now. It just is. I'm not even going to St. Alban's on Sunday mornings. I feel the need to hibernate with my heart, my soul, and my mind.

Maybe the hardest part of this 40+ year journey is the stroll through our past in photographs. I need to get all the loose pictures used in Judy's celebration of life returned to their proper albums, and there are hundreds of others that need to be sorted and organized.

It's also going to take a great deal of time. To get started, I just have to take *one step*. And then another. And then another. Nothing more, nothing less. I know I need to gird my heart for more tears and pain while also opening it with joy to the memories and smiles and warm sensations that will travel right alongside the pain.

I promise I will take that first step this week.

God, please help me as I walk down that memory path through hundreds of pictures.

Surrender

No More

Kissing you tenderly
On the cheek, forehead; early morning
"Goodbye Princess"
No more.

Hearing your voice, your melody,
Breaking up my work day.
Bringing me smiles.
"See you soon."
"Me Too, You"
No more.

Journey home to our cottage
Our sanctuary, ravine, and woods
To you.
"I'm at Tarklin Road"
No more.

Reader's Notes

_____

_____

_____

_____

_____

_____

_____

_____

_____

_____

_____

_____

_____

_____

_____

_____

_____

_____

Spring 2018

It's now been more than 16 and a half months since Judy became perfectly fulfilled in the presence and radiance of God.

Took another step forward today by attending a retirement reception for a Hide-A-Way Hills employee at The Lodge. I knew I would run into other Hide-A-Way Hills people, some who would ask, "How are you?" with *that look*. And others who would see me and look past me because they weren't sure what to say.

Both of these things happened. Both types of people, trying to do their best as they are able and/or to protect their own hearts.

Went to a visitation today for Donna's husband, James, who died Monday night. He died of ALS, along with Alzheimer's disease, two of the most evil diseases, as Judy would say. I don't know Donna very well, but I felt a need to go support her and her grief in my small way.

As I came up to her in line, we hugged. I said, "I'm so sorry for your loss."

I saw several Sisters who have been important in our lives at the visitation, including Amanda. "Can we meet soon about Wellstreams?" I asked her as I was leaving. Her response surprised me.

"Oh my gosh! Yes!" she exclaimed. "How about we go get a drink now if you're not going somewhere in particular. Can we do that?"

As I got in the car after I closed her door for her, I said, "I've never been picked up at a funeral by a woman asking me out for a drink." We both laughed. Roared, actually.

We toasted Judy and Amanda's husband, Tom, with her beer and my Manhattan. Amanda said she believes Wellstreams would be good for my spiritual growth, whether or not I become a spiritual director. She told me once again how honored she was to witness Judy's incredible growth as a spiritual director.

Based on my question about any possible obstacles, she said I would need to open up to other beliefs, thoughts, and processes, which I will. I learned that from Judy.

She texted Tom to ask him to join us for dinner. He declined, telling us to have fun and enjoy our dinner and each other's company.

Over dinner we shared stories about how we met our true loves, joked with our crazy waiter, and enjoyed being together. It was an unusual evening for me—out for dinner with Judy's dear friend, a woman, and enjoying it.

Amanda's comments and demeanor have always reminded me of Judy, from the moment Judy first introduced me to Amanda as her spiritual director. I'm convinced Judy was with us, laughing with us. The love between Amanda and Tom reminds me of us. All four of us, heavenly blessed.

Stopped by Sweeny's Pub on this St. Patty's Day for a Guinness or two. Charming old corner pub with many locals/regulars starting their celebrations in the early afternoon. Heavy wooden bar, fun music, Irish decorations everywhere, and peanut shells on the floor.

Enjoyed them and tossed my shells on the floor as instructed. Their DJ of sorts, a man close to our age, was playing a wide variety of classic rock, rock, and even some hip-hop. Eric Clapton's "Cocaine" blasted out of his speakers, and I smiled, remembering our afternoon beach time at Panama City when we lived in Florida. "Cocaine" blasted from powerful speakers at a beach bar overcrowded by spring break college students while we were beaching as 24-year-old young marrieds. That song always brings that special memory to my mind and heart with a smile, our Tallahassee years, our early marriage years. Such an incredible, special time.

We had each other completely then, with few distractions. Barnaby's Pizza with their twisted dough crust and open kitchen. Florida State football games. Wakulla Springs. Destin. Picking Judy up every afternoon at her "Pierced Earrings Booth" manager job at the mall and from the law firm where she was a receptionist. Bread at the Second Act restaurant. Friday or Saturday night dancing at quaint nightclubs. Parades with the Florida State marching band and the Florida A&M marching Rattlers.

Judy surprised me with tickets to the FAMU senior banquet where Woody Hayes was their guest speaker. She had just started taking night classes at Tallahassee Community College. I smiled as I recalled the time when I carried my long wooden umbrella around their buildings one night, searching for Judy because she was late and I was worried about her. There had been multiple murders by Ted Bundy at an FSU sorority house, so I prowled the campus until Judy came out of the building; she had stayed late to talk to her professor.

I remember how bad she felt when she saw me standing there with my umbrella. How tightly she hugged me. And how we laughed when she figured out why I had an umbrella with no clouds in the sky. In later years she called me her protector, still giggling about my umbrella. And then I'd say, "Well, I would have used it if I needed to!"

I told Sister Noreen about Judy's gentle monologue to me and my recent cheerful memories of our two years in Tallahassee. I guess she could sense my deep loneliness for Judy, my intense longing. Maybe, most likely, the Holy Spirit had alerted her to my mood and emptiness.

On this visit, Sister Noreen graced me with one of the most precious gifts I've ever received. She led me in a guided meditation to envision Judy, her presence, her voice and words of comfort, her closeness.

At first, I was unaware she was starting a meditation. Her closed eyes and gentle voice coaxed me into the path she was painting for both of us. I believe God used her vulnerable, wise heart to guide me, to give me a taste of healing, and to feel Judy's presence.

As I breathed calmly and deeply, she guided me to envision a picture of the two of us. Our selfie picture of us sitting on the Tiki Hut bar's outdoor picnic table by the bay in Sarasota quickly came to me. Judy was snuggled behind me. I could feel her body against my back and still can. We're both smiling with the hut behind us, her long, red, wavy hair framing her gorgeous face and green eyes over my right shoulder. A moment of pure joy.

Sister Noreen then guided me to rest and remain in that moment with Judy. Her closeness, the feel of her, our joy in a place that was so special to us.

She then asked me to be open to whatever Judy wanted to tell me in this holy meditation.

With my eyes still closed and the image of us at our beach picnic table anchored in my heart and mind, Judy said, ever so clearly, "I'm here."

It was Judy. I know because I had no preconceived notion or desire of what I wanted to hear from her, or if I would hear anything.

"I'm here."

Clear, soft words, *in Judy's voice*. Tears of joy welled up in my closed eyes. Her presence, her voice, her assuring words. Heaven was in that small room with Sister Noreen.

Finally, she guided me to be open to Judy's presence in our room with us. Almost immediately I sensed her with my heart's eye, sitting in a chair between us, wearing blue jeans and her yellow linen blouse over her white camisole. Her legs were crossed, and a smile adorned her eyes and face. She was with us, through the veil. I was thrilled.

After Sister Noreen calmly brought us back to our room, she asked me what I felt.

"I felt . . . joy!" I replied.

"Did you hear anything from her?" she asked.

"She said, 'I'm here,'" I said.

"Did you sense her presence with us, between us?

"Yes," I said and then proceeded to tell her the details of Judy's presence right there in that room with us.

"Thank you, God," she exclaimed quietly, as tears trickled down her cheeks.

God gifted both of us via Sister Noreen's guided meditation. She was God's vessel.

Had the pleasure of lunch with June today. She returned a few days ago from seven weeks in Kennebunk. It was a time of deep reflection for her as she visited her nana, repainted several rooms, snowshoed, wrote, journaled, attended centering prayer sessions, and listened to God in her quiet alone time.

We exchanged many emails while she was there in which I tried to channel Judy's talent for listening and responding. June's love of Maine and serving people in need reminds me of Judy.

This morning, as I was filling my water glass in our kitchen, I looked up just in time to see a bluebird land in the tree just outside my window. It looked right at me, as if to convey Judy's words, "I'm here." Judy saw many more bluebirds than I ever did. I paused and smiled as tears welled up in my eyes.

Met June at Franklin Park Conservatory and surprised her with a membership card because she had expressed a desire for a quiet place to be in nature. She said she was spoiled by her recent seven weeks in Maine and how much writing and reflection time she had there.

I also bought a membership for myself before she arrived. We spent about three hours walking and talking and listening to each other and to God. Once again, I felt myself channeling Judy and her listening skills to be present with June because she is struggling with various life transitions.

I suggested she connect with Amanda regarding spiritual direction. June believes God is stirring things up in her about serving others, spending quiet time with God, drinking in beauty and nature, about less anxiety and more peace, more releasing. I hope she meets with Amanda.

The following is another conversation/letter with Judy:

Me: Judy, I'm sorry, so sorry if I have in any way, ANY WAY, held you here, interfered with your complete transition, caused you any hurt, if that's possible, in heaven.

Judy: Roy, your journey is your journey. God and I have walked with you, never pushing, never anxious. Always beside and within you. We will always be with you, yet now in different ways. There is an emerging taking place within you, one that God is creating for you. You know this; you feel it. You wrote about us "releasing" you and you "releasing yourself."

God has placed people in your life, hearts and souls who were not there until recently. You see them, feel them. Cherish them, lean into them gently, carefully, completely.

God and I will still be with you, within your heart and soul as you walk and embrace your earthly life. We will still be with you when you join us in paradise.

Trust your heart. Trust your love. Trust the love of people in your life. It's real. God controls the timing, the people, your paths, your growth, and your adventures to come. God controls where you serve, whom you will serve, who will serve you, who will feed and encourage you, who will journey with you, who will help you "truly live" again.

God and our love and life together equipped you to do new and different things. To learn and grow and be open to new experiences. New "whats," wheres," and "whos"—a *whole* new life. Your sensitivity is God's gift. Yes, it is glorious—and painful at times.

It's time for you to let God hone it differently, with tender hearts and loving teachers at your side. I will whisper to you; you'll know it's me; you'll see my wink, my smile, my touch, my hand with your soul's eye, your soul's senses. It's time now to open your heart and soul to experiences and people who have been brought to you.

It's time to touch and embrace life, to let life touch and embrace you. It's time to let your soul and heart be caressed anew, as you need and deserve. Our space, our room in your heart and soul, is always ours. Our experiences are always ours. You will always be able to recall them.

You are now emerging in new ways in God's world. Explore the growth of your spirit, your heart, your soul—and of what God is placing in your path of life and adventure. Release any hesitation; take the leap and float as a feather into God's arms, into the arms of new love, into new experiences of life and adventure God is placing in your path. Float on God's river. Trust the gentle current and let it carry you.

MTY BF,
Judy

I had lunch with June again today. I shared events of an equine session I attended recently, some of my recent writings, and a couple of Judy's journal entries, what they meant to her as she wrote them and how they seemed prophetic about her illness and her approach to death. I also shared how these entries seem to be Judy's words to me now—and how they could also be guideposts for June's transitions.

Our conversation flowed naturally and easily as always. Our friendship is deepening; we have become a deep resource for each other in our changing lives. We both recognize that this is happening.

June truly loved Judy. She saw in Judy a love of life, compassion, creativity, and wisdom. She was devastated when Judy died and pleaded with God not to let her die. She told me many times how much it hurt to realize that the great love affair, earthly marriage, and deep connection Judy and I shared was done, that we were separated by death in such a cruel way.

She also told me recently that she is concerned about "stepping on toes" as our friendship grows and deepens. I have openly shared with her many times how much her friendship means to me. I also thanked her for her love for Judy, her respect and affection for our marriage and relationship.

June, Where is this going?

After dinner yesterday I went to Starbucks to write, think, listen, and pray through my pen. I wrote about many recent conversations and events. Emails with June. The equine event I attended. These all began to flow together as a continuum, a river.

God's river, the image Judy loved, spoke about often, and trusted.

When I got home, I couldn't even think about going to sleep. A glass of wine in the calmness of our screened porch called me to come, sit, be. My racing heart and anxious soul continued to agitate.

Then a new calmness washed over me as questions arose from the darkness within me:

Are you releasing me? Are you asking me to release myself?

I was completely shocked by these questions, and yet I felt at ease with them. I listened, in total peace, to these questions. Then more questions started to emerge. Questions about being released. Questions I had never considered. Then they came faster and faster. I went to our computer just after midnight as the following poem came to life.

Are You Releasing Me?

Are you asking me to release myself?
From what?
Our past, us, our love (never)
This swamp of pain, my desire for you to return
From what cannot be, ever again

Are you releasing me?
Are you asking me to release myself?
To what?
Must I release myself to live?
To explore, to emerge, to hear whispers,
To be. who I am now, who I am to become?

Are You Releasing Me? *(continued)*

Are you releasing me?
Are you asking me to release myself?
To where?
Do you see it? Are you guiding me?
Will you journey with me?
I'm scared of . . . losing you, forgetting you, your essence.

Are you releasing me?
Are you asking me to release myself?
To whom?
Is there a Who somewhere?
Will I know, will I open myself?
Will I be afraid of Who, if Who exists?

Are you releasing me?
Are you asking me to release myself?
Are you God? Are you . . . You?
Are you both releasing me?
. . . to life?

What is Blossoming?

This is where that poem that Judy and God wrote from deep within me surprised me at first with its openness. A flower bud or a cocoon, opening to reveal God-granted life and beauty, even as the flower and the butterfly don't know what awaits them, who will feed them, who will receive them, love them, be loved by them.

They open, trusting God, trusting eternal love, trusting the process. Unknown and unrevealed to them. They begin to bloom, to fly . . .

How many times, God? How many times does Judy have to die? How many of her deaths will I experience, live through? How many times will a piece of me die?

Since its inception our Always We Begin Again nonprofit (AWBA) board ran beside Judy and me as she led, guided, and passioned AWBA into the lives and souls of people from coast to coast.

In the summer of 2015 we put AWBA on hiatus, believing that Judy was experiencing only anxiety episodes. Life and passing of the calendar proved us wrong. For over 18 months I have harbored a desire to reignite this flame that burned within her, within us, to tip her lighted candle to ignite the candles we now hold and carry that light to people who need to be served.

This afternoon the AWBA Board came together to explore the "rebirthing of AWBA." Our chalice full of love for Judy ran over its brim as we talked, listened, prayed, spoke from our hearts, and discerned. All in love, all with the love of Judy and the love of one another.

After a great deal of discussion, Deb read one of the tenderest and most courageous letters I have ever heard, a letter she had written to Judy the previous day. We each absorbed Deb's words and compassion and knew the right decision was to "close AWBA with dignity."

With AWBA's closing I felt Judy die all over again, along with another piece of me. Of course, I knew AWBA had gone home with Judy—while Judy was much more than AWBA, AWBA *was* Judy. Still, it felt as though a piece of her that was still here was now being taken away.

"I feel strongly that this is right," someone said with compassionate eyes, then asked me, "Do you feel good about it?"

"It's right, *and* I don't feel good about it at all," I replied. "It hurts too much."

The organization that is AWBA has ended. The body that was Judy has ended. Both were holy gifts from God to us and many others. I grieve for both.

A chilly, gray, windy day. Arrived at the cemetery early for Aunt Carol's funeral service so I could put fresh flowers in Judy's vase. Aunt Carol's gravestone with Uncle Gene is next to Judy's parents' gravestone, which is next to ours.

Mental images re-played within me of holding onto Judy's urn, not wanting to let it go. Of releasing and returning Judy's ashes to God's earth. Of realizing that her body was truly gone. It still seems as though it all happened yesterday.

The tent for Aunt Carol's service covers all three gravestones. As I watched her casket being lowered into the ground, I thought of Uncle Gene, her loving, hurting, blessed husband who now will have to walk this earth alone. Then I pictured Aunt Carol dancing in heaven.

I thought about how Aunt Carol's tent would soon be taken down and all the people and their cars will be gone. Fresh dirt will still whisper that a cherished wife recently flew home to heaven.

"I don't think I can cry anymore. I have no more tears," Aunt Carol's oldest granddaughter said, just above a whisper. This is her first experience with death. How heavy it weighs on Judy's cousins and Uncle Gene. They are in deep, seemingly bottomless pain. Such love, such grief.

Overheard an innocent comment to Uncle Gene that knocked my sensitivity radar off the charts. A white-haired friend shook Uncle Gene's hand, offered his condolences, and then said, "Well, now you're in the club."

Obviously, a widower. Uncle Gene didn't need to be reminded so abruptly of that, as his stricken expression confirmed.

I sense a shedding, a releasing, like a lobster releasing the shell that no longer fits.

Did some gardening at our cottage with June. Afterward, we sat and talked for at least three hours. Something feels so right as I listen to her, as I hear her voice.

A carpet cleaner came today to remove stains from our bedroom carpet, stains from the last four months of Judy's life as I cared for her. Until now, I could not bear to have them removed.

It's time.

Found Judy's expressive arts journal in her studio by accident—which, of course was no accident. Several entries and mandalas seemed to be speaking to me from Judy. Prophetic words and images about her last years and for me, now.

I am overwhelmed as a torrent of new and conflicted thoughts, wonderings, and feelings swirl. Plans never before considered. Becoming different. Something new emerging.

What is happening? I'm a tangled entwinement of wonder, emotion, and confusion. What is emerging?

Suddenly, I recognized it.

Hope. Life. Love.

Love is an Infection

Love is an Infection. It Changes Everything.
Grief is an Infection. It Changes Everything.

It all belongs.

"Just Go With It"

Just Go With It

COLLABORATING AUTHOR'S NOTE

To say that it was a privilege and an honor to work with Roy and Judy (albeit posthumously) to bring *It All Belongs* into being would be the mother of all understatements. This raw, tender, funny, sweet, heartbreaking, inspiring, and oddly uplifting journey stole my heart from its very beginning. However, it wasn't until I began sifting through their journals, absorbing Judy's art, sitting with Roy's poetry, and unraveling their intricate layers of thought, emotion, exploration, philosophy, theological referencing, and spiritual meandering that I found my heart and theirs inextricably linked by this exquisite juxtaposition of separate-yet-connected journeys. In bringing forth its own brand of soul-deep comfort to readers of any circumstance, this story offers a deep frequency of connection around elements core to every human life. We all live, love, grieve, question, seek—and, sometimes as we navigate this journey called life we make lasting impact on the lives of others with whom we share a path. This is one of those stories. How fortunate I am to be able to help share it with countless other searchers in need of its timeless message of hope.

It All Belongs

Love, grief
  Joy, sadness
    Laughter, sobs and tears
New life, illness
  Growth, death
    Temporary here, forever in heaven
Pain, hope
  Fear, Trust
It all belongs.

LIST OF JUDY'S IMAGES

LIST OF JUDY'S IMAGES *(CONTINUED)*

LIST OF JUDY'S IMAGES *(CONTINUED)*

LIST OF JUDY'S IMAGES *(CONTINUED)*

LIST OF ROY'S POETRY

It All Belongs